THE
CHALLENGE
TO
GREAT
COMMISSION
OBEDIENCE

MOTIVATIONAL MESSAGES FOR
CONTEMPORARY MISSIONARIES

JERRY RANKIN

B&H
PUBLISHING GROUP
Nashville, Tennessee

Ten-digit ISBN: 0-8054-4521-8
Thirteen-digit ISBN: 978-0-8054-4521-3

Published by B&H Publishing Group,
Nashville, Tennessee

Dewey Decimal Classification: 266.023
Subject Heading: FOREIGN MISSIONS

Scriptures used include: NASB, The New American Standard Bible, © the
Lockman Foundation, 1960, 1962, 1963, 1968, 1971, 1972, 1973, 1975,
1977; used by permission, NKJV, New King James Version, copyright ©
1979, 1980, 1982, Thomas Nelson, Inc., Publishers, NIV, New International
Version, copyright © 1973, 1978, 1984 by International Bible Society, and
KJV, King James Version.

Some Scriptures throughout are paraphrased combinations
and/or the author's interpretations.

1 2 3 4 5 6 7 8 9 10   11 10 09 08 07 06

Dedicated to the thousands of Southern Baptist missionaries I have had the privilege of appointing to overseas service in appreciation for their obedience to God's call to fulfill the Great Commission and disciple the nations around the world.

CONTENTS

FOREWORD

The auditorium was silent except for the penetrating voice of the speaker whose words held captive the attention and imagination of his hearers. This was a moment they had long anticipated, and tonight he did not disappoint them. In descriptions so vivid it seemed as if they were there with him, he took this eager, attentive band on a journey around the world. This time it was not the scenery or the native customs that held them captive. It was the graphic picture he painted of this world's lostness and its need for messengers of hope, bearers of the gospel. Seated before him were the families and friends of candidates, present for the moment they had so long awaited, their appointment to a life of service as missionaries of the Southern Baptist Convention.

"So go ahead," intoned Baker James Cauthen, president of the convention's Foreign Mission Board. "Take your belongings, your clothes, your furniture and whatever else you think is necessary." Then fixing on them with his steely eyes that could not disguise the compassion residing in his heart, he continued. "But take them in your hand, not in your heart, for only your Master belongs there." He knew well enough what was ahead for those over whose heads he would soon pray and whose hands he would warmly shake as they were commissioned as missionaries.

Years have passed, and now Dr. Jerry Rankin serves as president of that same mission organization now called the International Mission Board of the Southern Baptist Convention. It is likely that no individual in modern history has preached at more commissioning services or to more candidates. During the tenure of his leadership, the ranks of missionaries in this remarkable body have swelled to include more than five thousand individuals presently in over 180 nations of the world. On the pages that follow, you'll be reading some of the messages he has delivered at those commissioning services.

On the surface this book appears to be a simple compilation of commissioning messages preached by Dr. Rankin over a twelve-year period. But they are alive with the passion of his heart and the fervor of his convictions!

Audiences affect the preacher more than one might imagine. A bullet fired into a snowbank comes quickly to a halt. And many messages forged with a hot heart on the anvil of prayer have received just that kind of cold, resistant reception by an indifferent congregation. That was not the case as these messages were preached and, now, as they are written. The spirit of the preacher and author joins with that of the listeners to produce messages that are white-hot with conviction.

An underlying theme in all these messages addresses issues of concern to many readers. "What is it to be called out as a missionary, and how can I discern that call from either eager desire or momentary impression?" For those asking these and similar questions, this book will bring clarity and understanding. And for those genuinely sensing God's call to missions, there is a refreshing dose of both biblical precept and personal illustration that will build your faith.

Neither can you escape one other emphasis with which each of these messages resonate: Missions is every believer's business. At any given moment you are to be either going, helping go, letting go, or covering those who have gone with your prayers. You'll discover that missions is something you can do—by God's grace. You'll come to the end of this book asking the Lord to show you just what role you are to play in sharing the gospel with the unreached of the world.

Here's a suggestion—no, a challenge. Put yourself among the ranks of those called out to serve in the remotest corners of the globe. Sit with them in the seats of honor, surrounded by your family, friends, and members of a caring church. Look up to a platform bedecked with flags representing all the peoples of the world, lean forward with this book in hand. Now listen as God speaks to your heart through these messages.

—Tom Elliff
Senior Vice President, IMB

PREFACE

In the 160-year history of the International Mission Board (previously Foreign Mission Board) of the Southern Baptist Convention, more than eighteen thousand missionaries have been sent out to proclaim the gospel and advance the kingdom of God around the world. Over half of them have been appointed in the last thirteen years in which I have been privileged to serve as IMB president. This phenomenal growth, which surpassed five thousand active missionaries in 2001, can only be attributed to God stirring in the hearts of His people, calling them to sacrificial service overseas. The number appointed exceeded one thousand in both 2001 and 2002, and currently more than three thousand candidates are in the process for long-term career and associate service. In addition, hundreds of short-term missionaries are sent out each year for two- or three-year assignments with the International Mission Corps or the Journeyman or Masters program.

This remarkable development is not an isolated phenomenon but is linked with what God is doing to open doors of opportunity all over the world. A few years ago we would never have dreamed of having residential missionary personnel in the Soviet Bloc of Eastern Europe, but the iron curtain fell, and literally thousands of missionaries and volunteers have swept into a region long prohibiting religious freedom. Creative access platforms have virtually eliminated the concept of closed countries, and previously unreached people groups are systematically being engaged with a gospel witness.

When doors to the communist world began to crack open, it was recognized there was one remaining formidable barrier to global evangelization—the Muslim world across Northern Africa and the Middle East. But ever since the tragic events of September 11, 2001, missionaries throughout the region are reporting that their friends and neighbors are expressing disillusionment with their Islamic faith and are asking questions for the first time that reflect a search for the hope and security that only Jesus can provide. Indeed, God seems to be using the chaos, warfare, political disruption, and natural disasters common throughout the world to create an awareness of spiritual needs that is accelerating the evangelistic harvest.

In the last few years an evangelistic witness has been planted among more than one thousand new people groups that were previously ignored or neglected. Missionaries, working in partnership with national Baptists, have been reporting an average of more than a thousand new believers a day being baptized around the world. Church planting movements have seen the annual growth in new churches being planted go from four thousand to more than twenty-one thousand in just these initial years of the twenty-first century.

In response to God's activity overseas, more and more people are exploring the possibility of missionary service. Realizing one dare not assume such a role apart from the calling and anointing of God, they are asking, "What is a call to missions? How can I know if God is calling me?" Hence, the introduction to this book, dealing with this topic, will be of interest to individuals as well as pastors and church staff guiding members to discern God's will. The messages selected for this volume are many of those I have used to challenge new missionaries at the time of appointment. Based on the admonition of Scripture, the missionaries are charged to be the kind of people who do the things that will enable them to effectively fulfill the Great Commission.

While designed uniquely for commissioning new missionaries, pastors will find the message outlines a valuable tool for challenging their own congregation. It is tragic that many churches never have a missionary called to overseas service; perhaps that is because pastors seldom preach the call to missions that is inherent throughout Scripture. Each message is based on a passage of Scripture and outlined with specific points of application. Each message is packed with mission illustrations that pastors and others will find useful in any context.

It is my desire that these messages will become a resource for widespread use. I hope they will equip pastors to have a new perspective on God's Word and add a new dimension to their preaching. The messages would be relevant for commissioning a volunteer team going out from a church and for ordaining or installing church officers.

My application of these messages has been for new missionaries preparing to leave the comforts and security of home and family to serve God around the world. However, they would be relevant to calling all Christians and church members to a mission lifestyle and challenging them to a greater commitment to living for the Lord and witnessing to the lost around them.

I am grateful for the opportunity and privilege of knowing and working with such a large host of missionaries. They have been the inspiration of these messages and the source of insights into missionary life. The testimonies of their devotion and sacrifice have provided the illustrations throughout this volume. Staff in the Office of Missionary Personnel, who conscientiously guide candidates through the appointment process, deserve more credit than they usually receive in facilitating the appointment of such large numbers of personnel. I appreciate the staff in the Office of Mobilization, especially in Events Coordination; they arrange and program the appointment services to be one of the most inspiring and exciting events that Southern Baptists have the privilege of attending.

Each message in this volume stirs memories of a particular appointment service and a group of missionaries beginning their pilgrimage of obedience to the Great Commission. I pray that they will inspire others to go and all of us to be equally obedient to the mandate of our Lord to disciple the nations.

—Jerry Rankin, President
International Mission Board, SBC

THE CALL TO MISSIONS

Commissioning new missionaries is an experience that occurs every other month—six times a year. In my thirteen years as president of the International Mission Board, there have been more than eighty missionary appointment services. Emotions are stirred by a procession of candidates following a colorful parade of flags, accompanied by the powerful strains of a familiar mission hymn. They include young couples just out of seminary with their lives before them as well as older families in mid-career who have put their vocation on the shelf to go to the mission field. There are single men and women who, in their devotion to God's call and the need to reach a lost world, have turned their backs on prospects of marriage to plant their lives in isolated outposts.

They come from a diverse background of locations all across the country, many reflecting the ethnic diversity that has become America. Though many come from the pastorate and church staff experience, in almost every group there are businessmen, doctors, engineers, teachers, policemen, building contractors, accountants, attorneys, and others. The numbers have grown significantly since my own appointment group of sixteen in 1970, to exceed, on a couple of occasions, more than one hundred. Including those approved for short-term assignments, the twenty-first century began with more than one thousand new missionaries being sent out by the International Mission Board in 2001 and 2002. All of them have been screened regarding moral character, doctrinal beliefs, educational and ministry experience, and approved to represent Southern Baptists as missionaries.

In spite of the diverse backgrounds and personalities, all of them have one thing in common: they have testified to a convicting sense of God's call to the mission field. In fact, that is the bottom line or the beginning point of becoming a missionary sent out by our churches to proclaim the gospel cross-culturally. Currently, more than three thousand candidates are in contact with the IMB, having expressed a testimony of that call and working to fulfill requirements for appointment. The International Mission Board identifies itself as a missionary-sending agency. Its basic strategy, as stated in its core values, is "to send and support gifted, God-called missionaries who, with mutual respect, accountability, and cooperation, carry out the Great Commission in an incarnational witness."

Jesus told us to go. He stated His basic purpose in Luke 19:10—"For the Son of Man has come to seek and to save that which was lost." Then He told His followers in John 20:21, "As the Father has sent Me, I also send you." The question each missionary candidate struggles with, and one that continues to confront a larger Christian community, is that of a call. What is a call to missions? How can one know unequivocally that God is calling one to missions?

As the parade of new missionaries file across the platform sharing their personal testimonies, it reveals there is no single, common, definitive answer to that question. The way God speaks into each life to reveal His will is as diverse as the personalities and experiences they represent. For some it was an impressionable moment as a child in GAs or RAs, or a time of dedicating one's life at a youth retreat. For others it was a growing awareness of the needs of a world without Christ and the conviction God wanted them to do something about it. Many express a conscientious response to the scriptural admonition to go, and the Great Commission became a personal mandate, compelling them to give of their life. More and more are returning from short-term volunteer trips and, having seen the needs and how God is at work, feel compelled to return and give their lives to join God on mission to reach the ends of the earth. Some point to an occasion of hearing a missionary speak or the influence of a friend or professor, but it would be impossible to identify specifically any one way that God calls one to missions.

It is interesting that we tend to relegate a call to missionary service to a special category requiring a mystical experience not expected of other calls. Most Christians readily understand that God's will is known through a commitment to His lordship and willingness to follow wherever He leads by means of circumstances, events, and other impressions. A dedicated layman may appropriately testify to being "called" to be a teacher, a doctor, a lawyer, or businessman without any distinct divine encounter. Certainly God uses one's interests and gifts to channel someone into vocational areas through which one can effectively serve the Lord. Even those in church vocations often gravitate in that direction through an interest in seminary studies and a somewhat vague "call to the ministry" without the location and role being clearly identified. But conventional wisdom treats a "call to missions" as something unique and distinct.

The issue is complicated by the prominent concept that everyone is a missionary. How often have we heard the expression that a person is either a mission field or a missionary; those without salvation in Jesus Christ are lost and are the object of mission efforts, wherever they are. But knowing Christ is accompanied by the responsibility to share Him with others and, hence, be a missionary wherever we are. There is some validity to that. We may not have the gift of evangelism, but everyone should be a witness. We may not be gifted and called to full-time vocational ministry, but everyone is expected to serve and minister as a member of the body of Christ. But is there a unique, distinct call of God for those who are to go as missionaries to cross-cultural, geographic locations away from one's home environment?

The Scripture seems to establish a strong precedent for such a call. Jesus was constantly calling people to come and be His disciples and to follow Him. On one occasion He sent out seventy disciples to be kingdom witnesses. But there was a special call to the Twelve who were to leave home and family and vocation to follow Him and give themselves fully to His kingdom purpose. Abraham clearly experienced that distinct call to leave his home and kindred to follow God even though he did not know where God would lead. That call was the foundation of missions as, in responding, he would become a blessing to the nations.

God appeared to Moses in the burning bush. He called Samuel as a boy in the night. He revealed to Jonah that he was to go to the despised city of Nineveh to represent God and call the people to repentance. Joshua, Gideon, Isaiah, Amos, and Jeremiah had a call that was to a distinct ministry and task. Some testified, as Jeremiah, that God had even planned that call before he was born—"Before I formed you in the womb I knew you, and before you were born I consecrated you; I have appointed you a prophet to the nations," (Jer. 1:5). Paul, in retrospect, acknowledged, "He who had set me apart, even from my mother's womb, and called me through His grace, was pleased to reveal His Son in me, that I might preach Him among the Gentiles" (Gal. 1:15–16). But one usually doesn't recognize that providential call until after the fact, when one has come to the point of responding, following God's will, and seeing the evidence of His hand upon one's life.

Paul had the most prominent mystical experience of all as he met Jesus on the road to Damascus; his call was accompanied by a blinding light and an audible voice. Few today would testify to hearing a voice or seeing a vision in which God revealed His will, though a specific mystical experience is not uncommon. God seems to create a knowledge and awareness of a need, prepare our heart and attitude to be receptive, and then through a sermon, an experience, or in private devotion speak to us with an unquestionable impression that we interpret as a call. Most would recognize, once that call is discerned, that God in His providence has had His hand upon them and determined that purpose and direction even before they acknowledged His lordship.

So, what is the basis of such selectivity? Does God single out an elite few to go overseas as missionaries while others remain exempt from the responsibility of taking the gospel to the nations? Jesus concluded the parable of the wedding feast in Matthew 22:14 with an interesting statement. He said, "Many are called, but few are chosen." He was obviously referring to those who had been invited and called to the wedding feast—to enter the kingdom of God—but not all responded to the invitation. Those who did respond were the "chosen" ones. He said to His disciples in John 15:16, "You did not choose Me, but I chose you, and appointed you, that you should go and bear fruit." It was not by virtue of their initiative and choice that they had become His disciples, but they were "chosen" by Christ. We often find ourselves being diverted by Calvinistic speculation as to why some are chosen and others are not, but that is to miss the point.

There are 195 references in the New Testament alone to the call of God. The people of God are identified as the *ekklesia*. This is interpreted as *assembly* or *church* but literally means "the called-out ones." First Peter 2:9 says, "You are a chosen people, a royal priesthood, a holy nation, a people belonging to God, that you might declare the praises of Him who called you out of darkness into His marvelous light." While that may express a general call that involves all born-again believers, are there those to whom God has given special talents and gifts for the purpose of sharing the gospel across cultures?

The call of Isaiah would be helpful to our understanding of who is called or chosen. In the sixth chapter of Isaiah, the prophet testifies of his encounter with God, and in verse 8 he says, "Then I heard the voice of the Lord, saying, 'Whom shall I send, and who will go for Us?' Then I said, 'Here am I. Send me!'" It was not a personal call that Isaiah heard; it was a generic call. He had come into God's presence and seen Him high and exalted. He recognized His lordship and that God had every right and claim on his life. He had experienced God's cleansing and anointing of his lips. He had come into an intimate relationship with God so that he could discern the yearning and the will of God seeking someone to go and represent Him to a people in darkness. Isaiah did not wait for God to tap him on the shoulder and say, "You're the one; I'm calling you." He did not respond to God's call, coerced to do something that was not his choosing, conscripted into service against his will. No, he took the initiative and invited God to send him. When he understood the need and clearly discerned God's will and desire, there was no alternative but to offer himself and say, "I'm available; let me be the one."

Why did Isaiah hear that appeal and offer himself as one distinct among others of God's people? Oswald Chambers gives us some insight here in speaking on this passage in his classic devotional book, *My Utmost for His Highest.* "The few who prove themselves the chosen ones are those who have come into a relationship with God whereby their disposition is altered and their ears unstopped. . . . They can hear that still small voice. It is not a matter of singling out Isaiah and saying, 'Now you go.' God did not lay a strong compulsion on him, but in the presence of God there was no other response but to say, 'Here am I. Send me!'"

There seem to be three steps that are prerequisite in discerning a specific, personal call to missionary service. The first is obviously an awareness of God's kingdom purpose and desire for His people to proclaim the gospel literally to the ends of the earth. Second, is a recognition of the needs of a lost world and the consequences of those who do not know the salvation God has provided through Jesus Christ. And third, is a relationship with God that is expressed in an availability to go—a willingness to offer oneself and follow God's leadership in that direction.

Our confusion regarding God's call is often created by an egotistical and self-centered perspective on God's will. I once heard Henry Blackaby speaking to a group of students who were in a critical time of preparation for what they would do with their lives. They wanted to know, as so many young people do, "How can I know God's will for my life?" Dr. Blackaby readily pointed out that they were asking the wrong question. He said that the appropriate question was, "What is God's will?" When we understand and discern God's will, then we can begin to discern how His purpose for us fits into it.

There can be no question about God's kingdom purpose and desire to bring a lost world to saving faith in Jesus Christ. This was inherent in the call to Abraham through which "all the families of the nations would be blessed," (Gen. 12:3). It was expressed through the psalmist, "All the ends of the earth will remember and turn to the LORD, and all the families of the nations will worship before Thee. For the kingdom is the LORD's, and He rules over the nations" (Ps. 22:27–28). It was expressed in the call to Israel to be His chosen people. They were to "proclaim good news of His salvation . . . tell of His glory among the nations, His wonderful deeds among all peoples" (1 Chron. 16:23–24). In Psalm 67:1–3 we read that God chose to bless them, to be gracious to them and favor them, but it was for a purpose, "That Thy way may be known on the earth, Thy salvation among all nations."

We are God's people, and He says to us, as He did to Israel in Isaiah 49:6, "It is too small a thing that you should be My Servant to raise up the tribes of Israel and to restore the preserved ones of Jacob; I have given You as a light to the nations that you should be My salvation to the ends of the earth." If God's desire and purpose for His people was not clearly evident, it became explicit with the coming of Jesus. He explained to His disciples in Luke 24:46–47 that His coming, His death and resurrection was to give us a message of hope and redemption for the nations. "Thus it is written, that the Christ should suffer and rise again from the dead the third day; and that repentance for forgiveness of sins should be proclaimed in His name to all the nations, beginning from Jerusalem." We tend to have an egotistical theology as if Jesus' death on the cross was just about us—to save us from our sins and give us assurance of eternal life in heaven. But it is about God's love for the whole world and His desire that none should be condemned but all might hear and respond to that message of repentance and salvation.

Romans 10:13–15 puts it in perspective. What Jesus did on the cross was for the whole world; the Scripture affirms that "whoever will call upon the name of the Lord will be saved." But then we are confronted with the question, "How then shall they call upon Him in whom they have not believed? And how shall they believe in Him whom they have not heard? And how shall they hear without a preacher? And how shall they preach unless they are sent?" Lest we think the use of the word "preach" relegates this mission responsibility to an elite category of clergy, the word literally means "to proclaim"—something we are all called to do. So who are the chosen ones? Who are those who are to be sent?

Let us examine some of those biblical models who were called. Abraham's call was (1) a call to leave the security of his home, family, and country; (2) it was a call to follow God by faith wherever He would lead; and (3) it was a call accompanied by a promise that God would go with him, guide him, and bless him. Moses was called in a unique encounter, but it was evident God had been preparing him for that call all his life. It was a personal call, a call to a specific task, and a call that was once again accompanied by the assurance God would be with him and equip him with all that he needed to fulfill God's purpose. Jonah was selected and called personally to go to a specific people and location. He was called to the task of going and preaching, just as Isaiah was called to "go and tell."

Often after an appointment service or mission conference someone will say to me, "Dr. Rankin, I would be willing to go as a missionary, but God has not called me." I'm afraid I have never been able to respond to such a statement tactfully. What I want to say is, "Do you have the same Bible I have? To whom do you think the Great Commission was given—just a handful of disciples on a hillside in Galilee or just an elite few among all of God's people?" When the IMB reached five thousand missionaries in 2001, that number represented only .03 percent of Southern Baptists, less than one out of three thousand born-again church members. And we tend to rationalize that if we haven't had a burning bush or Damascus Road experience, we are exempt. We can sit contentedly in our pew, enjoying the amenities of our American lifestyle, following our own plans and pursuit of the American dream with no responsibility for taking the gospel to the ends of the earth!

It is amazing how we can justify an unwillingness to hear God's call. There is a lost world in which researchers indicate more than 1.3 billion people have not even heard of Jesus. And the Bible reveals that God desires that none would perish but that all would know that Jesus came and died for them. Someone needs to go and tell them of God's love. Yet some would reason that they would be willing to go and meet that need, but they don't because God has chosen not to call them. I don't think so! The reason many never sense that call is that we have been deceived to think He calls only a select few. When all the time, as Oswald Chambers explained it, it is a matter of the disposition of our heart in which our ears are not sensitive to God's still small voice pleading, "Whom shall I send and who will go for Us?"

Once Jesus came and died, purchasing redemption for the sins of a lost world, the imperative of God's will became very clear for His people. Jesus said that the gospel of the kingdom was to be preached in all the world as a witness to all nations (Matt. 24:14). His final mandate to His followers was to go and make disciples of all nations (Matt. 28:19). He promised the power of His Holy Spirit for what purpose? That we might be His witnesses, even to the end of the earth (Acts 1:8). As someone expressed our lack of compliance with God's command, "What part of 'go' do you not understand?" Can anyone say, "I am exempt from involvement in God's mission, or this part of God's will doesn't apply to me"?

I received a letter a few years ago from a former pastor who had retired early due to health reasons and given himself to a prayer ministry. He said that he received the requests from our International Prayer Strategy Office and prayed faithfully for me and our work including systematic prayer for our missionaries around the world. He indicated that he had become aware of the massive numbers of unreached people groups that were yet unengaged with the gospel and the need for many more missionaries to be called out. He explained that he always chose a passage of Scripture to guide and affirm whatever he prayed for, and he had been praying Matthew 9:38 where we are told to pray that the Lord of the harvest will thrust out laborers into the harvest. Then he wrote, "Tell me, Dr. Rankin, why isn't God answering my prayers? Why isn't He doing what He promised? Why isn't He calling out the laborers that are needed?"

I was not sure how to answer him; I had been wondering the same thing myself. Then I happened to read an article by an eighteenth-century missions advocate who expressed the answer to our dilemma. He wrote, "God is calling out the laborers that are needed to reach a lost world, but the laborers are not responding to the call because of a closed mind, a calloused heart or a reluctant will." Most Christians are aware of the Great Commission and the need to evangelize a lost world but never apply it to themselves because their minds are closed to the possibility that God could call or use them. The task is something far removed from their home, business, family, and lifestyle and considered irrelevant to who they are and what they are doing. Many are closed to missionary service because they do not feel qualified or adequate for the task, forgetting that it is not ability but availability that God is able to use.

Few would ever admit that they are not sensitive to God's call because of a hardened heart that is calloused and indifferent to the needs of a lost world, but that is the case. Eternity is long and hell is real for those who do not know Jesus Christ. But we are indifferent to the fact that multitudes are dying everyday and entering a Christless eternity, not because they have rejected Jesus or have no spiritual needs that would lead them to embrace the gospel but because no one has cared enough to go and share the way of salvation. All we have to do is turn on our newscast to see a world in turmoil, conflict, despair, and spiritual darkness. But we wipe the images from our mind as easily as we turn off the television, never acknowledging that Jesus is the answer, and we are the ones that have the solution to a lost world.

But most likely we never hear and respond to God's call because of a reluctant will that is unwilling to trust God to lead us and use us. It is tragic that we have to term a response to God's call as a decision of "surrender" to His will. It does mean giving up our own selfish plans and ambitions, but the natural inclination of every Christian should be to willingly and joyfully place our lives in the Father's hands and count it a privilege of following wherever He leads. When we accept Jesus as our Savior, there should be no other desire except to serve Him and be obedient to His lordship. It is at the point of a surrendered will that most Christians struggle with God's call, rationalizing how to be obedient without sacrifice or denial of material comforts. Negotiating with God, expressing a willingness to serve Him where we are without having to go to the other side of the world. We seek to justify disobedience by questioning whether or not God is really calling us. But I assure you it is not Satan that is breaking your heart over a lost world and stirring your emotions with an inclination to walk the aisle and lay your life on the altar to go wherever God leads. That's your Lord speaking to your heart in the still small voice of His Spirit, and if He is Lord, your response is not optional.

It must be acknowledged that God usually brings one to a sense of prevailing conviction and "oughtness" regarding a personal call to missionary service, but also, especially initially, it will be accompanied generally by an element of uncertainty. That is because God requires an element of faith. Faith to follow is not reflected in clearly defined instructions and directions. In their book, *Run with the Vision*, Bob Sjogren and Bill and Amy Stearns make an interesting observation. "We don't sit and wait for a personal edict from heaven. . . . It's tough to steer a car while it's still parked. God's guidance to a particular ministry is more often a case of hearing His direction while we are moving on what we already know about His great plan. 'Whether you turn to the right or to the left, your ears will hear a voice behind you, saying, "This is the way: walk in it"' (Isa. 30:21)."

Obviously, God can call anyone He chooses for a particular task, including missions. And He can call in any way He chooses through the diverse personalities, experiences, and impressions He brings to bear on His people. He speaks through circumstance, through Scripture, and through the counsel of friends and the church to bring about a distinct impression of a call to missions. So let's examine what is involved in God's call.

IT IS A CALL TO KNOW GOD.

Like the invitation to the wedding feast, God calls whosoever will to come. Jesus invites us to come to Him and in repentance and faith to receive Him as Savior and Lord of our life. That is not a call to a select few but to everyone who will believe. However, we need to understand that is not just a call to salvation. When we trust Jesus as Savior, He comes to indwell our lives, and from that point on the call is one to know Him in an ever-growing intimate relationship. We are called, as Isaiah, to an encounter with God in all of His fullness so that every day we experience the reality of His grace and guidance. We recognize His sovereignty over our life and receive the abundant, victorious life that comes from knowing Him.

In several of the messages in this book, I tell about a missionary who was denied entry into his chosen field of service. During an interim period before his visa was finally granted, he and his family accepted several interim assignments in other countries. Later, reflecting on this experience, he commented, "We never knew where we would be from one month to the next this last year and a half. But one thing God has taught us is that He calls us, not so much to a place as to Himself." That is a call to everyone, and it is foundational to whatever vocational call we sense from God.

IT IS A CALL TO YIELD TO HIS LORDSHIP AND FOLLOW BY FAITH.

We fail to discern God's call because we want to know all the specifics about what we are to do, where we are to go and how we are to serve. We ask God to reveal His will and purpose for us, and then we decide whether or not that's what we are willing to do. But God doesn't play that game. He doesn't reveal His will only for you to reject it. His will is not a road map that shows the way to your ultimate destination because following God is a matter of faith. It is only when we sign a blank check, make an open commitment and truly yield our lives to whatever He wants us to do will He begin to reveal His calling. God seldom gives us the big picture. It is a matter of "followship"; we are called in submission to His lordship to be and become and do whatever He chooses. And that is a call for every believer.

Is this not the way it was with Paul? When Jesus appeared to him on the road to Damascus, Paul responded and asked, "Lord, what will you have me to do?" God didn't reveal at that time that He would lead him to the nations; He simply said to go into the city and to a certain house and it would be told him what he must do. Paul was obedient, and later Ananias revealed that God was calling Paul as an apostle to the Gentiles. God leads step-by-step because He wants us to follow by faith.

My wife, Bobbye, has often reflected on the time she was in high school and desperately wanting to know God's will for her life. One night during a youth revival she heard the evangelist say, "Young people, do you want to know God's will for your life? I can tell you." Bobbye sat up in her pew, alert to finally get the word on God's will for her life. The evangelist continued, "God wants you to be a witness for Him; that is God's will." A little disappointed that she still didn't know the vocation and direction she should go, the reality of that statement began to sink in and shaped what her life was to become. God's call is not so much to a place or a vocation as it is a call to be His witness wherever we are. It is a call to grow in Christian character. It is a call to serve God and others. If we respond to that call, we don't have a problem following when God opens a door of opportunity to move to another location. We see a new job offer as the hand of God enlarging our potential for kingdom impact. And if there is an impression that God could use us overseas, there is no reticence to follow His leading.

IT IS A CALL TO FIND OUR PLACE IN GOD'S LARGER MISSION TASK.

As Rick Warren begins his book, *The Purpose-Driven Life*, we need to discover that it is not about us. We tend to have a self-centered approach to the matter of God's will and whether or not He is calling us. A call to missions comes from an understanding that missions is God's basic purpose. This is what God is doing in the world, so He would not have a purpose for us personally that is disconnected and irrelevant to His plan to extend His kingdom to the ends of the earth. No one is exempt. It is a matter of discovering how we fit in God's overall plan.

Obviously God wants everyone to be a kingdom person and an influence where we live—witnessing and ministering to others, worshipping and serving Him. His will is to use us to bring about the lordship and reign of God in our home, our community, our church, and our nation. Everyone is called to pray and intercede for the nations and peoples of the world. Everyone is called to give and support missions through conscientious stewardship of the blessings God has given us. God calls us to be sensitive to opportunities for participation in mission trips, projects, and ministries through which we can extend our witness beyond our community and comfort zone. But the call to go, to be one who is chosen to plant his life on the mission field, comes from a willingness to find one's place in God's mission. We cannot excuse ourselves and compromise by saying, "I'll give, pray, and go on an occasional mission trip, and be unwilling to offer my life."

Certainly everyone is not called to go as a missionary, but everyone should be willing to go and even explore the opportunity to go. If it is God's will, it will be affirmed by one's church, by practicing one's spiritual gifts, and by recognizing a focused place and need that fits. I have often mused over the fact that Jesus told us in Matthew 9:38, "Therefore beseech the Lord of the harvest to send out workers into His harvest." Isn't God sovereign and capable of calling out the laborers whether we pray or not? Certainly, but perhaps He tells us to pray for laborers because He wants to convict us through our prayers that we are to be those laborers! Dr. Baker James Cauthen, former president of the Foreign Mission Board, used to say that everyone ought to be willing to go until God closes the door. We tend to have an inverted approach to our missions call and, instead of proceeding to go until God closes the door—and He will if it is not His calling and purpose—we say we are willing to go while all the time we are planning to stay!

For those who are not qualified or to whom God does close the door, that does not negate the call to missions. He calls some to go, but He calls others to send and to mobilize. If one stays at home, his influence as an advocate for missions should result in multiplied others being sent to the ends of the earth in lieu of going himself.

IT IS A CALL THAT IS ACCOMPANIED BY A VOLITIONAL RESPONSE.

God doesn't coerce anyone into being a missionary. He is not the author of a call where someone reluctantly responds out of a burden of guilt as if someone has to do it. The call of God will find a joyful response. One who hears and senses the call of God will receive it humbly, counting it a privilege that they would be chosen to be one that could take the gospel to a lost world. But it is a call that requires a decision and response.

Many people never have confirmation of a call because it was never met with a conscious decision to trust God and follow as He leads. Often after an appointment service an elderly person will speak to me and acknowledge that years ago they had felt a call to missions. They go on to explain that they had been diverted due to a spouse that did not share their call, or once they delayed responding, due to the demands of a job and a growing family, the call was never fulfilled. Many question the call or continue wondering whether or not it is God's will because of indecisiveness. A call to missions will be confirmed by a conscious and confident response in saying, "Yes, here am I."

That intentional response is also a recognition that God provides the resources and equipping needed. Many are deterred in a call to missions because of a low self-esteem or a feeling of not being qualified or adequate for the task. In fact, those who feel most unworthy and inadequate may be the most qualified, for they are the ones to whom God can entrust His power. God does not call the qualified; He qualifies the called. He equips every Christian surrendered to His will with the power of the Holy Spirit. Paul discovered this important principle. That is why he was used so effectively in spite of the fact he considered himself the least of the apostles and unworthy to be called an apostle. It was in his weakness that he was made strong in Jesus Christ. We must never forget that principle and realize a lack of ability is no excuse or justification for not responding to a call to missions.

Remember that the Great Commission is framed by two very important verses. In Matthew 28:18 Jesus said, "All power is given me in heaven and in earth." In the next verse (it begins with "Go therefore') He tells us to go and make disciples of all nations. Then He closes by reminding us that He goes with us, in all that power and authority, when we go in obedience to His call. When a missionary goes and plants his life among a people who are lost, there goes with him the indwelling presence of Jesus. It is His power that draws people to salvation through our witness and ministry. Obviously there are certain qualifications and educational requirements that are needed for effective missionary service, but missionaries don't respond to God's call because of their ability and skills; it is because of their confidence that Jesus goes with them when they respond with a commitment to go.

IT IS A CALL TO SUFFERING AND SACRIFICE.

This may be the point at which many struggle, rationalize away God's call, and never come to the point of obedient surrender. Make no mistake about it; the call to follow Jesus has always been a call to self-denial. The call to discipleship is a call to take up one's cross and die. That's not just a call to missionary service but to everyone. But it is easy to presume we have fulfilled that criteria in the comfort zone of an American lifestyle and dedicated service in our church fellowship. A call to missions brings the reality of suffering and sacrifice to the forefront. And many forfeit the privilege of being the ones to take Christ to a lost world because of their unwillingness to embrace possible suffering and inconvenience. Many reject the joy and reward of following Christ in obedience because of a conditional surrender that draws a bottom line regarding what one is willing to do or where one is willing to go. The call to missions is not so much a call to serve in a foreign country as it is a call to go all the way with Christ.

Why would one readily give up the security, comforts, and success of life in America and even go to a place of danger and risk? It is because of a commitment to a higher priority. Paul expressed that priority in Philippians 3:10, "That I may know Him, and the power of His resurrection and the fellowship of His sufferings, being conformed to His death." The call to missions is a call to know Christ and experience the fullness of His resurrected power, but with that call is a willingness to embrace the sufferings of Christ and die to all selfish ambition and desires. First Peter 2:21 expressed it, "For you have been called for this purpose, since Christ also suffered for you, leaving you an example for you to follow in His steps."

Jesus told His disciples that they would be hated and even killed for His sake, but Romans 8:18 puts it in perspective when Paul observed, "For I consider that the sufferings of this present time are not worthy to be compared with the glory that is to be revealed to us." The call to missions is not an easy call. It is not one that can be negotiated to provide for assurance of comforts and safety. One is venturing into Satan's territory, and the principalities and powers of darkness will not readily relinquish their control over the kingdoms of the world. The call is to suffering and sacrifice; but just as Jesus endured the cross for the joy that was set before Him, the joy of a lost world knowing Jesus is worth it all.

So, what is a call of God? It is a call to salvation and to know Him. It is a call to obedience and holiness. It is a call to abide in Christ and glorify Him as a kingdom person. It is a call to be His witness wherever we are.

But what about a missionary call? How can one know with certainty God is calling you to missionary service. No one can give you a formula. No one can interpret God's will for you. But it may be an oversimplification to say that if you are sensing God may be calling you to missions, He probably is. If not, He will make it evident as you follow Him by faith and willingly offer your life to Him.

A call to missions will be characterized by a sensitivity to a lost world and the need for someone to go. It will grow out of a surrendered heart that is committed to the lordship of Jesus Christ in one's life. It will come in the context of witnessing, serving God in obedience and seizing opportunities to fulfill His mission where we are. And it will be confirmed by one's church fellowship in recognition of the gifts God has given us. But never forget, it always involves an element of trust—making ourselves available and following as God leads. Proverbs 3:5-6 says, "Trust in the LORD with all your heart and do not lean on your own understanding. In all your ways acknowledge Him, and He will direct your paths."

For many, the needs of a lost world have been a primary factor in their call, but it has got to be more than just a response to need. For some, it has been a desire to be obedient personally to what our Lord has commanded us to do, but it must go beyond just a sense of obligation to God's will. God will use many factors, experiences, and influences to reveal His call, but it has to be motivated by a heart for God and His heart for the nations. A love for God will result in a devotion to serve Him and live for Him that will know no boundaries and impose no contingency clause on wherever He leads and whatever He leads us to do. An intimate relationship with God will lead one to have His heart for the world that will project one out of a narrow, self-centered provincialism and a willingness to say, "Wherever you lead, I'll go."

1

FULFILLING THE GREAT COMMISSION

Matthew 28:19–20

If there is any verse of Scripture a good Southern Baptist knows, next to John 3:16 or the 23rd Psalm, it would be the Great Commission in Matthew 28:19–20. Having completed His earthly ministry and finished His atoning work on the cross, the resurrected Lord gathered His followers on a hillside in Galilee for final instructions prior to ascending to the Father. He said, "Go, therefore, and make disciples of all nations, baptizing them in the name of the Father, the Son and the Holy Spirit, teaching them to observe all things I have commanded unto you; and, lo, I am with you always, even to the end of the age."

Although we are familiar with the Great Commission, it is sad that so few Christians feel any responsibility for fulfilling it. Oh, we know this reflects God's desire to evangelize a lost world and extend His kingdom to the ends of the earth, but we tend to just relegate it collectively to our mission programs. Most church members feel they have been obedient by supporting missionaries through the Cooperative Program and Lottie Moon Christmas Offering, sending someone else to do the work. But you are being appointed because you have taken personally the command of our Lord to disciple the nations. Some of you did not let the familiarity of this passage become a trite cliché; God's Spirit convicted you that it was your responsibility to go. You responded in obedience, and that's why you are here, on your way to a foreign country to make disciples. So I want to remind you of the purpose, the power and the promise of the Great Commission.

THE PURPOSE OF THE GREAT COMMISSION

Contrary to the perception of many people, as well as many sermons, including some of my own, Jesus does not command us to go in this passage. The mandate to go into all the world is a necessity if we are to be obedient to disciple the nations and be His witnesses to the ends of the earth. You have been called to go, and for you personally there is no other alternative but to be obedient to that call. That's why you are leaving a business in Texas, a pastorate in Mississippi, or family in North Carolina or Georgia. You are going to places like the Ukraine, Russia, India, and countries we cannot name publicly because God has told you to go. But in the Great Commission Jesus uses a participle that in effect says, as you are going, this is what you are to do. When He says to baptize and to teach, He once again uses a participle to explain what you do to make disciples.

There is only one transitive verb in this passage, and it clearly and explicitly reflects the purpose of the Great Commission. That is the command to make disciples. Disciples are students or learners, those that become true followers of Jesus Christ. For one to become a disciple, he is to be baptized. Administering water baptism does not provide salvation or make one a Christian. But Jesus made it clear that a disciple is one who openly and publicly identifies with the death, burial, and resurrection of Jesus Christ who makes salvation possible to all who come to Him in repentance and faith.

You may not be aware that the International Mission Board does not report professions of faith in our work around the world. We have many volunteer teams going overseas who return reporting thousands of professions of faith. We would like to think that everyone who lifted their hand in response to a public invitation or prayed the sinners prayer was genuinely born again, but we can't really know whether or not there was understanding of that decision and a sincere repentant heart; we can only be faithful to proclaim the message and invite people to respond. But we can assume that when one crosses the line to step away from cultural religious traditions, the darkness and bondage of sin or futile works-based personal efforts to find salvation and publicly confesses that through the testimony of baptism, he is a follower of Jesus Christ; it is the first step to becoming a true disciple. Last year we rejoiced that our missionaries reported more than 600,000 new believers baptized around the world.

Also a part of the task of making disciples is teaching obedience to what Jesus commanded, how one is to live as one who identifies with the Christ life. As a new missionary I was perplexed by this responsibility, stated by Jesus as, "teaching them to observe all that I commanded you." Upon leading a new group to accept Christ and be baptized, I would wonder how in the world

I could teach them everything that Jesus taught. They had no background whatsoever to understand the Christian life. What is the first priority? What should I teach them first? I tried to outline all the lessons for a new Christian, the things that Jesus taught, and realized it would take years. I finally realized what Jesus was saying was to teach them obedience. I gave them Bibles and instructed them to read them, believe what it said and do what it taught, and that took care of it.

But baptizing and teaching is how we fulfill the Great Commission. What is its purpose? The very nature of a transitive verb demands an object, and the object of the imperative verb "make disciples" is quite clear. It is all nations. But the word Jesus uses for "nations" isn't one that means the geopolitical countries portrayed on our maps. The expression in Greek is *panta ta ethne*, which literally means all the peoples. We often say the world is not a pancake; it's a waffle. If you had pancakes for breakfast and poured syrup on them, it probably flowed all over that smooth round surface; but not so with your waffle. Waffles have all those little squares separated by ridges, and if you want syrup all over your waffle, you have to be very deliberate to pour it in every little square. Well, the world is not a smooth homogeneous group of people who are all alike; even each country is a matrix of languages and cultures.

For example, missionaries have labored many years in Pakistan and poured the syrup of the gospel among the Punjabi people, but the Sindhi, Baluchi, and Pashtu are yet to be evangelized. We have had missionary work in Nigeria for 150 years; and there are more than a million Baptists there, mostly among the Hausa and Yoruba, but we have identified over two hundred people groups like the Fulani and Kanuri that have not become disciples of Christ. I just returned from a two-week trip to South America where missionaries have been working more than one hundred years. There are strong churches in almost every Latin American country. In one of our meetings, the regional leadership gave a report that indicated more than four hundred tribes and people groups, isolated in the Amazon jungles or remote valleys of the Andes, have yet to hear the gospel.

This is the purpose of the Great Commission. We have diluted it to make it apply to whatever we do in witness and ministry, but the purpose is to make disciples, followers of Jesus from among every tribe, people, tongue, and nation. And we can do that only by going to where they are. The mission and purpose of the International Mission Board is "that all peoples may know Him." I often ask myself in considering the abundant resources and manpower of Southern Baptists, "By what criteria should any people be denied access to the gospel when we have been so richly blessed?"

You have answered the call to go, but never forget the purpose for which you go is to make disciples. When I was on the field as a missionary in Indonesia, we would always give our report at our annual mission meeting. We would report on the number of baptisms, the number of new churches that had been planted in the previous year, how many mission points had been started and other activities. One year someone in the group asked, following my report, "How many disciples did you make this year?" I had to hesitate; though I had recorded the number baptized, how many had truly become followers of Christ, living in obedience to His teaching, emulating His lifestyle? I wasn't too confident of that answer. But it is the disciples that will multiply your witness, win others, start churches, and extend the kingdom of God far beyond what you could do. God is sending you to the peoples and nations to the ends of the earth to make disciples. That is His purpose.

THE POWER OF THE GREAT COMMISSION

It is an awesome task to be confronted with the responsibility to fulfill the purpose of the Great Commission as you go as a missionary. It requires planting your life among people within a strange culture, learning a new language, and possibly accepting a deprived lifestyle where you will not have many of the amenities you have come to take for granted here in America. You will encounter opposition and antagonism across the Muslim and Hindu world. You will confront restrictive government policies in China and former communist countries. You will encounter indifference among cultural Catholics in Latin America and secular humanists in Europe. But you must never forget that the Great Commission is framed by two very important verses.

In Matthew 28:18 Jesus says, "All authority has been given to Me in heaven and on earth." Now let that sink in for just a moment. There is no authority in all the universe that exceeds the authority of Jesus Christ. He has the power to do whatever He plans and determines to do. And He tells us what that is in the following verse. We are to go and make disciples of all nations. But we do so in His power and authority. It is not because of your education, language skills, or personal abilities that you will be able to make disciples of those who have never heard of Jesus or have no interest in following the Christian faith. You will have an extensive time of orientation before you go to the field and an initial time of language study and training once you arrive, but that is not sufficient to guarantee that you will have results and success in bringing people to Christ. It is the power of Christ that indwells the message of the gospel, the message you go to proclaim.

I continue to be amazed at reports of Muslims coming to faith in Christ. When we lived in Indonesia, the largest Muslim country in the world, we saw new believers who were rejected by their family, ostracized by their community, lost their job, even had their life threatened. Why would they turn their back on their culture, society, and religion to become a follower of Jesus? There was no explanation except the power of the gospel. Never forget that you are inadequate for the task. It is not because of who you are that God has chosen and called you, but you can go with confidence because you go in the power of Jesus Christ.

THE PROMISE OF THE GREAT COMMISSION

Not only did Jesus say, "All authority has been given to Me in heaven and on earth," He frames the Great Commission by adding in verse 20, "And lo, I am with you always, even to the end of the age." That's the promise of the Great Commission. When you go in obedience to God's call, He goes with you. When you go and plant your life among a people group overseas in order to fulfill His purpose to disciple the nations, He goes with you, in all that power and authority. It is a promise of His presence. He has said, as God said to the children of Israel, "I will never leave you nor forsake you" (Josh. 1:5 NIV).

I heard one missionary express it this way. He said the two most important words of the Great Commission are "go . . . lo." He went on, "No lo: no go." He grasped the significance of what you should realize as you are appointed to missionary service. You do not go alone, but Jesus goes with you. If He does not go with you, you have no business going to a foreign land, venturing into Satan's territory, and presuming to be His witness to a lost world. Upon hearing this, someone pointed out that this was similar to what Moses said as he faced the challenge of the people of Israel moving out to go to the promise land. In Exodus 33:15 he said to God, "If Thy presence does not go with us, do not lead us up from here." You could paraphrase this as, "No lo, no go, signed Mo!" He recognized they had no business going from their camp in the wilderness if God did not go with them.

You are here being commissioned because of your obedience to God's call, and you can be assured of the promise of the Great Commission, that His presence will go with you and empower you and use you to fulfill His purpose to disciple the nations.

2

A LIGHT IN THE DARKNESS

Isaiah 60:1–3

Our Global Research Department is constantly mapping the nations and people groups of the world as a tool to keep us focused on our task of discipling the nations. Identifying those that are yet to have access to the gospel and unreached people groups helps us to avoid complacency, taking pride in impressive statistical growth, and keeps us pushing to the edge in order to fulfill the Great Commission of our Lord. Recently they designed a world map on which the relative contrast between lostness and evangelized was portrayed in varying shades of gray. Areas and people groups where the gospel had been proclaimed and churches established were almost white; those that had yet to hear of Jesus were almost black with most of the world somewhere in between. As you stood off and looked at that map, yours eyes were drawn to what appeared to be a jet-black center of a target representing Central and Southern Asia.

I just returned from a two-week trip to South Asia with a group of pastors. Though I had worked in this part of the world for many years, I cannot return without being overwhelmed by the massive numbers of people, the poverty and suffering. If we had the same population density of India, there would be three billion people in the United States. Bangladesh is a little country the size of Arkansas with a hundred and forty million people. Can you imagine what that would do to our economy and lifestyle? Although there is a growing middle class and no lack of beautiful scenery, the impression is one of a strained infrastructure where aesthetics and comforts have given way to a struggle for survival. Yet the greatest impact of such a place that leaves one emotional and broken is the lostness and spiritual depravity of those in bondage to their cultural heritage.

In the Hindu holy city of Varanasi, we gazed on literally thousands of people bathing in the polluted waters of the Ganges River, believing it would bring them cleansing from sin. We saw the priests chanting over bodies being cremated and ashes being sprinkled in the water in hopes of a sequence of endless reincarnations that would bring one hope of enlightenment. It was impossible to become numb and indifferent to the ubiquitous scene of worship and sacrifices being offered to lifeless idols. Being there during the Muslim fasting month of Ramadan, the futile devotion of followers of Mohammed could not be ignored as they flocked to their mosques to pray to a punitive god who provides no assurance of their eternal hope. Our last morning in Nepal we prayer walked at a temple where people were observing an annual ritual of seeking favor from a syncretistic collection of Hindu and Buddhist images. The burning incense, cacophony of clanging bells, sprinkling of holy water, and kissing the shrine all testified to the darkness and hopelessness of people without Christ.

The Bible uses an expression to describe these people that is not appreciated by adherents of other religions. They are referred to as those dwelling in darkness. That appears condescending to those who think they are enlightened and grasp the way of truth. It appears to be arrogant to those who think that all religious expressions and beliefs are simply diverse roads that lead to God. It is offensive to the sophisticated rationalism of postmodern attitudes that contend there are no absolutes, and whatever one chooses to believe will do.

MOST OF THE PEOPLE OF THE WORLD LIVE IN DARKNESS.

What is darkness? It is simply the absence of light. If Jesus is the light of the world, then where there is no knowledge of Jesus, the people are in darkness. This is not something that we have contrived as Christians to put us in a position superior to others. It was Jesus Himself who said in John 8:12, "I am the light of the world." In John 12:46 He said, "I have come as a light into the world, that whoever believes in Me should not abide in darkness."

You know what it means to be in darkness. Have you ever experienced being in a room without windows when the electricity went off? Do you recall the pitch-black darkness around you as you groped for familiar surroundings, struggling to put your hand on a flashlight or find the candles and matches, desperate to bring light back into your world? To be in the dark means being unable to see; it means being thrust into uncertainty, insecure and directionless, not knowing where to go or how to get there. Why are children often afraid of the dark? Not being able to see, it conjures images of the boogey-man, threats and dangers that must be avoided and appeased. Can you imagine living your life in the dark? As one new believer in this part of the world said, "When you are born in the dark and live your entire life in darkness, you don't even know what light is."

That characterizes most of the people of our world. Speaking of the belief in millions of gods and idol worship in India, a local Christian explained that people are desperate to appease the spirits and the pervasive pantheon of gods lest they are harmed or punished. There is no love, no peace, no assurance, no praise, nothing but darkness of the life and of the soul. One billion people in China, even with the responsiveness and harvest taking place in that land, are still in darkness. One billion people in India and South Asia are living in darkness. One billion Muslims across Northern Africa, the Middle East, and into Asia worship in darkness. Multitudes following the rituals of cultural Catholicism in Latin America, secular humanism in Europe, and in bondage to animistic fetishes and superstitions in Africa are all dwelling in darkness. Why? Because they have chosen the hopelessness and futility that leads to death? No. It is simply because of the absence of light.

JESUS CAME AS THE LIGHT OF THE WORLD.

There are testimonies of this fact throughout Scripture, but I especially like the proclamation in Isaiah 60:1–3, "Arise, shine; for your light has come, and the glory of the LORD has risen upon you. For behold, darkness will cover the earth, and deep darkness the peoples; but the LORD will rise upon you, and His glory will appear upon you. And nations will come to your light, and kings to the brightness of your rising." Darkness covers the earth and a deep darkness is over the people, but Isaiah spoke of that day when the Lord's glory will appear and nations will come to His light.

The apostle Paul explained that this was our own personal experience as those who were once lost but have now been saved. Colossians 1:13–14 says, "For He delivered us from the domain of darkness, and transferred us to the kingdom of His beloved Son, in whom we have redemption, the forgiveness of sins." That light did not come through our own works and efforts of religious piety. Second Corinthians 4:6 explains, "For it is the God who commanded light to shine out of darkness, who has shone in our hearts to give the light of the knowledge of the glory of God in the face of Jesus Christ."

But when Jesus identified Himself as the "light of the world," it was truly a light that was to illuminate all the world with the knowledge of God and His redemptive love. It was something that was meant to shine not only in our hearts, but it was intended to dispel the darkness in Africa, India, and the uttermost parts of the earth. It was more than two thousand years ago when the Light came; why does darkness still cover the earth? It is the very nature of light to overcome darkness. When you turn on the light switch upon entering a dark room, the light and dark do not struggle to see which will prevail and overpower the other. The mere presence of light dispels the darkness. That is why Jesus changed the metaphor in Matthew 5:14 to say to His followers, "You are the light of the world."

YOU ARE TO CARRY THE LIGHT INTO THE WORLD.

It would be a distortion to say to missionaries being appointed that they are the ones who have the responsibility of taking the light to a world in darkness, for all of us who have come to the light and know Jesus Christ have that responsibility. There is darkness all around us in people that do not yet know Christ as their own personal Savior. But you are the ones God has called to leave your comfort zone, the warmth and support of your church fellowship where there is an abundance of light, to go to the dark corners of the world. You are going to Russia and the republics of Central Asia where communist policies for generations propagated an atheistic ideology that has kept people in darkness.

You are going to plant your lives to light a candle in the midst of the pervasive darkness of India, the Middle East, the African heartland, and Latin America. Some of you are going to Western Europe, a continent that once knew the light, but the light has grown dim and is floundering in the deepening shadows of lostness.

How do you penetrate the darkness that is so widespread? How do you bring light to hearts that have been darkened by generations of cultural and religious practices that have barricaded the countries and peoples of the world behind a wall of darkness? You will go through several weeks of orientation and training before you leave and upon arrival on the field. You will learn communication skills and gain an understanding of the world views and beliefs of the people to whom you are being assigned. You will be trained in culturally relevant ways to witness effectively. But the answer is very simple. What is it that will dispel the darkness and bring light to a dark world? It is a story—yes, a simple story. The story of God who was born in a manger in Bethlehem and became a man. It is the story of a Savior who lived and died on the cross and rose again to pay the penalty of sin and reconcile us to God. It is your story and testimony of how you found a new life in Jesus Christ. That story, the good news of the gospel, is what will cause the light to shine in the midst of darkness.

It is expressed so well in a familiar hymn we don't often sing these days.

We've a story to tell to the nations,
That shall turn their hearts to the right,
A story of truth and mercy,
A story of peace and light.

But I especially want to remind you of the chorus:

For the darkness shall turn to dawning, and the dawning to noonday
bright,
And Christ's great kingdom shall come on earth, The kingdom of love
and light.

All over the world the darkness is turning to dawning as unreached people groups are hearing the gospel for the first time. Last year mission strategies were initiated among 192 unreached people groups who heard the gospel for the first time. Churches were started among the Gujjar, Mishaba, Ditammari, and many others. The light is dawning among the Kabyle Berber in Northern Africa, Iraq, and Afghanistan and all across the Muslim world. But in other places the dawning is turning to noonday bright.

Several years ago I coordinated our work in South Asia and remember our early missionaries to Nepal initiating work among the Tamang, the Rai, and the Lomi people groups. On my recent visit I had the privilege of meeting with our IMB personnel in that country and asked how the work was going. Who is currently working with these peoples? I was told no one is because they have all been evangelized, and they are spreading the gospel throughout the Himalayan valleys to other people groups. In another South Asia country there is reported to be over 400,000 Muslim background believers who have been drawn to the light that is now shining brightly.

Isaiah indicated that the light would come and gave us the promise that the glory of the Lord will appear and nations will come to your light. We can be confident that Jesus, the Light that has come into the world, will draw those from every tribe, people, and tongue and nation to the light. And that is why you are being appointed. It is to carry the light by telling the story to the ends of the earth. But make no mistake about the nature of the task and the challenge that entails. Paul described it in Acts 26:18 in his testimony before King Agrippa as one of opening their eyes, turning them "from darkness to light, and from the power of Satan unto God." You will do that as you realize it is not about your assignment, your job description or platform, but it is in faithfully telling the story of Jesus and lifting Him up before a world in darkness.

3

THOSE OF WHOM THE WORLD IS NOT WORTHY

Hebrews 11:32–38

In the past year and a half four IMB missionaries were killed in Iraq, three missionaries were murdered at our Baptist Hospital in Yemen and another died in a terrorist bombing in the Philippines. It is not very comforting to be reminded of our vulnerability as you are being appointed to be dispersed all over the world. The victims of these incidents were missionaries, but they are a relative few among a multitude of national believers who have had to suffer for their faith. Christians numbering in the thousands have been massacred in Indonesia, imprisoned and tortured in China and other communist countries, and even martyred throughout Muslim countries.

The questions invariably emerge from grieving families and a skeptical public: "Why do missionaries go to places of danger? Why do they put themselves at risk in places their witness is not welcome?" In the volatile world in which we live, however, it is no longer because of their Christian witness but simply the fact we are Americans that makes us vulnerable to global terrorists. There is not sufficient time to explain why missionaries go to places such as Iraq and Yemen, as we have tried to do in media interviews. Very simply, however, it is because Jesus is the answer to the hatred, turmoil, and oppression throughout our world. It is not Western diplomacy, military might, or UN peacekeepers, but the gospel of Jesus Christ that holds the answer for a world in need, hope for people in despair, and salvation for those in the darkness and bondage of sin. We go because our Lord told us to go, and obedience is not optional.

It is amazing that no one questions the obligation of those serving in the military to follow their orders and to be deployed wherever their commander chooses to send them. We may not agree with military engagement by our country overseas, but we would never question the commitment of the soldiers who follow their orders to go, even though their lives are at risk. Yet we readily evaluate whether or not we will be obedient to our Commander in Chief who deployed us to go into all the world and share the gospel. He did not qualify His Great Commission mandate by saying we are to go but only if it is safe to do so or only to those places where no danger is involved. Some of you are going to places that entail risk; no, all of you are going to places where your safety cannot be guaranteed. You would not have the assurance of safety even if you were to stay at home. But you go in obedience to God's call, not out of concern for yourself but that a lost world would know Jesus.

That was the conviction of Larry and Jean Elliott in transferring to Iraq after twenty-five years in Honduras. It was the calling of Karen Watson and David and Carrie McDonnall, who in the last year found themselves so driven by love for the Iraqi people that the passion of their lives was to reach out to them, providing for their needs and demonstrating the reality of God's love. Many beautiful testimonies have been shared by their coworkers and by families, and it was said on more than one occasion that these were those "of whom the world was not worthy."

That expression comes from Hebrews 11:38 toward the conclusion of the familiar roll call of faith found in that chapter. It tells us that by faith Abel offered a more acceptable sacrifice, Enoch walked with God, Noah built the ark, Abraham followed God, Moses left the luxuries of Egypt to lead the people of God, and by faith the children of Israel passed through the Red Sea. We are told of Isaac and Jacob and Joseph, of Gideon and Samson and David, and others "who by faith conquered kingdoms, performed acts of righteousness, obtained promises, shut the mouths of lions, quenched the power of fire, escaped the edge of the sword, . . . [and] put foreign armies to flight" (Heb. 11:33–34). What was it that made these unworthy of this world?

FOCUS ON A GOAL AND REWARD BEYOND THIS LIFE.

It was because their lives were not focused on this life but on something of eternal significance. They were "looking for the city . . . whose architect and builder is God . . . a better country, that is a heavenly one. Therefore God is not ashamed to be called their God; for He has prepared a city for them" (Heb. 11:10, 16).

Our missionaries who were victims of terrorist gunfire in Iraq were not focused on the values and things of this life. Their passion was not about where they were going in life and attaining success and recognition. They had been trained and were very conscientious about issues of security, but their own safety and comfort was not the compelling priority of their lives. They understood the despair of people who were suffering; they comprehended the excessive darkness of hearts without Christ. They recognized the eternal consequences of those who had no opportunity to hear of God's love, and by faith they followed God and were obedient even unto death. They, like Moses and Abraham and others, recognized they were strangers and exiles on earth, and they stayed focused on that promise of reward; for them, it was that day when there would be people, including Iraqis, from every tribe and people and tongue and nation gathered around the throne and worshipping the Lamb of God.

When Carrie McDonnall, the one survivor, regained consciousness a week after the incident and was told that her husband David and the others had died, she said, "We have got to quit treating this life as home." She didn't expound on that statement but apparently realized that as long as we look on this life as home, we will be caught up in its values, seeking material comforts, worrying about our future, how our investments are doing, building our homes, preparing for a comfortable retirement, seeking fulfillment in things of the world. Carrie and these others realized that there is something more important, more lasting and more valuable. There is something worth giving your life for, and, yes, worth dying for. How can you be one of whom the world is not worthy?

LIKE ABRAHAM, FOLLOW GOD BY FAITH.

Abraham did not know where God was leading, but he followed by faith. That is not like the world. The world would say plan your life and follow your plan. Determine what you want to do. Pursue that which will bring you personal success and fulfillment. That's the course that is valued and worthy of the world. But "by faith, Abraham, when he was called, obeyed . . . and he went out, not knowing where he was going" (Heb. 11:8). Parents have a problem when they see you making this kind of decision. They love you. They sincerely want what is best for you. They have invested in your education to enable you to be a successful doctor, teacher, or business man. They have even celebrated your call to ministry and have taken pride in your serving the Lord in a church here in America. But to leave it all to go overseas doesn't make a lot of sense. And here you are going to Russia, and India, and China. You are going to plant your lives in places like Kazakhstan, Lebanon, Syria, Ethiopia, Angola, and Cote d'Ivoire. Some of you don't even know where you will be living, but you are obeying God's call to Latin America, to Africa, Asia, and Europe; you have said, "I'll be the one to engage that unreached people group." You don't know how and where you will end up, but that doesn't matter. Your only concern is obedience and a willingness to trust God and follow Him by faith.

The world is not worthy of that kind of attitude. They don't understand it. It just doesn't fit our postmodern, self-centered philosophy and lifestyle that says it's all about me. It's not a matter of where you are going or your place of assignment. If you are to be one of whom the world is not worthy, you will not get locked into a predetermined location but will follow by faith wherever God leads, wherever an open door of opportunity emerges, and will keep your eyes on Him.

LIKE MOSES, REJECT PLEASURES AND RICHES TO IDENTIFY WITH THE PEOPLE.

Some of you have already come to the point of selling the beautiful home of your dreams. You have walked away from lucrative businesses and promising careers. That's not the kind of decisions that get applauded by the world. You are going to places that will require an austere lifestyle. Many of the amenities we take for granted here will not be available; your children will not have the social outlets that are so valued by the world's standards, reflected by soccer moms shuttling kids from ball games to band practice to church fellowship in a hectic pace of keeping up with social pressures and expectations.

Larry and Jean Elliott's three children all testified to the wonderful legacy their parents had left them, a model of devotion and obedience to Christ. Larry had left a prominent engineering career to go to Honduras. His skills led him into relief work, drilling wells to provide pure drinking water, rebuilding homes and schools in the aftermath of hurricane Mitch, providing sanitation to destitute and neglected villages. He gave his life for the sake of the people of Middle America, but it was primarily that they might have an eternal hope in Jesus Christ. I can assure you there is one thing the Elliott children have not had to do in the aftermath of the death of their parents. They have not had to deliberate on what they will do with a massive financial inheritance. Larry and Jean chose the risks, and they chose to live among the impoverished people of Honduras and those suffering in Iraq. They chose a meager missionary salary instead of the riches and treasures of an American lifestyle, for they, like Moses, were looking for a greater reward.

FINALLY, DO NOT SHUN SUFFERING AND DEATH FOR THE CAUSE OF CHRIST.

We are told of these heroes who won the prize; they conquered kingdoms, escaped the sword, and obtained the promises. But there were others of whom we are told that also by faith "were tortured, . . . experienced mockings and scourgings, yes, also chains and imprisonment. They were stoned, . . . sawn in two, . . . put to death with the sword . . . destitute, afflicted, ill-treated"—"not accepting their own release, in order that they might obtain a better resurrection" (Heb. 11:35–37). You can only read this passage with deep emotion and reverence. The Scripture tells us they could have avoided these consequences of their faith, but they chose not to accept their release that they might obtain a better resurrection. They did not seek to avoid suffering and death for their own benefit or simply that they might have a martyr's crown but that their witness would bear fruit, and there would be a greater resurrection of those who believed because "they did not love their life even to death" (Rev. 12:11).

We need to explode a prominent and often quoted myth that the safest place on earth is the center of God's will. Would we conclude that these victims in Iraq were not in the center of God's will? Why do some die while others do not; does God in His providence sort out, like the tares and the wheat, those that are in His will, placing a hedge of protection around them, while others are left vulnerable to the forces of an evil and fallen world? Not at all; in fact, Jesus said, "In this world you shall have tribulation" (John 16:33). He told His disciples, "An hour is coming for everyone who kills you to think that he is offering service to God. And these things they will do because they have not known the Father, or Me" (John 16:2–3). No, you are not exempt from danger and suffering, and possibly death, just because you are going in faithful obedience as a missionary. God does not put a hedge of protection and safety around you because you have answered His call. In fact, He does not guarantee that you will see response and success in your witness because of your commitment. Your call is to obedience—period—not for the sake of results, not for the assurance of safety but only for His glory and for His purpose to be fulfilled.

At Karen Watson's funeral a friend reflected that they could tell something was happening in her life after each mission trip she went on. Finally, last year she resigned her job, sold her house, sold her car and all her earthly possessions. She packed what was left in a duffle bag and headed for Iraq. Now, a year later, her friend reflected, all that was left was her duffle bag, her Bible, and her devotion to Christ. Was it worth it? Karen had written a letter and left it with her pastor to be opened and read in the unlikely event of her death. It was a two-page letter that began, "Since you are reading this letter, it is apparent I will not be returning." She continued, "There are no regrets. My calling is to obedience, suffering is expected, and His glory is my reward." She was one of whom the world was not worthy.

I challenge you to be one of whom the world is not worthy by focusing on values beyond this life. Follow in obedience wherever God would lead even though you do not know where you are going and what the consequences will be. Consciously choose to reject the comforts, riches and material values of this world in order to identify with the suffering, the lost, and the people for whom Christ died. And do not reject the suffering that may accompany your calling.

4

CONTINGENCIES FOR
EFFECTIVE WITNESS

Psalm 51:10–13

Missionaries come from a wide variety of backgrounds and go to fill a diversity of assignments. In addition to evangelism and church and home responsibilities, they are appointed to administrative roles, business management, as teachers, engineers, and doctors; they work in theological education, music, youth ministries, and sports. Just as the channels of mission service and skills that are needed are endless, the locations and opportunities have also vastly expanded in recent years. Missionaries are going not only to South America, Africa, and Western Europe; but they are gaining access to unreached countries in Central Asia, Eastern Europe, China, and all across the Muslim world.

Regardless of your mission field and assignment, your calling and task are basically that expressed by David in Psalm 51:13, "Then will I teach transgressors thy ways; and sinners shall be converted unto thee." You are going to fill a strategic assignment, but wherever you are or whatever you do, you are to reveal the truth of a living Savior through your life and witness and influence. You could be doing what you are going to do vocationally here in the US and serve the Lord effectively in your church, but the reason God has called you to a foreign field is because people are lost and need to be converted through the proclaimed message of Jesus Christ.

Even though David was king of Israel, he realized his purpose was more than a political one of leading the government and administering the nation of Israel. It was God's purpose that he also provide spiritual leadership that sinners would be converted and transgressors know the way of God. He was not only to be a witness; he was to model what it meant to follow the Lord and live for Him, so if any of his people went astray his life would be an example and influence them to follow God's statutes and ordinances.

The core values of the International Mission Board state that our basic purpose is "that all the peoples of the world would have the opportunity to hear, understand, and respond to the gospel in their own cultural context." All over the world, we are receiving reports of unprecedented harvest. The number of baptisms recently surpassed 500,000 for the first time. We are hearing of breakthroughs in the Muslim countries and in World A, where people have not had access to the gospel until recent innovative strategies began to be implemented; multitudes of people separated from God by sin are being converted, and churches are being started. As Paul observed in Colossians 1:6, "All over the world this gospel is increasing and bearing fruit."

Note that David states this purpose as an obvious conclusion. He begins verse 13 (of Psalm 51) with "then" and says, "Then will I teach transgressors thy ways; and sinners shall be converted unto thee." Now I took the same homiletics course in seminary many of you did, and I know that an exegetical sermon is supposed to proceed verse by verse according to the text, but I am going to reverse that pattern and look at the Scripture in reverse. Certain prerequisites must obviously be satisfied before David could fulfill his spiritual task. So notice the contingency expressed in his prayer in the preceding verse.

ONE MUST HAVE THE JOY OF THE LORD IN ORDER TO WITNESS EFFECTIVELY.

In verses 12 and 13 (Ps 51) he prays, "Restore unto me the joy of thy salvation . . . then will I teach sinners thy ways and transgressors will be converted." We cannot be successful in our witness without reflecting the joy of our salvation. The world does not know this kind of joy, a joy that comes from a salvation provided by a loving and merciful God. It is a distinct contrast with the fear and superstition-dominated religions of the world. But if we have lost the joy of our salvation, the effectiveness of our witness is vastly diminished. We can talk about joy and victory; but unless the world sees that as a reality in our life, our testimony loses credibility, and our words become empty rhetoric.

David had not lost his salvation, but he had lost the joy of his salvation. Many things bring joy into our lives. We can all remember the joy of finally graduating from college and seminary even though the illusion of being finished with the pressure and discipline of studies was short-lived. You remember the joy of a wedding day or when your first child was born and many other significant events. I have just discovered the joy of our first grand-child (pictures are available)! But there is no greater joy than a loving and merciful God touching us with His grace in salvation. I can still remember the joy and peace as a ten-year-old boy in knowing my sins had been forgiven, though I must admit that I have not always had that joy.

As we were traveling in South America this summer, we had the privilege of participating in meetings with our missionaries in which Henry Blackaby was speaking. We saw God move in conviction and renewal among our mis-sionaries. One first-term missionary testified that he had lost his joy and con-fidence through his year of language study when he was unable to preach and witness; he requested prayer that the zeal for sharing Christ would return. A missionary named Carol said, "My name means 'song of joy,' but I have allowed Satan to take away my song, and I want it back."

When you get on the mission field, Satan will do everything he can to take away your joy. Jim and Sharon McPherson arrived in Chad to find the temperature 120 degrees and no electricity for fans or cooling. You will be in situations like a new missionary in Belarus who said they had become immobilized by fear and paranoia due to their house being burglarized and constant harassment by the immigration authorities and police. And when you lose that joy, you have lost an essential element in your witness. But why had David lost the joy of his salvation?

ONE MUST HAVE A SENSE OF GOD'S PRESENCE IN ORDER TO HAVE ABIDING JOY.

In Psalm 51:11 David prayed, "Cast me not away from your presence; and take not Thy Holy Spirit from me." He had lost a sense of God's abiding presence as if he were on his own and God's Spirit had been withdrawn. Have you been there? That is an awful condition to be in—trying to serve God in your own strength, seeing no evidence of God's divine power in your life and ministry, struggling to implement programs and find effective methods without an evidence of God's anointing. No wonder David had lost the joy of his salvation.

I don't have to remind you how susceptible you will be to the same experience. When illness comes, or the kids are having difficulties in their adjustments, life begins to unravel, the motivation is just not there, and you will find yourself praying, "Lord, what am I doing here?" You will find many alternatives rushing in to claim your time instead of witnessing to those who are lost and of leading them to the way of truth.

I have found that it is so easy to lose that sense of God's presence through failure to nurture the discipline of beginning each day with Him. Someone expressed this in a poem called "The Secret." (Ralph Cushman's "I Met God in the Morning")

> I met God in the morning
> When my day was at its best,
> And His Presence came like sunrise,
> Like a glory in my breast.
>
> All day long the Presence lingered,
> All day long He stayed with me,
> And we sailed in perfect calmness
> O'er a very troubled sea.
>
> Other ships were blown and battered,
> Other ships were sore distressed,
> But the winds that seem to drive them
> Brought to us a peace and rest.
>
> Then I thought of other mornings
> With a keen remorse of mind,
> When I, too, had loosed the moorings
> With the Presence left behind.
>
> So I think I know the secret
> Learned from many a troubled way;
> You must seek Him in the morning
> If you want Him through the day.

God has come to indwell your life in the person of the Holy Spirit, and He never leaves you. He is always there. But His presence is meaningless if you are not aware of it and unless you learn to practice the presence of Christ through a consistent devotional time and praising Him throughout the day. It is the only way to be overflowing with the joy of His salvation that will make your witness attractive and effective.

ONE MUST BE CLEANSED OF SIN IN ORDER TO HAVE A SENSE OF GOD'S PRESENCE.

Why did David lose a sense of God's presence? He had prayed in verse 10, "Create in me a clean heart, O God; and renew a right spirit within me." He felt separated from God because he had allowed sin to come into his life. Although he had fallen morally and committed adultery, he realized that the problem was in his heart. He failed to keep his heart clean and pure.

One day as I was returning from the village in Indonesia, I stopped at a favorite food stall that served delicious fried noodles. I had been out all day and was famished. As I was enjoying the tantalizing taste of those noodles, I noticed out of the corner of my eye one of those noodles moved. As I looked more closely, I realized it wasn't a noodle but a worm! Suddenly I lost my appetite for those noodles. It was a big plate of delicious noodles, and that worm was so tiny, but its presence contaminated the whole plate of food.

How quickly a small sin hidden deep within one's heart will render one's witness ineffective—when we fail to live a separated life of holiness or harbor an inappropriate attitude or spirit that is not Christlike. Many missionaries have become resentful of their situation, their deprived lifestyle, and look for comfort and entertainment in the things of the world. A root of bitterness will grow out of relationship problems. You feel sorry for yourself because no one recognizes or seems to appreciate the sacrifice you are making or because financial support from the International Mission Board seems inadequate.

In Psalm 139:23–24 David reflects the lesson he learned from this experience and prays, "Search me, O God, and know my heart; try me and know my ways, and see if there be any wicked way in me." When you allow your heart and attitude to become unclean, you lose a sense of God's abiding presence. And when you feel separated from God, you lose the joy of your salvation. And when you lose the joy of your salvation, you cease to be an effective witness leading others to the Lord.

So may you walk in holiness, with a pure heart and Christlike spirit and attitude, constantly aware of God's abiding presence, overflowing with the joy of His salvation and be the effective witness God has called you to be.

5

Serving in a Dangerous and Chaotic World

Acts 4:24–30

The world to which you are being sent is one that is being convulsed with conflict and tragedy that would have been unthinkable a few years ago. We are still reeling over the events of September 11, 2001, that shook the comfort zone of Americans and shattered our sense of security. The world has been thrown into an atmosphere of fear and suspicion. Tension and uncertainty have shattered confidence in the future. Our economy is in disarray, international alliances have been disrupted, and we find our world engaged in warfare against an elusive terrorist enemy.

It is into this kind of world you are being sent, and I do not believe it is a mere coincidence that at such a time as this you are the largest group ever to be appointed in the 156-year history of the International Mission Board. You could not foresee what would be happening when some of you responded to a call to missions several years ago. You responded in obedience to the conviction God placed in your heart to recognize that there was the potential within your life to touch a lost world cross-culturally. You could not have known at that time that it would be a world that was so desperate for a message of hope, a world that was longing for someone to reveal a God of love and mercy, more than ever.

As we send you out to be dispersed to this world, it is not without risk. In fact, Jesus never assured his followers of a safe, comfortable environment because of their faithfulness to His call. To the contrary, He assured them of tribulation. He said they would be hated. He called them to take up their cross and deal with the matter of dying before they go but assured them that God would be glorified regardless of what they encountered. But the kind of world we live in today is not without precedent. The early believers in the book of Acts also experienced this kind of hostile environment in which they were hated. There were those, with the same determination of modern-day terrorists who sought to eradicate the world of this fledgling Christian movement. Religious leaders and government authorities collaborated in a strategy that resulted in the apostles, missionary witnesses of the first century, being persecuted, harassed, put in prison and martyred. Notice the prayer of the church as they prayed in this situation in Acts 4:24–29:

> And when they heard this, they lifted their voices to God with one accord and said, O Lord, it is Thou who didst make the heaven and the earth and the sea, and all that is in them, who . . . through the mouth of our father David Thy servant didst say, "Why did the Gentiles rage, and the peoples devise futile things? The kings of earth took their stand, and the rulers were gathered together against the Lord, and against His Christ." For truly in this city there were gathered together against Thy holy servant Jesus, whom Thou didst anoint, both Herod and Pontius Pilate, along with the Gentiles and the peoples of Israel, to do whatever Thy hand and Thy purpose predestined to occur. And now, Lord, take note of their threats, and grant that Thy bond-servants may speak Thy word with all confidence.

Their response is very relevant to you today. Their prayer reflects the issues of dealing with a dangerous world and a hostile environment that would threaten your witness as you are dispersed throughout the world. Notice that they (1) recognized the consequences of a sinful world, (2) reflected their confidence in a sovereign God, and (3) renewed their commitment to a saving word.

THEY RECOGNIZED THE CONSEQUENCES OF A SINFUL WORLD.

They were asking the same question we ask today. Why do the nations rage? Why is there such evil in the world? Why do the peoples of the earth, and even kings and rulers conspire against the Lord, against freedom-loving democracies and those who bring a Christian witness of hope and salvation? They observed that pagan Gentiles and Jewish religious leaders collaborated with political rulers, Herod and Pontius Pilate, against Jesus Christ, the Lord's anointed. Why should it be any different today? We should not be surprised that governments place restrictions on a Christian witness. In the name of religion, missionaries who seek to feed, clothe, house, and minister to Afghan refugees are imprisoned and condemned. Persecution and harassment of those simply seeking to worship Jesus is rampant in China, Turkmenistan, Laos, and across Northern Africa. You are being sent to a world where Americans are vulnerable, branded as the enemy by those with distorted worldviews and perverted religious convictions.

What is the answer? Is this because of our inadequate Western diplomacy, our deficiency in security or our inability to understand cross-cultural world-views? No, it is because of our failure to fulfill the Great Commission. Two thousand years ago our Lord sent us to preach the gospel to every creature and to disciple the nations. What if preceding generations had been faithful to carry out that mandate? Can you imagine what kind of world we would live in if the Taliban in Afghanistan, Pakistanis, and Iraqis had all come to know Jesus as King of kings and Lord of lords? What kind of situation would we have in the Middle East if Israelis and Palestinians had all come to know the Prince of Peace and were worshipping Him together? But the tragedy is that we live in the consequences of a lost and fallen world, and it is because of our failure to be obedient and proclaim Jesus to those who do not know Him.

THEY REFLECTED THEIR CONFIDENCE IN A SOVEREIGN GOD.

But notice in the midst of these threats, opposition, and persecution, the believers affirmed their confidence and faith in God's sovereignty. They were reminded that He was the one who created the heavens and earth and everything in them. In fact, He had already spoken through David to reveal that these things would happen; it should not come as a surprise. They even affirmed that whatever was done by the enemies of their faith, whether Gentiles, Jewish religious leaders, or Roman rulers, that God was in control. They were doing only what God's hand allowed and what was predestined according to His purpose.

We could list a litany of tragedies and disasters over these last few weeks. Our nation has never experienced anything like the destruction and loss of life on Tuesday morning, September 11. We were already grieving as just the night before we had received word that a Journeyman, Genessa Wells, was killed in a bus accident in Egypt just two weeks prior to completing her term of service. Two weeks later I was leading a missions week at Florida Baptist College when the van carrying eleven students from a ministry engagement rolled over and three students were killed.

Did God know these things would happen? Absolutely! Even from the foundation of the world. He has not predestined such tragedies, but He has not relinquished His throne. What He has predestined is a way to use any and every event for His purpose, and His desire is to be glorified and to be exalted among the nations. I do not know the implications of all that we are experiencing. It is hard to see and anticipate how God can use the current global environment, but there is no doubt in my mind that He, who is sovereign over the nations, is shaking the heavens and earth. Just as we have seen incomprehensible events bring the disintegration of the Soviet Union and open the doors of China to an unprecedented harvest, I believe with all my heart that in the near future we will look back and see how God has used these events to break down the barriers of that last frontier of global evangelization—the Muslim world. Already missionaries throughout Northern Africa and the Middle East are reporting neighbors expressing a disillusionment with their Muslim faith that would be used to justify terrorist activity; they are asking questions that reflect a search for hope and security that only Jesus can provide. We must be confident that God can and will use the tragedies and dangers and chaos of our world to create a spiritual hunger and enable His purpose to be fulfilled.

They renewed their confidence in a saving word.

And He has called you at such a time as this, to join more than five thousand Southern Baptist missionary colleagues, to go forth proclaiming the word of life. You are to live out in an incarnational witness the life-changing message of salvation and hope, to declare that Jesus is the way, the truth, and the life. And what should be your response to the dangers and uncertainties that you face? How should you approach a hostile culture that may not welcome your witness? How should you react to the threats and intimidation that you are likely to encounter? Just as these New Testament believers did.

They did not pray that God would remove these threats and dangers and restore them to their comfort zone. They prayed, "Now, Lord, take note of their threats, and grant that Thy bond-servants may speak Thy word with all confidence." In other words, they recognized this was an unprecedented opportunity for witness. God is giving you a unique opportunity, as a result of the turmoil and threats in our world, to share a message of hope, to proclaim that security is found not in cultural and religious traditions but only in our Lord Jesus Christ. God has called you, and we are sending you out, to speak the word with confidence.

And notice that when you do, you can expect God to extend His hand to demonstrate His power through signs and wonders through the name of Jesus (Acts 4:30). Never forget that it is not your abilities and skills, but it is only the power of God that will change lives and draw people to Himself. And He is dwelling within you. As you go to plant your life in a foreign culture among people who are lost, He goes with you. When you proclaim the gospel with confidence and live out the reality of a living Savior in your life in an incarnational witness, you earn credibility for sharing a verbal witness. It is through that bold and confident witness that God is able to work and demonstrate His power.

And finally, in verse 31, we read that when they prayed, they were "filled with the Holy Spirit." Notice the consequences of that. They "began to speak the word of God with boldness." You are going to encounter a lot that will intimidate and even frighten you. Just the stress and challenge of learning another language and adapting to a deprived lifestyle in the midst of another culture can be overwhelming. You will find yourself in crowded cities of millions of people, congested traffic and among those who will be antagonistic to an American presence and a Christian witness. There will be a natural tendency to withdraw, and, in timidity and fear opt for discretion rather than boldness in sharing your faith. But God does not send you without the empowering of His Holy Spirit. Appropriate that through prayer. Devote yourselves to priority time on your knees. God will manifest His presence and give you boldness to take the risk, seize the opportunity, and be His witnesses, even to the uttermost ends of the earth.

You go out into a hostile world that will not necessarily appreciate and embrace your witness. Recognize it is because of a sinful world without Christ. But reflect upon your confidence in God's sovereignty and that He will use the circumstances and tragedies of the world to accomplish His purpose. Renew your commitment to God's saving word and go to proclaim it boldly and in confidence.

6

HERE AM I, SEND ME

Isaiah 6:1–9

It is a historic occasion as we commission these who have responded to God's call to share the gospel throughout the world. Those being sent out join a multitude of Southern Baptist missionaries dispersed among people groups in 184 countries and follow a legacy of others who have given their lives to claim our world for Jesus Christ.

Jesus articulated a sequence of stories about the kingdom of God prior to His crucifixion. In Matthew 22:14, at the conclusion of the parable of the feast, the Gospel of Matthew records Him saying, "Many are called, but few are chosen." The passage is apparently in reference to those who are invited to the wedding feast and to enter the kingdom of God, but many reject that invitation. Let us not be diverted by the various Calvinistic interpretations regarding those who are chosen, but focus on the obvious that many were called—they had the opportunity to be chosen—but rejected the invitation.

Jesus told His disciples and those who had left their home, their family, and their vocation to follow Him, that they had been "chosen." You have heard God's call and been chosen to serve Him in places such as Malawi, Mexico, Chile, Germany, the Ukraine, and Yemen. Why have you been chosen in lieu of others? Why have you, who are relatively few compared to the needs of a lost world, heard the call when others have not? Certainly the call of God is not for a select few, but for everyone who has been given the privilege of knowing Jesus Christ. The Great Commission was not intended for just a handful of disciples on a hillside in Galilee or for only five thousand among sixteen million Southern Baptists. As Oswald Chambers says in his devotional book, *My Utmost for His Highest*, "Whether or not I hear God's call depends upon the state of my ears and the disposition of my heart."

Note with me, if you will, the call of Isaiah. In chapter 6, verse 8, Isaiah said, "I heard the voice of the Lord, saying, 'Whom shall I send, and who will go for us?'" It was not a personal, individualized call to Isaiah; it was a generic call for whoever would respond—whom shall I send, and who will go? But Isaiah heard it as a personal call, and replied, "Here am I. Send me!" He was not responding in reluctant submission, heels dug in, conscripted into service contrary to his own aspirations and plans. He was inviting God to send Him. "You need someone to go and preach repentance and hope to a people whose hearts are hardened, ears dull, and eyes blind; well, here I am. Why not send me?"

You have heard that call of God saying, "Who will go to Ethiopia and tell a people emerging from years of atheistic Marxist domination that there is hope in Jesus Christ?" You have heard God calling, "Who will go to the massive cities of China and, through creative channels of witness, propagate the message that the 1.2 billion people there can be invited to the wedding feast of the Lamb?" Several have heard God calling, "Who will take the risk to go and minister among the weary, suffering refugees in war-torn Croatia and tell them of my love?" You have heard God calling, "I have opened the Hindu kingdom of Nepal to a Christian witness; who will go to these people, for centuries in bondage to spiritual darkness and oppression, and tell them that Jesus will set them free? And who will go to the fields white unto harvest in Latin America? Who will sow the seed on the hardened soils of the Muslim world? Who will seize the opportunity in the Ukraine, Germany, and throughout the gospel-deprived nations of Europe?" You are being commissioned tonight because you have heard that call and said, like Isaiah, "Here am I. Send me."

Why have you heard a call that others have not heard? Why have you been chosen among many whom God is obviously calling? Again Oswald Chambers provides some insight into your call and Isaiah's. He says:

> The few who prove themselves, the chosen ones, are those who
> have come into a relationship with God whereby their disposition
> is altered and their ears unstopped. They can hear that still small
> voice. . . . It is not a matter of God singling out a man and saying,
> "Now you go." God did not lay a strong compulsion on Isaiah, but
> he was in the presence of God and there was no other response
> but "Here am I, send me."

You are responding to God's call because you have had an encounter with Him.

The first thing I want you to remember is that you are going to the mission field, not necessarily because you have an affinity for foreign cultures or because you are such a talented and gifted individual or your education and experience is so exemplary. It is because you have had an encounter with God. You have recognized, as Isaiah, that God is on His throne, high and lifted up. His throne is the symbol of might and power and authority, and your response to His call is not optional. Although the credentials you bring to missionary service are impressive, they confirm you are here because of the nature of the one who calls—because of His grace and power—not because of your own merit.

Never forget in times of difficulty and hardship, when it seems no one cares, why you are there. When the children are sick, mail from home is lost, or your security is shattered by violence and warfare, you are not there because a friend or pastor persuaded you to go or because the International Mission Board enlisted you. It is because you have seen the Lord and discerned His heart for a world in darkness and need. It is in response to His lordship and call that you have been divinely chosen to go.

You are responding to God's call because He has cleansed your heart.

Isaiah was able to hear God's call and was chosen because he had allowed God to cleanse his heart and life. When he came into God's presence and was exposed to His holiness and His glory, Isaiah recognized his own sin and uncleanness. But he was touched by divine cleansing and told, "Your iniquity is taken away, and your sin is forgiven."

In efforts to pinpoint that specific call of God that resulted in my becoming a missionary, I can recall many experiences and impressions that God used to confirm that call. However, I invariably find myself all the way back to my salvation experience as a ten-year-old boy. When I came under the conviction of sin, I suddenly understood why Jesus had died on the cross. When I received Him as Savior, I had such a sense of joy and peace that my sins had been forgiven, I can recall thinking, "I wish everyone in the world could have the experience of knowing Jesus." When you personally experience God's marvelous grace in cleansing and forgiving us of sin and making us whole, it should result in our hearts being open and compelled to proclaim His love and tell of His grace to others.

You have been chosen because of a personal redemptive experience, and that experience is needed by a lost world. God will use you to the degree that you keep your heart cleansed and pure. You may not be tempted and attracted by the allure of the world, but it will take a deliberate effort to keep your mind and attitude pure and holy before the Lord. Even missionaries easily succumb to pride and self-centeredness that harm relationships or to attitudes of bitterness or self-pity that sabotage effectiveness. You have been cleansed and made worthy to be chosen; maintain that pure and holy walk with the Lord.

YOU ARE RESPONDING TO GOD'S CALL WITH ASSURANCE THAT YOU ARE ANOINTED FOR WITNESS.

I would also have you note from the experience of Isaiah that he heard and responded to God's call because his lips had been divinely anointed (Isa. 6:6–7). You are going to fill a diversity of assignments. Many are going to do direct evangelism and church development, but others are filling assignments in literature and publications, as a business manager, a teacher, a nurse, in theological education, and in church and home ministries. Regardless of your role, you are going because people are lost and need to know Jesus. You are being appointed tonight to proclaim and communicate the message of salvation with the anointing God has placed on your life.

Many of you have already had experience overseas and know something of the challenge you will encounter. However, if you are a typical group of new missionaries, you are a little anxious about language learning and communicating cross-culturally. How do you convince a Muslim the truth of Christianity in a language you have never spoken before? I dare say there are many others who have considered going as a missionary and would be called of God but are convinced they could never learn another language or relate cross-culturally. Don't forget the Lord who calls is the one who equips you and partners with you. He will anoint your lips and enable you to learn the language, to speak the truths of God's Word, and to witness with power.

YOU ARE RESPONDING TO GOD'S CALL BECAUSE OF A KINGDOM VISION.

Finally, Isaiah heard the call of God personally and was chosen because he had a kingdom vision. His eyes were lifted beyond a vision of King Uzziah's kingdom to see the nation of Israel as the kingdom of God, and God said, "Go, and tell this people," (Isa. 6:9). Habakkuk saw that kingdom when he said, "The earth shall be filled with the knowledge of the glory of the

LORD as the waters which cover the sea" (Hab. 2:14). John saw that kingdom when he saw a multitude that no man could count from every tribe and people and tongue and nation gathered around the throne (Rev. 7:9). Jesus came announcing that kingdom and has called you to proclaim the gospel or good news of the kingdom around the world.

I challenge you to go with a vision that sees the people of Africa and Latin America being a part of that kingdom. Go with the conviction that Jesus died for those numberless multitudes in China and throughout Asia that they might become a part of His kingdom. Believe that the power and providence of God are adequate to call those in the Muslim world of North Africa, the Middle East, and South Asia to the saving knowledge of Jesus Christ and become heirs of His kingdom. For it is that kingdom vision that will inspire, motivate, and sustain you in fulfilling God's call.

Now to others who have rejoiced and supported the missionaries that are being appointed, you have heard this challenge to those who, like Isaiah, have said, "Here am I, Lord, send me." Would God be calling you to join them, that a lost world might know your Savior? I often hear people say, "I would be willing to go as a missionary, but God has not called me." By what criteria can anyone consider themselves to be exempt from God's kingdom purpose to "declare His glories among the nations and His salvation to the ends of, the earth?" Are you called, but not chosen, simply due to your own lack of response and unwillingness? When our Lord called His disciples, there was no irresistible compulsion but just a matter-of-fact invitation, "Follow Me."

Like Isaiah, have you been cleansed of your sin and been given the privilege of knowing Jesus? For what purpose? Is it not to join God in making Him known to a lost world? Are you reluctant to yield your life in surrender to an uncertain pilgrimage because of a sense of inadequacy? Realize that God's anointing comes with surrender to His will. He does not call because of who you are and what you have to give, but He chooses the willing heart and then provides all that is needed in equipping and empowering to fulfill that call. Many are called, but few are chosen because few are willing to lay on the altar their own plans and ambitions, their own comfortable lifestyles, and follow God by faith.

Isaiah put his hope in King Uzziah—a man; he looked to the success and grandeur of an earthly kingdom for his security and prosperity. When Uzziah died he was devastated; his hope was gone. But it was then that he saw the Lord. It is often when our worlds crumble around us that God is able to reveal Himself and His will. Have you been holding on to a "King Uzziah" for your hope and security—perhaps aspirations of a successful pastorate, a church position that would provide recognition and influence, or financial security in a fragile economy? Have you been disillusioned by denominational events or had your own faith shattered by the actions and behavior of others?

Would not God have us see Him in His power and glory and authority—a vision that brings the will of God and everything into proper perspective? Some will never have that vision of God and His kingdom and hear that call to missions until Uzziah is put in his casket. What have you been holding on to as your hope and security in life—education, position, or family? What has kept you from hearing and responding to God's call? I would challenge you tonight to put your Uzziah in the casket. Bury the things you have been holding on to so that you can see God and hear His call. But remember who it is that calls. When God calls, the response is not optional. Will you say, "Here am I, Lord, send me"?

7

MORE THAN CONQUERORS

Romans 8:31–39

Each time missionaries are appointed, there is so much about which we need to be reminded from God's Word. I have a desire to share lessons from my own experience over the years and the experience of others who have gone before you. However, one passage of Scripture stands out in my mind as encompassing the heart of what every missionary or volunteer facing service overseas should understand.

In Romans 8, Paul reaches a peak of inspiration as he speaks of our redemptive relationship with Christ. There is no condemnation to them which are in Christ Jesus. The Spirit of Him who raised Christ from the dead shall also dwell in you. We are the sons of God and joint-heirs with Christ. We know that all things work together for good to them that love God and are called according to His purpose. But I especially want to call your attention to verses 31–39 of that chapter.

> What shall we then say to these things? If God be for us, who shall be against us? He that spared not his own Son, but delivered him up for us all, how shall he not with him freely give us all things? Who shall lay any thing to the charge of God's elect? It is God that justifieth. Who is he that condemneth? It is Christ that died, yea rather, that is risen again, who is even at the right hand of God, who also maketh intercession for us. Who shall separate us from the love of Christ? shall tribulation, or distress, or persecution, or famine, or nakedness, or peril, or sword? As it is written, For thy sake we are killed all the day long; we are accounted as

sheep for the slaughter. Nay, in all these things we are more than conquerors through him that loved us. For I am persuaded, that neither death, nor life, nor angels, nor principalities, nor powers, nor things present, nor things to come, Nor height, nor depth, nor any other creature, shall be able to separate us from the love of God, which in Christ Jesus our Lord.

There is so much that could be drawn from this passage, but I want to focus your attention on two questions and a declaration that are vital to every believer but particularly to your success on the mission field.

THE FIRST QUESTION IS: "IF GOD BE FOR US, WHO CAN BE AGAINST US?"

There will certainly be a lot of things that will come against you overseas. You are probably already a little apprehensive about cross-cultural adjustments and learning a new language. Some of you are going to countries that do not readily welcome a Christian witness. Nationalism is intense in some parts of our world to the point that your American identity will be a barrier to acceptance. You have never seen bureaucracy and red tape like you will encounter it in an endless, time-consuming process of renewing visas and work permits, buying groceries, and just surviving. You will feel that government authorities and all the dynamics of society are conspiring against you.

You will also experience the reality of spiritual warfare as never before. You will be overwhelmed by the needs and try to maintain a fatiguing pace of ministry in a year-round humid climate of tropical heat that will sap your energy. The stress of fulfilling your assignment, caring for your family, trying to understand and identify with local people will strain interpersonal relationships and challenge your servant spirit and Christlike demeanor that perhaps you thought was an entitlement of missionary appointment. As demanding responsibilities infringe upon your prayer life and devotional time, you will begin to feel loneliness and isolation and that all the forces of the universe are against you.

But Paul's rhetorical question has an implied answer. Because God is for you, there is nothing that can overcome you. God is on His throne; He is sovereign over the universe. There may be obstacles and opposition, but the Scripture tells us of the "surpassing greatness of His power" which is "far above all rule and authority and power and dominion and every name that is named. "All things" have been put "in subjection under His feet" (Eph. 1:19a, 21–22). Never forget this simple but powerful illustration:

if God went so far as to give His Son for us, shall He not also freely give us all things—all that you need?

In 1950 when our missionaries had to evacuate from China, it would have seemed that the communist government had won. God's purpose of evangelizing that great nation through one hundred years of Southern Baptist missionary efforts and the labors of many others appeared to have been thwarted. But it is evident in retrospect that that seeming defeat has now yielded a harvest that is continuing to multiply in China. God has not abdicated His throne.

In recent weeks missionaries have lost work permits and had to leave Zimbabwe and Zambia. In the last two years entire missions have had to be evacuated ten times from countries in Africa due to warfare and violence—places like Rwanda, Burundi, Angola, Liberia, and just this month in Sierra Leone. A disappointment? Yes. Discouraging? For the missionary, yes. But we are seeing a response to the gospel that is so phenomenal that researchers tell us Africa will probably be 50 percent Christian by the end of the century.

The psalmist says, "The Lord nullifies the counsel of the nations; He frustrates the plans of the peoples" (Ps. 33:10). "The Lord has established His throne in the heavens; and His sovereignty rules over all" (Ps. 103:19). Not too many years ago missionaries in Spain and Latin America ran up against formidable barriers in opposition and persecution in those Roman Catholic cultures, but it was just a matter of time until the gospel gained free reign. In some of those countries the population is already 20 percent evangelical believers; Brazil reported sixty-nine thousand baptisms and over two hundred new churches last year. Remember, God is on your side. He is for you, and nothing can prevail against you.

THE SECOND QUESTION IS: WHAT CAN SEPARATE YOU FROM THE LOVE OF GOD?

And you know the answer to that—absolutely nothing. You, doubtless, have already been through some difficult and trying experiences in which you have found the grace of God sufficient and His love unfailing. But you will have an opportunity on the mission field to know the depth of God's love in a new dimension as He enfolds you in His arms and cares for you.

In a time of tribulation and distress, a couple serving in Central Asia wrote that October was a month they could have done without. Twelve people were killed in their neighborhood in an attempted coup, water dripped into their kitchen only a few hours a day, and electricity was off more than it was on. There was no heating in their small apartment, and the wife had been sick most of the month. They did not have comforts, family, and a church support group to love them and pull them through, but they experienced God's presence and faithfulness in their time of need.

After Keith Stamps had been shot in Guatemala in January, we were in a prayer retreat with the missionaries. One was rather distraught and said, "I came here and was reconciled that I would probably get robbed at gunpoint, my house would be burglarized, my car would be stolen, and I would be left by the side of the road. But I never considered the possibility of getting shot." Jeff Polyglase returned to his house in Burundi after evacuating to the mission compound for safety overnight. Not only had thieves taken all their clothes, furniture, and belongings; they had stripped the house of light fixtures, doors, and windows. Nakedness? Maybe, but God's love is not dependent on our possessions. Famine? A missionary in Azerbaijan told me he would never take bread for granted again after standing in bread lines for hours to buy a few loaves when they became available. Another in Nepal said the family had survived for weeks on potatoes and cabbage, the only food available in the market in their city high in the Himalayas.

Social structures all over the world are deteriorating into anarchy and violence. Living in peril and under the sword of warfare seems to go with the territory, whether in our own country or abroad. Never forget that your greatest security is in God's abiding love and these situations are simply opportunities to know and experience the reality of that love.

Jan and Jim Johnsonius went to Argentina in 1991. While still in their first term, a head-on collision took Jim's life and left Jan in the hospital for two months. Jan testified that in that hospital bed God filled her with a peace and tranquility that was impossible to describe. She did not realize that the serenity she felt was physically visible to others; doctors and those in the hospital wanted to know the source of her peace. Jan said, "I was literally bathed in God's love." She said, "Contrary to the idea that time heals all wounds, I find the grief and pain still there, but it grows fainter because God's love grows stronger—an unending love, the depth of which I never truly knew before."

She said, "I do not understand why my husband had to die; he was so young. He had just begun his missionary service. But I do not see tragedy, only victory—victory in the lives of people changed forever because of his servant heart and witness. I see victory and the joy of a life lived fully for the Lord. It would have been a tragedy if Jim had not had a personal relationship with Christ as Lord and Savior, if he had not surrendered his life to full-time Christian ministry, if he had not answered God's call to missions. That would have been a tragedy." Jan's testimony reflects what Paul is really saying in

Romans 8. He declared, "In all these things we are more than conquerors through Him that loved us."

God has called you to a challenging lifestyle. He has called you to face danger and hardship, but He has called you to be more than conquerors as you carry the good news of eternal life. Wherever you go, whether to North Brazil, Burkina Paso, Eritrea, China, Lithuania, or Russia, you go as conquerors. The battle has been won. "The earth will be filled with the knowledge of the glory of the LORD as waters that cover the sea," (Hab. 2:14). There will be trials and opposition, peril and sword, but neither principalities or powers, things present or things to come can separate you from an all-powerful God and His prevailing love.

David and Mary Carpenter directed teams of volunteers in Albania through a summer of showing the JESUS film in over two hundred rural villages. It was a logistical nightmare, feeding the teams when food was unavailable, coping with attacks of dysentery when food was available, being stoned and chased away by Muslim villagers, generators malfunctioning, and transportation being undependable. But Mary reported, in spite of the trials and tears, twenty-eight hundred people came to faith in Christ. She said it was not a David and Mary Carpenter victory. It was not an International Mission Board victory. It was God's victory because the plan was right from the heart of God.

Ron Cansler arrived in Belarus last year and wrote, "We have become real missionaries in a strange and exciting land. We have survived culture shock, police searches, and hours in long lines waiting to get into offices that were empty when we got there. Former communist officials still harass believers, but God has enabled us to be here and will enable us to stay so that we can share with those who have long been deprived of hearing the gospel."

We send you to the mission field not for what you can do in your assignment as evangelists, seminary teachers, media workers, or business managers. You are being sent, not in hopes of success and personal victory but as more than conquerors because of the blood of Jesus Christ that was shed for the redemption of a lost world. You are more than conquerors in the power of the Holy Spirit through which you become His witnesses unto the uttermost parts of the earth. You are more than conquerors because all power and authority has been given to Him who sits on the throne and in whose name one day every knee will bow and every tongue confess that Jesus is Lord!

8

CALLED FOR THE SAKE OF THE GOSPEL

2 Timothy 1:8–9

As new appointees to overseas missionary service, you are joining a vast host of Southern Baptists who have responded to God's call. Many of you have already had cross-cultural experience through the Journeyman program or International Service Corps assignments. Some of you have had overseas experience on a volunteer trip or short-term assignment. But as new missionaries you are going out as the new kids on the block and will encounter many challenges and adjustments.

As I think of what you will face, I think of Paul exhorting young Timothy in his ministry to "let no one despise your youth, but be an example . . . in word, in conduct, in love, in spirit, in faith, in purity" (1 Tim. 4:12). Now many of you are not really young in age, but like Timothy you are going out as a novice and are young in terms of tenure. Don't let that deter you from being the example and witness you should be to those among whom you go to serve and a support and encouragement to your colleagues.

There is a lot of material in Paul's epistles to Timothy that is appropriate as a charge to those who go to the mission field, but I want to focus your attention on 2 Timothy 1:8–9.

> Therefore do not be ashamed of the testimony of our Lord,
> nor of me His prisoner, but share with me in the sufferings for the
> gospel according to the power of God, who has saved us and called
> us with a holy calling, not according to our works, but according to

His own purpose and grace which was given to us in Christ Jesus before time began.

You were called by grace for God's purpose.

I wish every Christian would understand this. God did not save us from sin just to deliver us from hell. He did not bring us to repentance and faith only so we could have assurance of eternal life in heaven. You were saved by God's grace for a purpose. Now I have read your biographical material, and it is evident some of you have experienced more grace than others in coming to this point!

I recently heard the testimony of a missionary I cannot name due to the sensitivity of his assignment at a mission conference. He and his wife are being used in a mighty way to evangelize an unreached people group in the horn of Africa. This missionary grew up on the streets of Houston and was into drugs and all kinds of trouble with the law. He had to get the courts to expunge his prison record when God turned his life around in order for him to leave the country for missionary service. You have probably not come out of such a background, but whatever your life was in the past, it is a testimony of God's grace that you are here tonight.

Like Timothy, some of you can thank God for His grace in giving you a godly mother and grandmother, a family that raised you in the nurture and admonition of the Lord so that obedience to God's will was the natural thing for you to do. Others of you did not have that kind of spiritual nurture and influence, but you experienced God's grace because He had a purpose for your life.

It's interesting that there are many who fully support you and rejoice in your appointment to missionary service but who think they are the recipients of greater grace because they are blessed by God with a comfortable life-style and are permitted to stay here in America. They think because they don't have to sacrifice to go and live in a congested Asian city or a forsaken, isolated African village that it is because of God's grace. But let me tell you, many whom God would call are forfeiting God's greater grace by remaining at home and refusing to consider missionary service.

Never forget that you are getting to go and share the gospel with those who have not heard. You are the ones who have the privilege of appropriating the fullness of God's blessings and power. You are not going just because of a personal choice or decision. You are not being appointed tonight just because your education and experience qualified you to be a missionary. You are going to fulfill God's purpose because by His grace you were chosen and singled out to be used to reach the nations.

Isn't it amazing that that grace, which redeemed you and reconciled you as a sinner to God, was prepared before time began? Likewise, before you were even born, God chose you by His grace and determined the purpose for which you are being commissioned tonight. As He said to Jeremiah, "Before I formed you in the womb, I knew you; before you were born I sanctified you; I ordained you a prophet to the nations" (Jer. 1:5).

YOU ARE CALLED TO A HOLY LIFE.

You were not just saved by grace and called to missionary service by God's grace, but that divine calling is a calling to holiness. Never think that your missionary assignment is just a matter of filling a job description, even witnessing and planting churches. That is what you are going to do, but you will never do it unless you walk in purity and holiness.

For you see, you are going to plant your life among people that are lost. What they see in you will determine their impressions of Christianity. Seeing a life of holiness and purity will earn credibility for your verbal witness. Remember that God has called you to be something as much as He has called you to do something.

I have heard countless missionaries tell about someone, often a casual acquaintance, approach them expressing a desire to become a follower of Jesus, even in the Muslim countries. Upon inquiry as to why they were taking that initiative, the person would explain that they had been observing the missionary's life; they had seen his integrity, his compassion, and the conviction of his witness. It was distinct from anyone they had ever known, even the religious leaders in their community, and it led them to the conviction that the faith of the missionary was the way of truth.

Ezekiel 38:16 makes a profound declaration regarding your call to holiness. God says, "In the latter days . . . the nations shall know Me, when I am hallowed in you . . . before their eyes."

YOU ARE CALLED TO UNASHAMEDLY TESTIFY OF THE GOSPEL.

You will be overwhelmed by the crowds and intimidated by the religious and cultural strongholds that hold the people in bondage. Many of you are going to places where missionaries are not welcome and where witnessing is forbidden. It will be easy to justify presence instead of proclamation as your task. But people cannot believe without the knowledge that results from a clear witness of the gospel.

Paul made clear to Timothy that "God has not given you a spirit of fear, but of power and love and of a sound mind" (2 Tim.1:7). When you are intimidated and find yourself afraid of the consequences, unwilling to take the risk, remember that attitude is not of God. God, who is sending you out as His witness, has promised to empower you. You will be motivated by a love for the people; and because of that love, you will desire for them to know your Savior. It is God who will give you wisdom and discernment to be discrete when appropriate and bold when needed. You have a treasure to share. You have had an experience for which the world is longing. Don't pay the price of sacrifice in going to a foreign land, leaving your mother and father, adjusting to austere circumstances, and then be hesitant to testify of the gospel wherever you go.

YOU ARE CALLED TO SHARE IN SUFFERING FOR THE SAKE OF THE GOSPEL.

I have known literally thousands of missionaries, and I know of no one who has not suffered in some way as a result of their calling and commitment to missionary service. For many it is just the loneliness and isolation that is difficult. For others it is the exposure to tropical disease, succumbing to strange allergies and an unsanitary environment. For some suffering has come from personal attacks and misunderstanding resulting in strained relationships with friends and coworkers. A few have been subjected to armed robbery, car jacking, litigation in foreign courts following a traffic accident or cancellation of one's visa, which disrupts plans and throws the future into uncertainty.

Paul was in prison when he challenged Timothy to "share with me in the sufferings for the gospel." You have no business being commissioned tonight unless you are willing to share in the sufferings of our Lord for the sake of the gospel. Going as a missionary does not obligate God to put a hedge of protection around you and your family. In fact, God seems to know that your most effective witness may be the faith you are able to exhibit in times of trial and suffering.

What impression does it make on an impoverished Third World nation to see you living comfortably in a Western style house with a secure income from abroad that can provide you and your family with any and every consumer good available? If warfare or ethnic disturbance comes, as it does so often, an American passport assures that you can leave and return home.

The testimony of a victorious life in Christ in the context of such a lifestyle doesn't make a strong impression. But let them see the reality of your faith when a child is sick, you lose a loved one at home, or lose all your material possessions in war or a fire or robbery and they will know that your faith and testimony are real.

This was something Paul confirmed over and over. In Philippians 1:29 he reminds us, "For to you it has been granted on behalf of Christ, not only to believe in Him, but also to suffer for His sake." His own testimony in Philippians 3:10 was, "That I may know Him and the power of His resurrection, and the fellowship of His sufferings." It goes with the calling. Paul wanted Timothy to realize that, and you should know it as well.

Paul presented a beautiful conclusion to these challenges in the verses that follow. He reminded Timothy of God's grace in his life and that he had been saved and called by grace for a special specific purpose, just as you have. He challenged him to walk worthy of that holy calling, just as you have been called to holiness. He charged him not to succumb to fear and not to be ashamed to testify of the gospel, and to be willing to suffer for the sake of the gospel.

Then Paul summed it all up in verses 11 and 12 of 2 Timothy 1 with his own testimony of being "appointed a preacher, an apostle, and a teacher of the Gentiles"—to the nations. He said, "For this reason I also suffer these things; nevertheless I am not ashamed, for I know whom I have believed and am persuaded that He is able to keep what I have committed to Him until that Day."

So go, understanding why you will go through stressful times of language learning and cultural adjustment. Don't be surprised at trials and hardships. Realize that you are going to encounter opposition and discouragement. Understand why it is necessary that the gospel of the Lord Jesus Christ be declared among the nations and be assured that He who has called you, to whom you have committed your life and ministry, is able to keep you, sustain you, empower you, and use you for that coming day when every knee will bow and every tongue confess that Jesus is Lord.

9

GO ALL THE WAY

Hebrews 3:8–11; 4:1

Doubtless, many of you have used the little Campus Crusade tract, "Four Spiritual Laws," to witness to others. It starts out with the fact that God loves you and has a wonderful plan for your life. That plan for you involved your coming to know Jesus Christ as your personal Lord and Savior. Now God's plan is unfolding to lead you to the mission field. Some would not see that as consistent with the full and abundant life promised in the "Four Spiritual Laws" tract. They would think, "Uh oh! He's got you now. You accepted His promise of an abundant life. He got you to make a commitment, and now He is sending you to a life of sacrifice and deprivation in the middle of nowhere."

However, I am certain that you are confident of God's blessings in even greater proportion because of your obedience to follow wherever He leads. I would wish that more would be open to that call and recognize that obedience, even to leave family and friends and a familiar environment here, is the path of greatest blessing. I am aware of the needs around the world, and in my zeal for missionaries to be called out, some have accused me of paraphrasing the "Four Spiritual Laws" to say, "God loves you, and I have a wonderful plan for your life." As a matter of fact, I would be quite willing to plan others' lives to fill the many needs we have overseas.

But now that you are being appointed a missionary, what is God's plan? Is this it? No, even now that plan is just beginning to be fleshed out. We kind of help you over the next few months by saying that plan involves crating your household goods, attending missionary orientation and then a proscribed period of language study. You won't have a lot of options in deciding what God's plan is for the immediate future.

However, after that, some you will find God's plan involves an exciting and fulfilling participation in reaping the harvest and facilitating church growth. For others God's plan will involve plowing the barren, rocky soil and laying the foundation in a difficult field or people group for others to harvest later. I can assure you that God's plan for most of you on the mission field will be a servant role with little recognition or acclaim. You will continually have to call forth that submissive spirit that brought you to this point in order to persevere. For many of you God's plan will involve hardship and heartache and trials in order for Him to reveal His Son in you.

I once was visiting with a new missionary who had recently arrived on the field. In our conversation he told about a call to missions at an early age. He said, "All my life I have had a goal of becoming a missionary. Now that I have seen that goal fulfilled, I am wondering what my next goal in life should be." I sat there incredulous. Your appointment as a missionary should not be seen as fulfilling a goal but only having finally come to the starting point of understanding and living out God's plan and purpose for you. My message to you tonight is, "Don't stop short but go all the way!" No matter what God's plan entails, your faithfulness and obedience will bring abundant blessing and enable God to use you just as He intends.

You will remember that God had a plan and purpose for the children of Israel. He expounded that call to Abraham and continued to reinforce it to Isaac, Jacob, and others who followed. In order for that plan to be carried out, He delivered His people from Egypt just as He has delivered you from the bondage to sin and from self-serving ambitions and personal plans which you may have had. It was essential in that plan for them to follow God to the land of Canaan. Going in to possess the land represented God's purpose, but also the fullness of blessing and provision for His people. The book of Hebrews, chapters 3 and 4, refers to that experience. God is imploring His people today not to harden their hearts but to go all the way in fulfilling His plan and purpose.

> Today if you hear His voice, do not harden your hearts as when
> they provoked Me, as in the day of trial in the wilderness, . . .
> therefore I was angry with this generation, and said, "They always
> go astray in their heart; and they did not know My ways"; as
> I swore in My wrath, "they shall not enter My rest." Therefore, let
> us fear lest, while a promise remains of entering His rest, any one
> of you should seem to have come short of it. (Heb. 3:7–8, 10–11; 4:1)

You are familiar with how they were diverted in following God's plan.

They wandered in the wilderness and stopped short. I want to alert you to the fact that many things are likely to divert you from God's plan. If you aren't careful, like many others who have been where you are tonight, you will stop short of going all the way in fulfilling God's purpose in Brazil or Mali or Indonesia or Peru.

DON'T STOP SHORT BY BEING DISCOURAGED BY ADJUSTMENT TO NEW CULTURES.

Initially you will encounter a tremendous challenge of adjustment to a new culture. It will be difficult to find yourself in a situation where you cannot communicate. No one understands you. Not only can you not preach; you cannot even buy gasoline or bread. You will feel humiliated trying to learn to speak like a preschooler and embarrassed by the mistakes that elicit laughter from those around you. When the electricity goes off and the heat and humidity are soaring or angry mobs are roaming the streets of your city, you will wonder as most other new missionaries have done at some time or other, "What am I doing here?" It will be easy to lose your focus and for God's plan to become obscure when you are struggling for survival. As someone has said, "It is hard to remember you came to clean out the swamp when you are busy fighting alligators!"

In these situations of adjustment and difficulties, you will find that it is easy to lose a passion for the lost around you. The motivation that led you to respond to your assignment in the first place and a desire to share Christ will diminish as your heart becomes hardened. You will resent the crowds that infringe on your space and privacy. Those who interrupt your schedule and take advantage of you as a foreigner will become an irritant instead of an object of God's love.

In the third chapter of Hebrews, we are told that the generation that wandered in the wilderness failed to enter into the promised land because of the hardness of their hearts. We are told in verse 15, "Today, if you hear His voice, do not harden your hearts . . . as in the day of trial." You will go through trials and feel you are in the wilderness, but do not let your heart become hardened to the lost people in that nation and city or people group where you serve and stop short of God's plan.

DON'T STOP SHORT BY BEING DIVERTED BY WORLDLY VALUES.

Second, you can easily be diverted from God's plan by succumbing to worldly values. That may seem improbable tonight because in this moment of inspiration and emotion of being appointed and sharing your call, you are reveling in the privilege and prospects of being used of God in a unique place of assignment. But the thrill of adventure and quaintness of your cross-cultural experience will diminish as communication from home grows slack and a feeling of loneliness and isolation sweeps over you. You will find yourself fantasizing about Wal-Mart and shopping malls, about your spacious, nicely furnished home that you gave up to follow God's plan.

Some of you will begin to write letters about the inadequate financial support from the IMB that is not keeping pace with inflation and the cost of living, forgetting that sacrifice has always been a part of fulfilling God's plan. Some missionaries have looked to a supply of movies and videos to fill a void of entertainment and recreation and find their walk with the Lord compromised by being exposed to a steady diet of worldly values characterized by sex and violence. The human tendency to champion your personal rights and opinions will create interpersonal conflicts with fellow missionaries and national coworkers and will become a barrier to the anointing of God's Spirit in your work and ministry.

In the last verse of 1 Corinthians 9, Paul recognized the danger of missing God's plan and purpose for his life; he said, "I buffet my body and make it my slave, lest possibly after I have preached to others, I myself should be disqualified." Then in the very next verses, he related how the children of Israel became disqualified from fulfilling God's plan. He said, "The people sat down to eat and drink, and stood up to play" (10:7). Instead of pressing forward to follow God and walk in holiness, they were diverted by the desire to enjoy life and have a good time. Then Paul points out that "these things happened to them as an example" (v. 11) that we should not stop short of God's plan and purpose.

DON'T STOP SHORT BY BEING DISTRACTED BY THE ACTIVITY TRAP.

You are also likely to stop short of God's plan by falling into the "activity trap." Like many other missionaries you will arrive on the field with a clear vision of what God wants to do. It is probably a vision of making a spiritual impact in your area of assignment, seeing a church planting movement launched that will touch the entire nation or people group or at least your city effectively evangelized. But then the ministries and strategies you employ will become so time-consuming that they become an end in themselves. You will become entrapped in busyness and keeping the activity, program, or ministry going, which may be worthy in itself; but one day you will realize it's not going anywhere. Since creative access platforms have emerged as a channel to gain entry among restricted and unreached people groups, many have become distracted by maintaining the platform and satisfied with presence rather than fulfilling the purpose for which they are there.

When Betty Hart responded to God's call to Chile, she sailed into the port of Antofagasta and from the ship saw the brown, desolate hillsides and the sprawling, dilapidated shacks and hovels of the city. She recalled saying, "God, with all due respect, you've got to be kidding!" But she got off that ship and stayed for thirty-one years, never losing the focus for which she had come. Working with local pastors and other missionaries she saw the churches grow and multiply, impacting northern Chile with the gospel. John Griggs is one of those unusual missionaries who went to Masvingo in Zimbabwe thirty-three years ago. He realized the limitations in what he could do personally but recognized God's plan for bringing him to that place. Starting with four churches, he poured his life into discipling, training converts, and walking alongside lay pastors in encouragement and equipping. He retired last year having seen more than twenty thousand new believers baptized and 361 churches started in that association.

Don't allow anything to cause you to stall or stop short in following God's plan. Stay focused on His providence and lordship. Like the cloud and the pillar of fire, He goes before you, leading the way. In Exodus 14 the children of Israel had started out following God, just as you have started out to follow Him. But they came to the Red Sea with Pharaoh's army in hot pursuit. And in verse 15 the Lord said to Moses, "Why are you crying out to Me? Tell the sons of Israel to go forward." You will encounter obstacles that seem impossible to overcome. You will come under attack by the enemy. You will not know what to do or which direction to turn, and God will say to you, "Don't just stand there fretting; don't stop short." Keep going forward following God's plan.

Be assured of God's promise for Israel as spoken through Jeremiah, "'For I know the plans I have for you,' declares the LORD, 'plans for welfare and not for calamity to give you a future and a hope'" (Jer. 29:11). God has a plan for your life that is yet to be fulfilled. You are only beginning to understand that plan and purpose. But you will stop short if you lose the focus of your call and allow your heart to be hardened. You will be diverted if you allow yourself to be influenced by worldly values, and God's plan will never be realized if you fall into the activity trap and substitute busyness for moving forward.

Basically there were two things that kept Israel from going forward, that caused them to fail in God's plan. In Hebrews 3:18–19 we read, "And to whom did He swear that they should not enter His rest, but to those who were disobedient? And so we see that they were not able to enter because of unbelief." It was because they were disobedient and because of their lack of faith and unbelief. Don't allow disobedience and failure to keep you from going all the way in God's plan for your life, even on the mission field.

10

THE SPIRIT OF CALEB

Numbers 13—14

Your testimonies have revealed that you have a pretty good grasp of the world to which God has called you. Some of you have been there, if not on a two-year ISC or Journeyman assignment, you have been exposed to the challenges of a lost world by going on short-term volunteer projects. You have seen the conditions of people without Jesus Christ. You are aware of the spiritual darkness and hopelessness of unreached people groups. And for many of you, the suffering and needs of our world were used of God to plant a call in your life to respond and do something about it. For others, you would not have chosen the lifestyle of a missionary, but God has been working in your life to lead you to a dedication and commitment to His lordship, and when He impressed you with a calling to share the gospel overseas, you were prepared to follow in obedience.

God desires for the nations to know Him and to be exalted among all people. His plan of redemption through Jesus Christ was not just for you and me. We learned to quote as a child, "God so loved the world," and you have come to realize that it is literally true. God does not desire that any should perish, but that all should come to repentance. His passion and desire for the salvation of the world is why He has told us to disciple the nations; it is why He is sending you to be His witnesses to the uttermost ends of the earth. In fact, our mission task is not unlike the calling to God's chosen people, Israel, to go into the land of Canaan and possess the land. In Psalm 2:8, God says, "Ask of me and I will surely give the nations as Thine inheritance, and the very ends of the earth as Thy possession." That should remind us all that our primary strategy is to pray. As the director of our prayer strategy office has often said, "The battle for the nations will be won on the knees of God's people; we send the missionaries in for the mopping up exercises." He is calling you and others to go, but He has called all of us to pray for the nations until the strongholds of Satan, the barriers of resistance, are broken down and God's kingdom is extended to the ends of the earth.

But you are the ones who have been called to go. You are like that generation of the children of Israel who had left Egypt, crossed the Red Sea, and finally made their way to the borders of the promised land after a brief stop by Sinai to receive the law. Just as you do today, they understood the calling and purpose of God. They now faced the responsibility of fulfilling that task in obedience to God's purpose. In the thirteenth chapter of Numbers we read that they sent twelve spies into the land in order to scope out the territory and plan their strategy. They came back with their report in verses 25 and following:

> When they returned from spying out the land, after forty
> days . . . they brought back word to [Moses and Aaron] and to all
> the congregation and showed them the fruit of the land . . . [which
> truly] does flow with milk and honey. . . . Nevertheless, the people
> who live in the land are strong, and the cities are fortified and
> very large; and moreover, we saw the descendants of Anak there.
> Amalek is living in the land of the Negev and the Hittites and the
> Jebusites and the Amorites . . . and the Canaanites are living in
> the hill country, . . . and by the side of the Jordan.

A Discouraging Dilemma

First of all, they encountered a discouraging dilemma. They saw the giants and the strength of the people. They saw fortified cities. Instead of open frontier beckoning the people to come and settle, they discovered there were pagan tribes occupying the territory that would have to be displaced. They knew what God wanted them to do. They understood His promise to deliver the land into their hands, but they faced that discouraging dilemma and decided in verse 31, "We are not able to go up against the people, for they are too strong for us." It is not unlikely that you are going to be confronted with the same dilemma as you consider your mission task when you arrive on the field.

Massive Population. You will be overwhelmed by the masses of people who are strongly knit together by their culture and traditions. Collectively they are like giants in the land. I'll never forget arriving in Indonesia, the fourth largest country in the world, and living on the island of Java amid 120 million people in an area the size and shape of Tennessee. Later my work took me to Bangladesh, a little country the size of Arkansas, with 140 million people. Some of you are going to India, a country about the size of the US east of the Mississippi River; if we had the same population density as India, we would have almost three billion people in the United States. Can you imagine what that would do to our economy, our unemployment, our health-care plans and quality of life? Others are joining a growing influx of personnel in China. Do you realize not 1.3 billion minutes have gone by since Jesus walked upon the earth, yet there are 1.3 billion people in that country, most of whom have never heard of Jesus. Wherever you are going, you will find the worldview of the people reflected in religious convictions that harden their hearts and blind them to the truth of the gospel. There will be a tendency to just throw up your hands and say, "What's the use? We are just not able to reach them."

Fortified Cities. They saw the fortified cities that would have to be penetrated and overcome. You probably will not encounter literal fortifications, but the urban challenge will be overwhelming. I always considered myself a city boy even though my hometown of Clinton, Mississippi, just had fifteen hundred people when I was growing up. But, after all, I didn't live out in the country on a farm or ride a school bus into town. I knew Clinton really wasn't much of a city, but it was very close to Jackson, a massive city of 200,000 with expressways, skyscrapers, and shopping malls. I thought I knew what a city was until I traveled to Mexico City and Tokyo, each with twenty million people. The massive, multicultural megacities of Cairo, Istanbul, Jakarta, Bombay, Calcutta, and Karachi defy the most entrepreneurial urban strategists. You may be going to one of the 140 cities in China with more than a million people and face the challenge of planting the gospel for the first time among a cacophony of factories, traffic jams, and impenetrable apartment complexes. Others are going to cities fortified against the gospel for generations and hidden from the awareness of Westerners like Chongking, Dushanbe, Samarkand, Lhasa, and Tashkent.

People Groups. The spies were especially threatened and repelled by the tribal groups that occupied the land. There were Amalekites, Canaanites, Jebusites, Amorites, stalactites and stalagmites, and all those other tribes. Researchers have identified over two thousand major ethno-linguistic people groups that have yet to have access to the gospel. They have a cumulative population of 1.7 billion people. Some of you are going to places where people have been isolated culturally and geographically throughout history where missionaries have never been allowed. There are no churches there to present a Christian witness and no Scripture in the language for the people to read. How do you gain access to restricted people groups? How do you communicate the gospel in a way that will be understood and received? How do you precipitate a church planting movement among the five million Baluchi in Pakistan, twelve million Uigar in China, twenty-eight million Sundanese in Indonesia, or eight million Quashqai in Iran?

God has said to go up and possess the land, but one of your first reactions will be to succumb to discouragement and dismay and say like the majority report of the spies, "We are not able to go up against the people, for they are too strong; there are too many. The obstacles are too great." But there was another perspective expressed that day. In verse 30 we read, "Then Caleb quieted the people before Moses, and said, 'We should by all means go up and take possession of it, for we shall surely overcome it.'" What was the matter with Caleb? Didn't he see the masses of people, the giants, the fortified cities and all the tribes and people groups? Yes, but he saw them through the eyes of God!

A Dedicated Decision

A discouraging dilemma was countered by a dedicated decision. We can understand the difference by God's explanation in Numbers 14:24. He said, "But My servant Caleb, because he has had a different spirit and has followed Me fully, I will bring into the land which he entered, and his descendants shall take possession of it." What will enable you to go to Spain and Albania and Russia and claim them for God? What will enable you to reap a harvest for God in Ecuador, Malawi, Tanzania, and Myanmar? What will enable you to glorify God and exalt Him among the people of China, Egypt, and Senegal? You can fulfill the task and claim the nations for God only if you have the spirit of Caleb and follow God fully.

It is not a spirit that is readily discouraged. It is not an attitude where one is constantly thinking about one's own needs and the comforts and the security of your family. It is not a perspective that sees only obstacles and problems, but it is a spirit that is characterized by a vision, a vision that sees people turning to Christ, churches being planted and society being transformed. It is a spirit of faith that believes the gospel is the power of God unto salvation. It is a spirit that believes you are living in the day when Habakkuk's prophecy will be fulfilled "that the earth shall be filled with the knowledge of the glory of God like the waters that cover the sea." It is a spirit that sees the people, the cities, the tribes and languages in the context of Psalm 22:27 that "all the ends of the earth will remember and turn to the LORD and all the families of the nations" shall worship Him, for He is the Lord "and He rules over the nations."

Who is the person that will see the nations become God's possession? It is the one who decides to follow God fully. No compromise, no going halfway, no contingency clause is in your commitment. You have made a dedicated decision not just to be a missionary but to follow God fully, trusting in His provision. It is His faithfulness and grace that will sustain you, not the benefits and support of the International Mission Board. It is the guidance of His Spirit that will unfold His will and give you wisdom as you build relationships and implement strategies. It is faith to follow fully, even when you cannot understand where He is leading or why He would allow you to walk through those valleys of hardship and trial. Like Caleb, you will be among those who see the kingdoms of the world becoming the kingdom of God. Have that kind of spirit and follow God fully, and the victory will be yours.

A DANGEROUS DISOBEDIENCE

Forty years later when God replaced a faithless generation and the children of Israel were prepared to go in and possess the land of Canaan, we read in Numbers 32 that the tribes of Reuben and Gad wanted to stay on the western side of the Jordan. They had large numbers of livestock; God had prospered them, and they were comfortable where they had settled. They asked Moses for permission to stay and not cross over with the others to conquer the land. In verse 6 Moses asked, "Shall your brothers go to war while you yourselves sit here?" He went on to explain that they shared the calling and responsibility of taking possession of the land. He told them that their obligation would be fulfilled if they assisted in subduing the land; then they could return to their homes. "But if you will not do so, behold, you have sinned against the Lord, and be sure your sin will find you out" (Num. 32:23).

Like the tribes of Reuben and Gad, many Christians today clearly understand our Great Commission task. They know God has called us to be witnesses to the ends of the earth and to proclaim the gospel until the nations of the world become the kingdom of God. But they want to send you as missionaries to fight the battle on their behalf. God has blessed and prospered us in America, so we want to stay in our comfort zone and enjoy our families and our wealth rather than crossing over the oceans in obedience to our mission task. But no one is exempt. Whether through praying, giving, participating in short-term volunteer mission projects, or giving our lives, we all have a part in fulfilling God's mission. The sin to which the Bible has reference here is the sin of disobedience.

We are assured that everyone will be held accountable, and it is dangerous to be disobedient to what God has called us to do as His people. May all of us, like those of you being appointed, face the discouraging dilemma and challenge of a lost world not with a dangerous disobedience but a dedicated decision in the spirit of Caleb, a decision to trust God and follow Him fully.

11

ELIJAH: MODEL OF AN INCARNATIONAL WITNESS

1 Kings 17:1–39

Being commissioned as a missionary is a significant occasion for those being appointed but is equally meaningful for many others. The obedience to God's leadership of those going to the mission field brings a great deal of joy to those who have been a part of your life, especially those who have nurtured, influenced, and encouraged you in your walk with the Lord and counseled you in understanding God's will.

Becoming a missionary is the result of prayer and the confirming counsel of others as you come to understand God's call to an overseas assignment. It is natural that your focus is on what you will be doing and where you will be going. The International Mission Board will be doing all that we can to equip you for the task you face and to prepare you for the cross-cultural adjustments you will encounter. However, where you are going and what you will be doing is not the most important thing for which you are being appointed.

Why are you being sent as missionaries to every region of the world? Why don't we just rely on modern technology and find ways to broadcast the gospel to the non-Christian world? Would not it be sufficient to just publish Bibles and distribute them to everyone in the world? While these, and other methods, are certainly a valid channel for telling people about Christ, the most effective channel, and the primary channel, is the missionary living out his or her faith and verbalizing it as an incarnational witness in a cross-cultural context. That is why the primary strategy of Southern Baptists for fulfilling the Great Commission is to send and support gifted and God-called missionaries. Paul said to the Corinthians, "You are our letter, written in our hearts, known and read by all men; being manifested that you are a letter of Christ . . . written not with ink, but with the Spirit of the living God, not on tablets of stone, but on tablets of human hearts" (2 Cor. 3:2–3).

The Old Testament prophets were somewhat of an incarnational witness of God's presence among His people. I am especially impressed with Elijah as having characteristics similar to many missionaries. There were times when he could call the people to God with courage and boldness, but he would also become discouraged in the face of threats and insecurity. He could proclaim the word of God with conviction before the crowds and yet become despondent, feeling misunderstood and unappreciated. He reached the spiritual heights of serving God on Mount Carmel, but then we find him withdrawn, cowering in the cave of Horeb. He could react against sin with vengeance and then minister to a widow in tenderness. Like Elijah, you will find yourselves on the mountaintops and in the valleys, witnessing in boldness to the crowds and sometimes withdrawing in loneliness and self-pity.

We find Elijah appearing in chapter 17 of 1 Kings, and even his name was an incarnational reminder of God's presence and claim on His people. It is variously translated, "My God the Lord," or "Jehovah is my God." Can you imagine how Israel detested that name? They had turned away from God to serve Baal, and every time they saw him they had to spit out that name, "Here comes ol', you know, (and they had to say it again) Jehovah is my God," reminding them of the God they had forsaken.

You are going to serve in some strange places where people do not know Jesus Christ, places like northern Africa, Jordan, China, Bangladesh, and Kazakhstan. What are people going to know and think about Jesus when they see you?

I will never forget hearing one of our missionaries tell about an experience soon after their arrival in a Muslim country. Her husband was to accompany a pastor out to a rural village. She had presumed she would not be going since it is not common for women to get out in public and travel with men, but the pastor insisted she come along. He said of the women in the village, "They have never seen a Christian woman before." She described the awesome feeling she had in that village that was forever implanted in her conscious awareness from that day. They walked into the village, and she could see the women peering out from the darkened doorways; they had never seen a Christian woman before. What did they see? What did her life represent? It made an indelible impression on her on the importance of the life she must live out before them as a Christian.

As you go to the mission field, you will verbalize your witness, but what will they see in your life? They will see an American, and that unfortunately carries with it many negative connotations. What will they see? Will they see someone who confirms that Americans are wealthy because of your affluent lifestyle? Will the way you interrelate with your missionary colleagues, national coworkers, and just the general public confirm their perception that Americans are impatient, easily angered, and arrogant; or will they see the Spirit of Christ in you? Will they see love and compassion, joy, even in trials, and a victorious demeanor that will make them want to know what makes the difference and draw them to Jesus Christ?

Let's return to Elijah and note three things that characterize an incarnational witness.

FIRST, IT IS A CALL TO MAKE CHRIST KNOWN.

Elijah was God's representative to reveal Him to the people. In 1 Kings 18:21 he boldly challenged them, "How long will you hesitate between two opinions? If the LORD is God, follow Him." Just as Elijah appeared on the scene to call people back to God, you are called to proclaim Christ and call people to Him. You have diverse types of assignments. Many of you are going to plant churches. Others are responding to a request in music, youth work, media, or teaching English. You may be planning to serve as a doctor, a nurse, a school administrator, a treasurer and business manager, or as a computer specialist. But the reason God has called you there instead of here is because people are lost and need to know Christ. Jesus Christ is living within you, and by going you demonstrate the presence of Christ among people that need to know Him.

I pray that you will have a successful ministry in whatever you go to do, but never lose sight of the fact that your most effective witness may be to your neighbors, the government clerks, the man at the post office, and the vendor in the market. They are the ones who see you as you really are; they catch you when your guard is down. They are the masses who recognize the foreigner in their midst, but they see you and your behavior in the heat and traffic and pressures of life away from your pious demeanor in a Bible study or worship service.

Why is God sending you to Belarus, Bulgaria, and Romania? Because the people there know Christ only in the hollow ritual of their Orthodox faith, and God wants them to know a living Savior. Why is God sending you to Indonesia, Bangladesh, the Middle East, and North Africa? Because the Muslims there know Jesus only as a prophet subordinate to Mohammed, and God wants them to know Him as the way, the truth, and the life. Why is God sending you to Europe and Latin America? Because God wants them to discover that Jesus is not an irrelevant historical figure lost in the secularization of so-called Christian societies but a Redeemer who is calling all men to repent and receive eternal life. Why is God calling you to China and Hong Kong, to Korea and Japan, to Tanzania and Cote d'Ivoire? It is to reveal a living hope that sets people free from the fear and superstition of their animistic and oriental religions.

SECOND, IT IS A CALL TO BE A CHANNEL OF GOD'S POWER.

Elijah was not responsible for the fire that fell on Mount Carmel, but he had to be obedient to do what God told him to do; he was available for God to use when He chose to manifest His power. You do not plan a movement of God. You do not simply engage in power encounters at will. But as you walk in His presence, you will find God's power sufficient for anything you might confront. He sends you to be His witnesses to the ends of the earth because, as He promised in Acts 1:8, you have received the power of God's Holy Spirit within you. An incarnational witness means that you live out your faith in a way that allows you to be a channel of God's power.

THIRD, IT IS A CALL TO TRUST IN GOD'S PROVISION.

God had His hand on Elijah; He had called him to be an incarnational witness of His presence. And therefore He cared for Elijah and provided for his needs. There was a famine in the land, but God led him to Cherith and provided the water of the brook and commanded the ravens to feed him. When the brook dried up, God led him to Zarephath and caused a widow's oil and flour to be constantly replenished.

The key word is "there." It was there, where God led him, that God provided for his needs. As long as you are there, in the center of His will, can you be assured that He will provide for all your needs because God goes with you, indwelling you. Your witness will reflect your confidence and trust in His provision for your every need. Most of the world does not know that kind of God. They do not have a personal relationship with a living God that goes with them, lives within them, and gives grace for every need. Your call is to live out that kind of faith-walk that they might see the reality of a living Savior and God's faithful provision in your life.

In closing, let me offer one more analogy. What was it that allowed Elijah to represent God as an incarnational witness in the midst of opposition and hardship? What was it that enabled him to boldly call the people to repentance, to be a channel of God's power, and to trust confidently in God's provision?

You will recall that when Elijah first appeared on the scene in chapter 17 of 1 Kings, he declared three years of drought. That was obviously to bring Israel to their knees and to the point of being called back to God. But I think there may have been another purpose. It was an awesome manifestation of power for Elijah to call down fire from heaven and consume the water-logged sacrifice on Mount Carmel. You do not just walk into that kind of experience after a busy day at the office. Elijah needed three years with the Lord in order to know God in the kind of intimacy that would enable him to be a channel of His power (1 Kings 17:2). The first thing that Elijah did before he was used mightily of God was to repair the altar. First Kings 18:30 says, "And he repaired the altar of the LORD which had been torn down."

Some of you may need to repair the prayer altar that has been neglected in the busyness of seminary studies, the pastorate, and other responsibilities. You may need to repair the altar in your home of your family praying and spending time with the Lord together. You may get by successfully here in America by fulfilling expectations of ministry and conforming to all the programs, but I assure you it will not be sufficient where you are going. Only as you draw apart and spend quality time with the Lord will His presence and power be there. You go as an incarnational witness. May you rely on His provision and may the presence and power of Jesus be evident in you and the life you live before a lost world.

12

PAUL'S CALL TO THE NATIONS

Acts 9:15–16

Being appointed to missionary service is a pivotal moment in one's life that links the past and the future. It is an affirmation of your response to a call of God at some time in the past, and it is a time of rejoicing in the potential of the future as you fulfill that call in overseas service. You have come to this moment having testified of a call, and with a deep conviction you are going out in obedience to God's leadership.

In the ninth chapter of Acts, we read about Paul being called by the Lord Jesus Christ to proclaim the gospel to the Gentiles. At that time it was definitely a call to foreign missions though perhaps not as geographic as it was theological. The gospel was thoroughly embedded in the context of a Jewish heritage and culture, but Paul's call was an indication of God's timing to carry the good news to the nations. It was a rather dramatic experience and represented a total turn-around in his life. From being antagonistic to Christ, it resulted in a complete reversal of his life as he experienced salvation, yielded to the lordship of Christ, and surrendered to preach in one remarkable encounter with Christ.

I do not know of anyone who has had a call just like that; in fact, some have stated that they did not see a bright light or a burning bush but felt a growing conviction of a call to missions. For some it came through hearing or getting to know missionaries who shared the needs of people who did not have the opportunity to know Christ. I find it intriguing to read the testimonies of missionary candidates in their applications and biographical material. God spoke to some at a GA or RA camp, at a Baptist assembly program, at a world missions conference, or during a missions class in college or seminary.

It is remarkable how many had that call confirmed through an overseas experience while participating on a volunteer mission project. Indeed, it is difficult to be exposed to the lostness of a world without Christ and not sense a personal responsibility to respond by being available to go.

Now you are going, assigned to a specific place, a country or a people group. It may be to Zambia, Kenya, Morocco in Africa, or Indonesia, Taiwan, or Bangladesh in Asia, to Eastern Europe, Soviet Central Asia, or Latin America. You know where you are going, but you really do not know how God will work, how He will use you, or what course your missionary service will take. You simply know that God has called you, and you are confident that God will be faithful to equip you, to care for you, and to use you.

God did not really give Paul a picture of all that would happen to him. He did not reveal all the places to which he would be led, nor did He describe how he would be used. In fact, He told him to get up, go into the city, and he would be told what to do. There He had prepared Ananias to minister to him and reveal God's plan for his life. In Acts 9:15–16 we read, "The Lord said to [Ananias], 'Go, for he is a chosen instrument of Mine, to bear My name before the Gentiles and kings and the sons of Israel; for I will show him how much he must suffer for My name's sake." Right now you are just preparing to go where God has told you to go; you will probably find some missionary colleagues there who would presume to tell you what to do, but it is probably fortunate you do not know what all God has in store for you. So I want you to understand what it really means to respond to God's call.

IT IS A CALL TO FOLLOW AND TO TRUST.

It is not a call to a definite future. A call to Tanzania, Belarus, Romania, Peru—yes; but be reminded that your call is to follow Jesus and trust the future to him. Many missionaries arrive on the field and experience disillusionment, thinking, "This is not what I came to do." I do not think I have met a missionary who, once they found themselves in a cross-cultural setting, confronted with overwhelming needs, found themselves doing exactly what they perceived their assignment would entail. But never forget that while your call may be to a certain country and a specific job assignment, it is basically a call to follow Jesus and to trust Him.

A few years ago fifty-six veteran missionaries were denied visa renewals by the Indonesian government. They had been called there. They had planted their lives there, and it took quite a struggle before most of them began to realize that God was still in control. He had an alternative future for fulfilling their calling in even more effective assignments as a result of their years of experience in Indonesia. One missionary lived in fifteen different places while trying to get a visa to enter the country to which he had been called. Once it was granted he said in a testimony, "We never knew where we would be from one month to the next. But one thing God has taught us through all of this is that He does not call us to a place as much as He calls us to Himself!"

On his second missionary journey Paul and his companions felt led to go into Asia, but they were forbidden by the Holy Spirit. They tried to go to Bithynia, but the door was closed. So instead of going east and north, they found themselves going west to the city of Troas, wondering, "What in the world does God want us here for?" But there he received the Macedonian vision, and the gospel was spread in Europe for the first time. Paul did not seem to be upset or frustrated when the door was closed or plans were changed, for in his initial response to God's call he said, "Lord, what will you have me to do?" From that point on it was a matter of just following and trusting.

IT IS A CALL TO MAKE JESUS KNOWN.

God revealed this to Ananias in Acts 9:15. "Go, for he is a chosen instrument of Mine, to bear My name before the Gentiles and kings and the sons of Israel." Paul himself came to a clear understanding that this was the essence of his call. In Galatians 1:15–16 he wrote, "He who had set me apart, even from my mother's womb, and called me through His grace, was pleased to reveal His Son in me, that I might preach Him among the Gentiles."

Yes, he was called to Antioch, Derbe, and Lystra. God led him to Philippi, Thessalonica, Corinth, and Ephesus. But the place and the time of where he happened to be was only incidental to the purpose for which he was called, and that was to reveal Jesus Christ. The way he described his calling before King Agrippa in Acts 26:18 was "to open their eyes so that they may turn from darkness to light and from the dominion of Satan to God."

I hope you will realize, as did Paul, that God set you apart from your mother's womb for the purpose of revealing His Son. You did not hear and respond to that call until after you were saved and at sometime later in life. But realize that call came because God had His hand on your life. He knew the iron curtain would fall and the opportunity would emerge for Jesus to be made known in Eastern Europe and the former Soviet Union through your life and witness. He knew there would be a day when Christ could be proclaimed to the Afghans in a nearby country, and nations such as Bangladesh would be open for harvest. You may be going as a teacher, a business manager, a church planter, a homemaker, or a musician; but never forget that regardless of the place and regardless of the assignment, God has called you to proclaim Jesus.

But that is not all. Not only is the call to missions a call to follow and trust God's leadership and a call to make Jesus known, but Acts 9:16 also says, "I will show him how much he must suffer for My name's sake."

THE CALL TO MISSIONS IS A CALL NOT EXEMPT FROM SUFFERING.

Did you know this was a part of the call? It is not unlikely that you and your family will succumb to foreign germs and experience illness, be subjected to injury and possible bodily harm. However, it is not just physical suffering such as sickness and deprivation, but you will suffer emotionally on behalf of your children's needs, due to separation from aged parents, because of misunderstanding with colleagues or rejection by national coworkers with whom you came to serve. You do not relish those experiences, but you waste a lot of time trying to avoid them; and in doing so, in complaining and self-pity, you miss the blessing of God's grace.

I wonder if Paul would have followed through on his commitment if he had known it would result in being stoned, beaten, imprisoned, shipwrecked, and eventually martyred. Would you? Once he discovered that suffering went with the calling, he seemed to realize that a willingness to suffer for Christ's sake was a key to effectiveness and power. In Philippians 3:10 he said his desire was to "know Him, and the power of His resurrection and the fellowship of His sufferings." He seemed to understand that the inevitability of suffering went with fulfilling the calling.

In 1 Corinthians 15:32 Paul asks, "If from human motives I fought with wild beasts at Ephesus, what does it profit me?" You will not likely fight with tigers and lions (I once had to kill a cobra on the doorstep), but you will have to suffer brownouts in sweltering tropical heat, you will have to suffer isolation, you will have inconveniences and trials; it goes with the territory. Let me tell you, it is not worth it if you are there for human reasons. If you are there for personal comfort or for recognition, you will quickly decide it is not worth it and come home. But because Christ is the one who called you, because you were called to trust Him and to make Him known, you will never question if it is worth it. And because you are willing to pay the price in suffering, many will believe and inherit eternal life.

First Peter 4:12–13 says, "Beloved, do not be surprised at the fiery ordeal among you, which comes upon you for your testing, as though some strange thing were happening to you; but to the degree that you share the sufferings of Christ, keep on rejoicing; so that also at the revelation of His glory, you may rejoice with exultation." Miss Elizabeth Hale served for many years in China and Malaysia and remained on the field many years following retirement. When she finally returned to the States she would write letters of encouragement back to her friends and former colleagues on the field. Once she sent a form letter and in it made the comment, "Many of you are serving in places of great difficulty and hardship and therefore have an opportunity of knowing our Lord in a deeper, more meaningful way." Do not waste that opportunity; embrace it, and rejoice that you are counted worthy to suffer on behalf of our Lord Jesus Christ who called you.

Your call to missions was probably not a dramatic Damascus Road experience, but nevertheless it was very real and was a genuine call of God. You rightly understand that call to go to a certain place and fulfill a personnel request that fits your gifts and experience. But don't forget that it is basically a call to trust God and follow Him wherever He leads. It is a call to make Christ known. And it is also a call to suffer with Christ for the sake of the gospel. But be assured that God's grace is sufficient. His hand is upon you to guide you, to sustain you, and to use you to fulfill His will and calling for His glory.

13

OBEDIENT IN SPITE OF DANGER

Ezekiel 2:3–6

God has touched your life and brought you to this point of mission-ary appointment because of His grace. Each of you has experienced His grace in receiving Jesus Christ as your Savior. You are confident of His call and are trusting God's grace to empower and use you wherever you go. However, it would be unnatural if your excitement and resolve were not mixed with just a little anxiety and concern about the world into which you go. Certainly your families are concerned; in fact, some of them may not be sympathetic and supportive of you carrying their grandchildren to places where Americans in general, and Christians in particular, are not held in high esteem. The risks and dangers are real. In the past couple of years, we prayed for Dana Curry and Heather Mercer, arrested by the Taliban in Afghanistan, for Martin and Gracia Burnham held hostage in the Philippines, for those injured in a church bombing in Pakistan, and for colleagues vulnerable to a suicide bomber anytime, anyplace in the Middle East. The International Mission Board is not exempt from such dangers, for no mission organization has so many personnel deployed so extensively, sharing the gospel all over the world.

A few weeks ago the call came that I feared and had fervently hoped I would never receive. Three of our missionaries were murdered in Yemen. It was not the first time we have lost missionaries to violence, but it is amaz-ing that in 157 years of sending out almost eighteen thousand missionaries to the most dangerous places on the globe that so few have lost their lives to unnatural causes. We have had to answer the question, Why do missionaries go to dangerous places? It has to do with God's desire to reconcile a lost world to Himself. It has to do with God's love for the whole world, and He plants that love in our hearts. That has resulted in your giving of your life, sacrificing safety, security, and comfort to bring hope to those in despair, light to those in darkness, and salvation to those in bondage to sin. Why do you go? Because Jesus is the answer to a world filled with chaos and violence and hatred. The blood of Jesus was shed for those from every tribe and people and tongue and nation.

So tonight we are sending you to Asia, Africa, Northern Africa, and the Middle East, to Eastern Europe and volatile places in Latin America. You will receive training in security issues and how to respond and deal with crises and threats. We give a high priority to the safety and security of missionaries, but no human organization can guarantee your safety in our world today. Some places may seem more dangerous than others, but it wasn't many weeks ago when my neighbors in northern Virginia and Washington were living in fear of a sniper's bullets. Those who went to their offices in the World Trade Center on the morning of September 11, 2001, never dreamed they were in a place that was not safe. Helen Keller once said, "Avoiding danger is no safer in the long run than outright exposure. The fearful are caught as often as the bold." In response to this premise, someone said, "Whether you agree or not with the importance of spreading the gospel to every creature, there has to be something special about knowing what you feel called to do on this earth and being bold enough to do it."

That would characterize Bill Koehn, Martha Myers, and Kathy Gariety who were killed on December 30 in Yemen. Each of them testified time and time again that God had called them to Yemen. He had given them a love for the Yemeni people and a passion for them to know Jesus. They could not witness and preach openly, so they had to plant their lives among the people and engage in a ministry of love and compassion that the reality of their faith could be seen and the darkness penetrated. Martha had already been kidnapped several years ago. Bill was often threatened due to his profile as administrator of the hospital, yet he persevered for twenty-eight years, not seeing an abundance of fruit but confident the harvest would come some day. Kathy found it difficult to express and justify to her family why she kept going back; she could only say, "I know God has called me, and I will stay until He tells me to leave."

One week ago today I stood with the colleagues of these three in Yemen as we grieved their deaths together. It was an emotional experience to walk through the Jibla Baptist Hospital where they had treated forty thousand patients a year and to see the place they were killed. We gathered around Bill and Martha's grave, there on the hospital compound, and I was moved by those who were undeterred by this tragedy. Believing the impact of these deaths would be used of God to plant the seeds for the church in Yemen, they were resolved to stay and continue. I recalled the words of Jesus that unless a grain of wheat falls into the ground and dies, it stands alone; but if it dies, it will bear much fruit.

It is highly unlikely that you will be called on to suffer a martyr's death, but Jesus is calling you to take up your cross and die. It has been repeated many times in reflection, in testimony and in memorial services these past few weeks that a gunmen's bullet did not take the life of Bill Koehn, Martha Myers, and Kathy Gariety, for he could not take from them what had already been given. They gave their lives and died to self when they decided to follow Jesus as Savior and live in submission to His lordship and will. They died to selfish ambition, personal recognition, worldly success, and any desire to preserve an egotistical comfort zone when they turned their backs on medical and business careers in the States to go as missionaries. Each day they were in Yemen, they died to self and gave of their lives to God and the people to whom He had called them. Jesus sent out his disciples into a hostile world that did not welcome the Christian message. They were to be threatened, beaten, imprisoned, and martyred for their obedience. The call to follow Jesus, the call to be a missionary, has always been a call to die, a call to sacrifice, a call to take the risk. It has never been otherwise. It is the price of bringing a lost world to Jesus Christ.

In the memorial service for Bill Koehn at Cross Timbers Baptist Church in Burleson, Texas, pastor Scott Whitson, in his message, sought to explain why Bill had gone to Yemen and, with his wife Marty, had spent twenty-eight years there. Scott was an MK (missionary kid) who grew up in East Africa. He could understand. I want to share with you tonight the passage from Ezekiel 2 that Scott used in that memorial service. The prophet is explaining his call from God, beginning in verse 3:

> Then He said to me, "Son of man, I am sending you to the
> sons of Israel, to a rebellious people who have rebelled against
> Me; . . . And I am sending you to them who are stubborn and
> obstinate children; and you shall say to them, 'Thus says the Lord
> God.' As for them, whether they listen or not, . . . they will know
> that a prophet has been among them. And you, son of man, neither
> fear them nor fear their words, though thistles and thorns are with
> you and you sit on scorpions. . . . But you shall speak My words."

YOU ARE GOING BECAUSE GOD HAS CALLED YOU.

Why did Ezekiel go? Why did these who died go to Yemen? Would we dare be disobedient to God? At almost every appointment service, I have the sad experience of an elderly person coming to me and confessing that many years ago they felt a call to missions, but they got diverted by their career or stateside ministry or by a spouse that did not share their call. What is worth the forfeiting of God's will? Would we dare draw a bottom line beyond which we would not go and compromise His calling? "I'll serve you as long as I can do it here in the States, near my family." "OK, I'll go as a missionary as long as I don't have to go to an isolated place that requires a deprived life-style and risk to my family's health and safety." Would we dare bargain with God and dictate the limits of our willingness to follow Him and yet expect Him to bless us and empower us? You have said, "Wherever He leads I'll go." And for many of you it will be to places where the risks and dangers will be real. So why do you go? It is for the same reason that Ezekiel went—because God had called Him.

YOU ARE GOING IN ORDER TO SPEAK HIS WORDS.

Like the children of Israel in Ezekiel's day, the people to whom you are being called are rebellious and stubborn and obstinate. They have their own religion and cultural worldviews. They are not interested in your Christian witness; in fact, it may not even be allowed. God said they may not listen to you. So why did God bother to send Ezekiel? It was to proclaim His word that they might know one from God had been among them.

They may not accept the message, but they would not be without a witness. As I see the lostness of our world, I am continually plagued by the question, By what criteria should anyone be denied the privilege and opportunity of hearing and responding to the gospel?

Bill and Martha and Kathy were forbidden to proselytize and share their faith openly among the people of Yemen, one of the most backward, restrictive Muslim countries in the world. So did the people of Jibla know they were sent from God? Because of their presence among them, did they begin to comprehend a God of love in contrast to the punitive, far-removed God of their own fatalistic beliefs? One day a burka-clad woman in the hospital asked one of these missionaries, "How is it that your heart is so white?" In reply he said it was because Jesus had washed it clean. The lady then asked, "Who is Jesus? Does He work here in the hospital?" She and multitudes of others had an opportunity to know who Jesus is. It is apparent as the people of

Jibla turned out by the thousands and mourned the death of Bill and Martha and Kathy, they knew people of God had been among them, people who knew the true and living God and were now with Him.

No one can guarantee you will have results. You have no assurance that people will heed and respond to your message and ministry. You may never see the fruit of your witness, but we know that one day there will be a multitude that no man can count from every tribe and people and tongue and nation gathered around the throne of God. Your country and city and people group will be represented in that celestial throng because you go; they will have heard the word and known a prophet, a man or woman of God, was among them.

YOU ARE GOING IN SPITE OF THREATS AND DANGERS.

Like Bill and Martha and Kathy in Yemen, you may receive threats; but God says do not fear them or their words. One missionary there expressed their early impressions of arriving and the fear that overwhelmed him as he saw masses of Arab-dressed men, each with an AK-47 over his shoulder, a dagger in his belt, and a scowl on his face. You will go to radical Muslim countries and hear the call to prayer and people assembling at the mosque where they will hear radical imans slandering America and stirring up fanaticism. You will go to China and Central Asia and other places where agents of the government arrest and harass the pastors and close down churches. You will feel that you, like Ezekiel, are in the midst of thorns and thistles and sitting on scorpions when you find yourself threatened in the midst of riots and demonstrations in Venezuela or Peru, or live in sub-Saharan Africa where AIDS is rampant and life is being decimated all around you. But God has said, "I will not leave you or forsake you. I am the One who called you; do not be afraid."

Riots, strikes, and political demonstrations in Venezuela have created a vulnerable situation for expatriates as well as for the local people in recent weeks. The American embassy recently sent out a notice that it was not safe, and all nonessential American personal should evacuate. The family of one of our missionaries, expecting them to heed this alert and come to the States, asked them about their plans for returning home. They made it clear that they had no plans to come home. In fact, the husband explained there were four reasons why they were staying: "(1) We are essential personnel; if these people are to know God, it is essential we be here. (2) This is where God has called us, and we must give priority to obedience rather than our own well-being. (3) It is in times of crisis that people are most open to spiritual things and this is the time that they will most readily respond. (4) And finally, it's too cold in the States!"

Never forget you go because God has called you; it is not because Southern Baptists enlisted you, your church selected you, or the IMB has employed you but because God has called you. You go to be a witness and proclaim His Word that people might hear, understand, and respond. You have no assurance of response and harvest. You may be going to people that have hardened hearts and are blind to the truth, but they can never respond if they have never heard. And though you go to places of risk and danger, though you encounter trials, illness, misfortune and even threats, do not fear them or their words, but trust in God. He is your strength. He is your refuge. He is your stronghold. You go in His power, His protection, and His provision.

14

RAISING THE DEAD TO LIFE

John 11:38–44

In the eleventh chapter of John, we read the intriguing account of Jesus' raising Lazarus from the dead. Throughout the Gospel accounts of Jesus' ministry, we read of those who were sick or demon possessed coming to Jesus, and He healed them all. However, there are only three incidents in which Jesus raised someone from the dead—Jairus's daughter, the widow of Nain's son, and His good friend Lazarus. Jesus didn't go around raising the dead as a prominent part of His ministry. We don't know why He chose to do so in response to the death of these three. There is no question regarding His power to raise the dead, but whether to demonstrate His compassion, teach an object lesson for the sake of those around Him at the time, or to honor one's faith to believe in Him and His miraculous power, He raised these three from the dead.

The fact was evident that Jesus had something to teach Mary and Martha, His disciples, and the skeptical religious leaders about the power of God and the reality of a future resurrection. He could have arrived in time to heal Lazarus before he died, but His greater purpose was to demonstrate the glory of God.

YOU ARE CALLED TO RAISE THE DEAD TO LIFE.

It may be a startling comment for you to hear me say that your task is to raise the dead to life. Our missionaries have occasionally reported incidents of the dead being raised on the mission field. I don't know of any missionary who has prayed successfully for the dead to be raised, but several say they have witnessed it. Not much is said due to the prevalent skepticism in which these stories are received; the usual response is speculation whether the person resurrected had really been dead. Don't misunderstand me. We are not sending you out primarily to perform signs and wonders. But you do want to be available to the power of God's Spirit and demonstrate a faith that believes nothing is impossible with God. You will certainly be disappointed and frustrated if you presume that you will be able to physically raise the dead.

But you have been called to a world that is dead in trespasses and sins. Paul made it clear to believers in Ephesus, "And you were dead in your trespasses and sins" (Eph. 2:1). He was addressing this comment to those who had now become believers by the grace of God. He explained that prior to being saved they were separated from God, without hope, and, due to the condemnation of their sin, were spiritually dead and bound for hell.

That is the condition of most of the people in our world and certainly to those to whom you go as missionaries. If you and I were once lost and dead in sin until we came to repentance and faith in Jesus Christ as our Savior and Redeemer, how much more are those who have no knowledge of Him. Oh, there are those who presume people who follow other religions will be saved because of their sincerity in following their own cultural traditions. But the Bible tells us that "all have sinned and fall short of the glory of God" (Rom. 3:23), and "the wages of sin is death" (6:23). But when one comes to faith in Jesus Christ, they are literally resurrected to a new life, a Christ life that is eternal. The purpose for which you are going—the reason you are being sent—is to bring life to those who are dead in trespasses and sin through the message you proclaim.

YOU ARE CALLED TO ROLL AWAY THE STONE.

It was Jesus that raised Lazarus from the dead, but He asked others to remove the stone that covered the entrance of the tomb. "Jesus . . . came to the tomb. . . . And a stone was lying against it. Jesus said, 'Remove the stone'" (John 11:38–39). It is only Jesus that can bring new life to persons who are lost. It is only His Holy Spirit that convicts of sin and righteousness, enlightening one's understanding that Jesus is the way, the truth, and the life. But He has called us to roll away the stone. He could have rolled away the stone with a mere gesture, but it was something He had others do that He might do what only He could do!

You see, there are a lot of barriers to people receiving a new life in Christ. Like the parable of the sower, as you sow the seed of the gospel, some of it will fall on the hardened soil of resistant and closed hearts. But others will fall on rocky soil where it cannot take root until the stones have been removed. You will find a spiritual hunger wherever you go, and people will be inclined to embrace your message only to have their faith choked by the thorns of social pressure and distorted worldviews. It is not to disparage the power of the gospel message itself, but you will have to remove the stone in people's hearts in order for them to believe and experience that new life in Christ.

When we went to Indonesia, the largest Muslim country in the world, I envisioned the pages of Acts being reenacted with multitudes being saved once they heard my preaching. But they were largely indifferent and antagonistic to my witness. They had been taught that Jesus was just another prophet and that He really didn't die on the cross; it was an imposter. They were convinced I had it all wrong. They were convinced the Christianity I presented was characterized by the immoral lifestyle they saw in Western movies, something that was in no way attractive to them. There were some stones that had to be rolled away before they could discover and experience a new life.

Some of you are going to South Asia where Hindus will hear and respect your message and what you choose to believe, but there is a big stone of pluralism and tolerance in believing all religions are equal that needs to be removed. It is a challenge to remove the stone keeping Buddhists in Asia from being raised to new life, one that has convinced them for thousands of years that their eternal destiny is determined by accumulating "karma" through their own good works. Many of you going to Catholic cultures will find a stone of deception that needs to be removed, one that convinces them they are already Christians in spite of the fact they have never had a personal experience of repentance and faith. More and more you will find all over the world a humanistic philosophy of self-sufficiency that needs to be removed.

Let me suggest that you can remove the stone, the barriers that keep people from believing on Jesus, by the life that you live. You can raise people who are dead in sin to new life through the message you proclaim, but you must remove the stone through the life that you live. When you build relationships that allow them to see the difference Christ makes, when they see a genuine heart of compassion and love, when they see the purity and holiness of your life, then they will begin to understand the message you proclaim is authentic. Ezekiel 36:23 says, "Then the nations will know that I am the LORD . . . when I am hallowed in you before their eyes."

YOU ARE CALLED TO UNBIND THEM AND SET THEM FREE.

After the stone was removed, Jesus prayed to the Father and then called out, "Lazarus, come forth." And we read in John 11:44, "He who had died came forth, bound hand and foot with wrappings; and his face was wrapped around with a cloth. Jesus said to them, 'Unbind him, and let him go.'"

God is calling a lost world to salvation. But He is not calling them to repentance and faith just to keep them out of hell or add more numbers to His kingdom. He came to set them free from the bondage and power of sin. He came to give them an abundant life that is free from fear and superstition. He said, "You shall know the truth, and the truth shall make you free" (John 8:32).

How do you unbind them from all the clutter of cultural worldviews? How do you set them free from the fears and superstitions that have dominated their lives? It is by teaching the Word of God. I remember developing a pattern of teaching new believers. After a village group had come to the point of commitment to be followers of Christ and were baptized, I, either directly or through one of the local leaders, began a series of discipleship lessons and follow-up to their decision. Generally they had no understanding of what was expected and how to live the Christian life. They had no background for understanding what a church was and how they were to relate and function as the body of Christ.

It was amazing when we would come to the lesson on spiritual warfare and they discovered the reality of 1 John 4:4: "Greater is He that is in you than he that is in the world." Now you could tell the difference in their lives when they first became believers, but a notable change occurred when they comprehended the victory they had in Jesus Christ. They no longer had to fear the demons and spirits that had so dominated their lives and their village. In Christ they had been set free; and as they learned the Word of God and applied its truth, their lives became unbound from old habits and beliefs.

I recall leading a man to Christ who was a real reprobate. It took quite some time, but he truly gave his heart to Jesus. He was always getting in fights and made his living as a con man through fraud and dishonesty. A few weeks after he had become a Christian, he came to visit me and asked, "Is a Christian supposed to be happy?" I affirmed that we had great joy because our sins were forgiven and we had a new life in Christ. He explained that he was miserable and confused. His old friends had abandoned him. Every time he had an opportunity to make a killing by deception, something would not allow him to follow through, and he felt bad when he lost his temper now, something he had never felt before. I replied, "Praise God!" The Holy Spirit was creating a new creature, unbinding him from his old habits and way of life as he learned the truths of God's Word.

As you are faithful to witness and proclaim the gospel, people will be saved. Maybe not all of them, but it is the nature and power of the gospel to draw people to Jesus. And the message you proclaim will turn them from darkness to light and from death to life. The relationship you build and the life that you live will roll away the stone that keeps them from coming to Jesus. Then as you are faithful to teach and nurture and disciple new believers in the Word of God, you will unbind them from their old habits, superstitions, and worldviews and set them free to a victorious new life in Christ.

15

Overcoming Inadequacy and Frustration

1 Corinthians 2:1–5

In each appointment service I relive the emotion and nostalgia of my own appointment more than thirty years ago. I recall the excitement and confidence mixed with my naivety and not just a little dose of fear. The appointment service represented the "crossing of the Rubicon" in my life. There were no doubts about my call. God had strongly confirmed that in my pilgrimage of seeking His will. I was confident of His sufficiency and bolstered by the enthusiasm and support of the crowd that attended the commissioning service. I tried to ignore the anxiety about what I would be facing in the months that followed, and I suspect you are experiencing much of that same mixture of emotion.

It was much later that the reality of my idealism and naivety actually surfaced. I had been a successful pastor and gained experience through youth ministry and student work. I had been trained in evangelism, soaked up mission strategy in seminary classes, and had had short-term cross-cultural experience overseas. I was ready to take on the largest Muslim country in the world, confident that when I arrived in Indonesia the pages of Acts would unfold once again with multitudes being saved and drawn into the kingdom.

Well, as you already suspect, it didn't quite happen that way. It was humiliating not to be able to communicate and to have to revert back to a childlike process of learning to speak in another language. The oddity of my foreignness in the midst of a different culture was an object that shifted between humor and scorn. To be deprived of the accouterments of my comfort zone and support network left me vulnerable to loneliness and self-pity. Rather than a spiritually hungry people that welcomed my message of hope and eternal life, I found people who were antagonistic to a Christian witness or indifferent at best. My self-confidence, built from years of Christian growth, education, and successful ministry, evaporated as I encountered congested crowds of people and could not even communicate.

YOU WILL BE CONFRONTED WITH FRUSTRATION AND A SENSE OF INADEQUACY.

In those early years I found great comfort in Paul's testimony in 1 Corinthians 2:1–5. I had always had the image of Paul as a bold, self-confident evangelist, persuasive in his eloquence and able to weave impressive apologetics for the claims of Christ through his wisdom and theological understanding. But listen to what he says as he reflects on bringing the gospel to Corinth:

> "And when I came to you, brethren, I did not come with superiority of speech or of wisdom, proclaiming to you the testimony of God. . . . And I was with you in weakness and in fear and in much trembling. And my message and my preaching were not in persuasive words of wisdom." (1 Cor. 2:1, 3–4)

I could really identify with that, especially the struggle of trying to communicate spiritual truths with a limited vocabulary and lack of fluency. I remember in a presentation of the gospel trying to quote Romans 6:23, "For the wages of sin is death." The Indonesian word for wages is "*gaji*." Well, I had just learned the word for elephant which is "*gaja*" and used the wrong one! It made no sense whatsoever to my listeners to hear that an elephant would be the result of sinning! It was quite disconcerting to preach and have blank, puzzled expressions on the faces of the congregation punctuated by polite snickers and outbursts of laughter when I was saying nothing that was intended to be humorous.

Talk about standing in fear and trembling—on more than one occasion a Muslim villager, with his hand on his machete, would tell me that I was not welcome in his village with my Christian witness. When I would find an individual receptive to my testimony on the street or in the market, it would not be long before a disruptive mob would gather. I found my Western logic in presenting the Four Spiritual Laws or the Roman Road in which a sequence of logical premises led to an obvious conclusion regarding the claims of Christ did not fit their worldview and made no sense whatsoever. All of my education and theological studies seemed irrelevant in equipping me for the challenge I faced. Your experience may not be similar to mine, but it is not unlikely that you will encounter frustration and a sense of inadequacy.

YOUR WITNESS MUST BE A DEMONSTRATION OF THE SPIRIT AND OF POWER.

But what did Paul learn in this situation? He discovered an interesting paradox of the Christian life that it is in our weakness we are strong. It is when we come to the end of ourselves and recognize our inadequacy that Christ is able to reveal His power and use us. In fact, Paul understood that this is how it needed to be so that his words and testimony would be a "demonstration of the Spirit and of power, that your faith should not rest on the wisdom of men, but on the power of God" (vv. 4b–5).

That is the only thing that will draw people to Jesus Christ and that will influence them to embrace a life-changing faith. It is not necessarily fluent words and persuasive arguments but a life that demonstrates the power and reality of Jesus Christ. That's why God has called you to plant your lives in a foreign culture, in the midst of people who are lost. That's why you are being sent by the International Mission Board to places like Cairo, Zimbabwe, Istanbul and Kosovo, China and Nepal, Kazakhstan and Sumatra. It is to be an incarnational witness so that people might see the reality of a living Savior in your life, and so you would earn the credibility of a verbal witness that is not based on your abilities, training, and skills but an experience of knowing Jesus.

We must never forget that the Great Commission is framed by two very important verses. In Matthew 28:18 Jesus says, "All power is given unto me in heaven and in earth." Now let that sink in for just a moment. There is no power in all the universe that exceeds the power of Jesus Christ. He has the authority to do whatever He plans and determines to do. And He tells us what that is in the next verse. Therefore, we are to go and make disciples of all nations. Then He closes by reminding us that He goes with us, in all that power and authority, when we go in obedience to His call. Remember Luke's version in Acts 1:8. Being witnesses to the uttermost ends of the earth is predicated on having received the power of the Holy Spirit in our lives.

YOU MUST FOCUS ON KNOWING CHRIST AND PROCLAIMING THE GOSPEL.

It's obvious that I left out the second verse in reflecting on this passage, which is, of course, the key verse. Paul put it all in perspective when he said, "I determined to know nothing among you except Jesus Christ, and Him crucified" (1 Cor. 2:2). That's the heart of my challenge to you. It is the foundation of any success in your witness and ministry. It is the source of God's grace that you will need in your adjustments and transition—to keep your eyes on Jesus. All the gifts and experience God has poured into your preparation for this assignment, all the education and training you have received, the abilities and skills you bring to your role overseas are important. But they are meaningless apart from a relationship with Jesus Christ that keeps you mindful of His abiding presence and His sufficiency and power. The gospel "is the power of God for salvation" (Rom. 1:16). And you go equipped with that simple tool, a story, a message of God's love—to proclaim Jesus Christ and Him crucified.

We had finished a year of full-time language study and had been in our place of assignment for several months. I was convicted of a call to missions at an early age, and it seemed all my life had been a process of preparation for where I would be one day in culmination of that call. Suddenly we were there. There was no more getting ready, looking forward to, and preparing for eventually fulfilling that call—we had arrived. We sought to implement our well-honed strategies formulated in the artificial environment of seminary and missionary orientation. We busied ourselves in efforts to build relationships with neighbors. But nothing was happening. The longer we went with no results from our efforts, the more our frustration led to discouragement and discouragement to despondency. I remember one day coming home from a futile effort to witness in some villages and fell on my face on the floor and cried, "God, what are we doing here? Why have You brought us here? We have sacrificed and left family and a successful, fulfilling ministry in the States. We have committed our lives as fully as we know how. Why aren't You keeping your part of the bargain? Why don't we see any evidence of Your power?"

In that time of desperation, God led me in a time of prayer and fasting that changed my desire to see evidence of His hand at work through my ministry to a desire only to know Him in all His fullness. He led me back to the book of Acts where the witness of the apostles and early disciples were so effective, also in a hostile society and religious climate, not unlike I faced in Indonesia. Multitudes were being saved every day. And I realized all these ignorant and unlearned disciples, as they were described, were doing was lifting up Jesus in a bold, positive witness. I realized that is why God had brought me to Indonesia. There was dwelling within me the person of Jesus Christ. God wanted Him to be known by the people of Indonesia, and the only way they could know Him was for me to be there. We began to see open doors. People began to respond, seeds of the gospel were planted, and churches began to emerge in that remote area of East Java. There were many diverse opportunities and channels for witness and ministry, but our only reason for being there was to make Christ known in a bold positive witness.

You, too, will find yourself overwhelmed with fear in the face of cross-cultural challenges and dangers. You will feel so inadequate in the challenge of language study and cross-cultural communication. You will plead for wisdom to understand a worldview that is different. But if you keep your eyes on Jesus—determine only to know Him and the power of His resurrection—you will find people drawn to faith in Christ in ways that defy explanation.

In conclusion, I want you to notice God's assurance in verse 9: "Eye hath not seen nor ear heard, neither has entered into the heart of man the things God has prepared for those who love Him." This is not just talking about the glories of heaven by and by. You cannot imagine what God has prepared for you as you go to lift up Jesus in a foreign land, join an accelerating harvest or penetrate an unreached people group with the gospel for the first time. I still cannot understand how a Muslim in Indonesia could turn his back on his culture, religion, and society, be disowned by his family, lose his job, and perhaps his life threatened in order to embrace faith in Jesus Christ. It could not be simply because of my words or persuasive witness but only because of the power of the gospel.

We would never have believed the church growth and harvest that is sweeping China today, in spite of persecution and government restrictions. We would have never believed that some of the most outstanding church growth would be taking place in Cambodia, Cuba, Mozambique, Ethiopia, among the Azeris in Central Asia and Kabyle Berbers in Algeria. Our strategies twelve years ago did not foresee thousands of missionaries and volunteers that would be sweeping across the Soviet Union and Eastern Europe. Our eyes cannot envision nor our heart imagine what God is seeking to do in our world today through those who love Him and go in obedience to His call. Many of you have already served short-term assignments overseas. You know something of what to expect, but your eye cannot see nor your heart imagine what God has prepared for you as you go, determining to know nothing expect Jesus Christ and Him crucified.

16

THE PASSION TO KNOW HIM

Philippians 3:7–10

This summer I have had the opportunity to be with many of our missionaries around the world. We have been in annual meetings with personnel serving in Central and Eastern Europe, South Asia, and the Pacific Rim. We have had large contingents of missionaries attending stateside assignment conferences, and last month my wife and I had the privilege of traveling throughout several countries of West Africa. Like those of you being appointed tonight, our missionaries represented a diversity of personalities and assignments.

You are going places where God has led you to plant your life. He has gifted and called you to a particular assignment that is aligned with how He is seeking to work in a particular place and people group. As you have shared your testimonies, it is apparent that God calls in a variety of ways. But in spite of the diversity of backgrounds, the ways God has called, and the places of assignment, there is something that each of you hold in common—a passion to be obedient to God's call and to reach a lost world for Jesus Christ. It has got to be more than a sense of being conscripted into service contrary to what you may have chosen to do with your life. It is not a matter of Jesus giving us the Great Commission and your feeling that someone has got to do it. It has got to supersede a sense of guilt in responding to the needs and lostness of a world without Christ. There has got to be a driving passion in your life that motivates you to do what you are doing, a passion that inspires you to go to the edge and do whatever it takes in devotion and sacrifice.

Paul describes that passion in Philippians 3:10. He had already testified that it was not his heritage, his status, his reputation, or personal attainments that were the compelling passion of his life, but it was "that I may know Him, and the power of His resurrection and the fellowship of His sufferings, being conformed to His death."

KNOWING JESUS MUST BE THE PASSION OF YOUR LIFE.

Like Paul, the passion of your life must be to know Jesus. Didn't Paul already know Jesus? Hadn't He met him on the road to Damascus and called him as an apostle to the Gentiles? Hadn't Paul walked with Jesus and experienced His power and presence in an effective life of witnessing and planting churches? Yes, Paul knew Jesus. It was Paul that testified his life was "not I, but Christ in me." He gave one of the most graphic pictures of knowing Christ we have in the New Testament when he said in Galatians 2:20: "I am crucified with Christ, nevertheless I live; yet not I, but Christ who lives in me. And the life I live in the flesh I live by the faith of the Son of God, who loved me, and gave Himself for me." Yet Paul was never satisfied; he always wanted to know more of Jesus.

It is intriguing to realize that Philippians is one of the prison epistles, written toward the end of Paul's life and ministry. After years of walking with Christ, suffering with Him and finding His grace sufficient, seeing the evidence of His power, his desire was still to know Christ in all of His fullness.

I find that is a common factor in missionaries that persevere through trials and hardships. Those that seem to be used effectively have discovered it is not simply a matter of learning how to plant churches, how to communicate and share the gospel cross-culturally, and develop competency for fulfilling their assignment. They become obsessed with knowing Jesus, walking in close fellowship with Him, and experiencing the fullness of His grace and power day by day. For you can't make Him known if you don't know Him—really know Him in a personal relationship each day.

You will discover the more you learn of Jesus, the more there is to know. As you grow in your intimacy with Him, nurturing that early morning quiet time in His presence, you will find He reveals Himself in a deeper, more meaningful way. As you come to the end of yourself and go through the valley of discouragement and despair, you will experience the sufficiency of His grace in a new dimension. After a lifetime of walking with Jesus and serving Him, Paul continued to have a passion to know Him.

KNOWING JESUS MEANS EXPERIENCING THE POWER OF HIS RESURRECTION.

However, it is not only just a passion to know Him but to know the power of His resurrection. Certainly Paul had known the power of God in His life. He had seen God heal the sick, cast out demons, and even raise the dead. He had seen the power of the gospel penetrate pagan hearts and Jewish pride to bring people to saving faith. So what was it that Paul desired?

There is no greater manifestation of power than the resurrection of Jesus Christ. It wasn't just a matter of God bringing to life a dead body; the power of God overcame the death of all humanity. In the crucifixion of Christ, the sins of the whole world were laid on His shoulders and the penalty of that sin borne in His body. When Jesus arose from the tomb, God demonstrated His power over sin and death. He established His power, dominion, and authority over all the universe. Because of His resurrection Jesus could claim in Matthew 28:18, "All power is given to Me in heaven and in earth."

Because Jesus had come to live within him, Paul wanted to know the reality of that power. Doubtless he remembered the apostles reporting Jesus' promise as recorded in Acts 1:8 that they would receive the power of the Holy Spirit and become His witnesses. As a young Pharisee in Jerusalem Paul had witnessed what we read in Acts 4:33, "With great power the apostles were giving witness to the resurrection of the Lord Jesus." I have always felt it was just a witness that Jesus had arose, but their lives and the power of their message was evidence of the power of Jesus' resurrection. Paul wanted that power to always be evident in his life. It wasn't a desire for signs and wonders to be able to perform miracles and to preach with power. He wanted people to see the resurrected power of Jesus in his life day by day. But the only way to know that power was to die, to be crucified with Christ. And that will be the most effective testimony you can have—for people to see in you the reality of a living Savior.

That is why the International Mission Board is basically a missionary sending agency. There are a lot of things that can be done to share the gospel around the world, but Jesus told us to go. Why was that? Because when we go, He promises to go with us, and I think He realized the most effective way to win and disciple a lost world is to plant your life among them. Live with them, walk with them, let them observe the difference Christ makes in your life. We call this an incarnational witness, living out the gospel in flesh and blood, and that is what will give credibility to your verbal witness. It is what will draw people to Jesus when they see that His power is what enables you to live a holy life, a life that demonstrates compassion and a servant heart to those around you. It is a power that is demonstrated in faith to believe God as you pray for people and their needs.

KNOWING JESUS MEANS SHARING IN HIS SUFFERINGS.

Paul makes a strange twist in expressing his passion to know Christ and the power of His resurrection. He adds that it was also a passion to share in His sufferings, even to the point of being conformed to His death. He understood that the only way to know Christ was to go all the way with Him. You can't draw a bottom line and say I'll go this far but no farther. Too many people have said, "I want to know Christ; I want to serve Him and live for Him but not if it means going overseas as a missionary." You can go as a missionary but limit how God can use you by restricting where you are willing to live or by an unwillingness to entail risk or danger if that's what obedience to God's will means.

I heard someone describe how Paul may have responded to some of the situations we face today in getting the gospel to the whole world. Someone may say, "You can't go to that country because the government doesn't allow missionaries. Or you can't share the gospel among that Muslim people group; you might get arrested, or beaten, or stoned. You could even get killed!" I think Paul would say, "So? What's the point?" He didn't have a death wish or a martyr's complex; he just gave himself with abandon to Christ, whatever the cost. A willingness to entail suffering unleashed a power in his life and witness.

It was a principle he had discovered earlier in his ministry. Remember in 2 Corinthians 12 when he spoke of the suffering and affliction of that thorn in the flesh? He learned that God's power is perfected through his weakness. Therefore, he said, "Most gladly, therefore, I will rather boast about my weaknesses, that the power of Christ may dwell in me. Therefore I am well content with weaknesses, with insults, with distresses, with persecutions, with difficulties, for Christ's sake; for when I am weak, then I am strong" (vv. 9–10).

He discovered, as you need to discover early in your ministry, what it means to follow Christ in obedience. You have testified of a call to follow Christ to a certain country or people group, but let me remind you what Peter said that entails. Paul would agree with 1 Peter 2:21, "For you have been called for this purpose, since Christ also suffered for you, leaving you an example for you to follow in His steps."

Let me ask you a question as you prepare to go to the mission field. For most of you, you see this as a lifetime commitment. Would you rather have a life of comfort and ease, free from distress and difficulties and suffering, and never experience anything of God's power? Or would you rather give God an opportunity to manifest His power and grace in your life by being confronted with your own weakness and inadequacy? I wasn't on the mission field long until I was pleading with God to do something that could not be explained except by the power of His Spirit. I knew my abilities and programs and personal efforts would not cut it.

At the annual meeting in the Pacific Rim, I was sitting in a session with strategy coordinators, and seven of them gave reports on phenomenal breakthroughs and growth among their people group. It was very subtle and wasn't a point of emphasis, but everyone had experienced suffering. It was the trauma of an armed robbery, a family injured in a terrorist bombing, a debilitating illness, or a child critically injured; but the common element of suffering—the cost involved—seemed to be more than coincidental.

As I traveled across West Africa last month, I met missionaries who had embraced a lifestyle of suffering as much as any I have seen around the world. They are in impoverished, disease-ridden countries that the United Nations identifies as the worst quality of life in the world. Some of them live hours from any other missionary with no running water, phone service, or dependable electricity. Many go out to the villages and live in mud huts, cooking over an open fire. They don't talk about whether or not one has contracted malaria, but when they last had it and what they did to treat it. Why would they embrace a lifestyle of self-denial and suffering? For the sake of reaching a lost world? Yes, but that would not be enough to keep them there.

It is because they had the same motivation and passion expressed by Paul to know Jesus, to experience the power of His resurrection and the fellowship of His suffering. That's what it takes to survive on the mission field, and that's what it takes to reach a lost world. I pray that will always be the passion and desire of your life, that in your weakness God would find a vessel in which He can entrust His power.

17

BEAUTIFUL FEET

Romans 10:15

It is always thrilling to hear the testimonies of how God has touched the lives of new missionary candidates and how they have responded to His call. Those that are present for this appointment service are here apparently because of interest in and support of missions or perhaps due to a special relationship with someone being commissioned. But you may not have realized that you are attending a beauty pageant!

Your immediate response may be that this sure isn't like any beauty pageant you have attended before. You may have been impressed by the testimonies and occasionally thought, *That's a sharp guy*, or *that's an attractive couple*, but their appearance didn't make you think that you were attending a beauty pageant. But did you notice their feet? Romans 10:15 says, "How beautiful are the feet of those who preach the gospel of peace, who bring glad tidings of good things!"

We don't normally think of feet as being beautiful. In judging a person's appearance, we may observe that a lady has beautiful hair or hands, or even a guy may have a beautiful complexion or beautiful eyes, but not feet. To the contrary, our feet may be everything but beautiful. The first week we arrived in Indonesia, I took my wife and children to buy some sandals that could be readily made and were appropriate for that hot tropical climate. The sandal maker would put their feet on a piece of paper and draw the outline of the foot to get the size. We had not had any language study, but as he drew the foot of my wife, Bobbye, and exclaimed, "Aduh, besar!" I learned my first word—the word for "big"!

YOUR FEET ARE BEAUTIFUL BECAUSE THEY ARE OBEDIENT FEET.

If we asked these folks to take off their shoes, you would probably see some with little stubby toes, others possibly with ugly corns and calluses. But in God's perspective these feet are beautiful because they are obedient feet, going where God has called them. In Romans 10:13–15 we are told that "whoever calls on the name of the Lord shall be saved." That's really good news. There is no exclusion, no exceptions, and no contingency clauses; simply, whoever calls on the name of the Lord Jesus Christ shall be saved.

But then we are confronted with that sequence of questions, "How then shall they call on Him in whom they have not believed? And how shall they believe in Him of whom they have not heard? And how shall they hear without a preacher? And how shall they preach unless they are sent?"

I have been to India twice in the past year, and as often as I go, I never get used to seeing people bowing before idols representing the millions of deities they worship. In Africa multitudes are in bondage to superstition and spiritism, clinging to charms and fetishes as their only hope for protection against evil. You are going to proclaim good tidings of great joy that a Savior has come, and His name is Jesus, so they can call on Him in faith and be saved.

Some of you are going to unreached people groups that, amazingly, have never heard the name of Jesus. They have been isolated culturally and geographically in places where missionaries have never been allowed. They are lost in sin not because they have rejected Jesus Christ or because they don't want to be saved, but they have never heard of Him on whom they must call, and you are going to lift up the name of Jesus. But now they will have an opportunity to hear, to believe, and to call upon the name that is above all names because you go in obedience.

YOUR FEET ARE BEAUTIFUL BECAUSE THEY TAKE YOU TO SHARE THE GOOD NEWS OF PEACE.

Those going as missionaries are not unaware of the kind of world to which they have been called. Have you been keeping up with the news? There is turmoil all across the Muslim world because of tensions and conflict with Iraq. Economic deterioration in Asia has brought political upheaval along with rioting in Indonesia and other countries. There is continuing ethnic conflict between Tutsis and Hutus in Africa, Serbs and Albanians in Kosovo, Palestinians and Israelis, North and South Koreans, and other places all over the world. Thousands have died from floods in Bangladesh, drought in

West Africa, and earthquakes in Central Asia. These are being sent to a world that is desperate for peace.

Fred Levrets, who retired a couple of years ago from Nigeria and is now living in Abilene, Texas, told me a story of one of the lay preachers with whom he worked. Brother Andreas lived in a village on the remote fringes of where Fred served. Fred could only get out to the area every few months, but each time he returned he found that Brother Andreas had started a few more churches and baptized dozens of new believers. He asked him how it was that the people were so receptive. Brother Andreas replied simply, "The poor don't get much good news."

You are going to a world that doesn't get much good news. That's why your feet are so beautiful. They are taking you to proclaim the peace that only God provides through Jesus Christ. You are going to bring glad tidings that there is salvation from sin and hope in a hopeless world of poverty and suffering. You are going to bring light to a world in darkness. They cannot believe if they have never heard, but they can never hear unless someone goes to tell them. And that's why you are being sent tonight. The verse which Paul quotes comes from Isaiah 52:7. It says, "How beautiful upon the mountains are the feet of him who brings good news, who proclaims peace, who brings glad tidings of good things, who proclaims salvation, who says to Zion, 'Your God reigns!'"

Some of you will be going to villages in the Andes Mountains of Peru or to isolated valleys in the Caucasus Mountains of Central Asia to bring the good news of salvation. Some are going to do medical work or agriculture and development But as you minister to people, never forget that you are going to tell them how they can have peace with God, a peace that eradicates differences and discrimination, yet primarily a peace that bridges that chasm of sin and reconciles them to God. Many of you are going as teachers or through business platforms to join others in restricted countries that have succumbed to godless teachings that have brought despair. Go, and proclaim that God reigns; He's alive. And invite them to call upon His name, that name which is above every name.

YOUR FEET ARE BEAUTIFUL BECAUSE THEY ARE GUIDED BY GOD'S SPIRIT.

In 1998 David and Amy Jarboe from Oklahoma were appointed for Cambodia where they joined colleagues who were training church leaders and facilitating a remarkable church planting movement that has seen two hundred churches started in just six years. While they were at missionary orientation prior to their departure, I was eating at a table with the Jarboes and others when one of them said, "David, show Dr. Rankin what your Sunday School class gave you." David stood up, put his foot on the table right there in the midst of our food trays, and he was wearing some expensive hiking boots that would obviously serve him well in doing a lot of walking in any climate or terrain. He said, "My Sunday School class gave this pair of shoes to me," and he choked up as he continued. "They said they were going to pray for me every morning when I put these shoes on and every night when I took them off. They said they would be praying that everywhere these shoes went God's Spirit would bless my witness and bring people to faith in Jesus Christ!"

Because you go in obedience to share the good news of peace to a lost world, God promises to go with you. He will guide your steps, both literally and in the many decisions you will face. He will lead you through open doors of opportunity, and when you encounter resistance and barriers, He will give discernment. Paul trusted God to lead him, and one of the reasons he was so effective and was used so extensively was because he was confident that God guided his steps and showed him the way. When he tried to share the gospel in Asia and Bithynia and the door was closed, it did not bother him because God was guiding. He responded to the Macedonian vision and planted churches throughout Europe. And you can be assured that God will be guiding you as you walk by faith and follow obediently wherever He leads, realizing that wherever you go, it is to proclaim the good news of peace.

We won't ask our missionaries to take their shoes off and show us their feet, but they are all winners in our beauty pageant tonight. Their feet are beautiful; they are the most beautiful feet of all because they are going to declare the good news of salvation and peace to a lost world. But what about your feet? Are they beautiful? Why not? Is it because they are not carrying the gospel of peace to those hurting around you or because you have not been obedient to respond to God's call and go where He wants the good news of the gospel to be proclaimed?

Are there those who cannot call on the name of the Lord because you are unwilling to go? When our researchers calculated the total population of unreached people groups, which have been identified that are still waiting to hear the gospel, it came to 1.7 billion. How tragic! Jesus died on the cross to save them, but they can't call on Him because they have never heard of Jesus. They are still waiting for someone to be sent. How much longer must they wait? How many more will die and enter an eternity of torment in hell simply because no one reached them upon the mountains and in the valleys with the glad tidings of peace and salvation.

Who will go to the cities of Russia, Belarus, Moldova, and the Ukraine while a door of opportunity is still open? Who will respond to an unfilled request for a strategy coordinator to go to Jilin and Harbin in China? Who will go into the fields that are white unto harvest in Africa and Latin America?

You may rejoice in these that are being commissioned and think what a blessing this service has been; you may say, "I'm going to pray for them and support them, but these feet are staying right here!" If you are unwilling for your feet to walk through the sands of the African desert or through the war-torn streets of Bosnia or on the jungle trails of the Amazon, then how will people there hear the good news of peace?

One of these missionaries being appointed told of praying that God would send laborers into the fields of harvest around the world. God spoke to her and convicted her; He seemed to say, "How can you pray for laborers and not be willing to be one?" Paul goes on to quote Isaiah again in Romans 10:21, "All day long I have stretched out My hands to a disobedient and contrary people." Could that be you? Could God be stretching out His hand to you, calling you to go, but finding a disobedient heart and contrary response? Allow Him to make your feet beautiful by becoming obedient to wherever He will send them.

18

BE AN EXAMPLE OF THOSE WHO BELIEVE

1 Timothy 4:12–14

I know something of what you are going to face as you go as missionaries to a cross-cultural overseas assignment. As I think back to my own experience and those initial years on the field, I realize, in retrospect, that they were learning experiences. I went with a great deal of confidence and all the training available but discovered God had to teach me many things if I was to be useful over the long haul. I am always tempted to base my comments and challenge on those experiences, and there might be some profit in that, but I have discovered that God's Word is quite adequate for all you need to know.

A text that encapsulates my challenge to those of you being appointed is 1 Timothy 4:12. Paul is writing to encourage and challenge Timothy who had been sent to Ephesus. He had joined Paul on his missionary journeys and, in spite of his shyness, had been delegated to care for the emerging churches, nurturing the results of Paul's witness at Thessalonica and later at Ephesus. He says in verse 12, "Let no one look down on your youthfulness, but rather in speech, conduct, love, faith and purity, show yourself an example of those who believe."

Now all of you may not be able to identify with that because, relatively speaking, you are not exactly young! But you are young in tenure and experience as a cross-cultural missionary. Many of you have already served for two years as a journeyman or on an International Service Corps assignment. But as you go now to plant your life in obedience to God's call, you go as a novice. Most of you have been on short-term, overseas mission trips; you have been there for a brief period of time, seen the needs, shared your witness, ministered to people in need, and then returned home. You have not had the ongoing responsibilities that come from planting your lives and staying to live among the people to whom God is now calling you. You may be fifty years old but can relate to Timothy as being youthful in terms of missionary service.

What Paul is saying is, "Timothy, you must be an incarnational witness." We speak of Christ as God incarnate. John says in his gospel witness, "The Word became flesh, and dwelt among us, and we beheld His glory, glory as of the only begotten from the Father" (John 1:14). We cannot approach the significance of God becoming flesh in order to reveal Himself to us, but, in a sense, missionaries are to be an incarnational witness, living out their faith in flesh and blood. Your words may come across as simply teaching a foreign religion. Your verbal witness will ring hollow unless it is backed up by a life that reflects the reality of a living Christ. That's why the International Mission Board is essentially a sending agency. Jesus called us to go, and the most effective mission strategy to reach a lost world is to send God-called people who will plant their lives cross-culturally that others might see Christ in you.

But notice there are five ways in which Timothy is to demonstrate his faith as an example of those who believe. These five admonitions apply to you as well. Following these characteristics will give authenticity to your witness and provide a vivid, living example of the kind of life represented by believers who know Jesus Christ. God may anoint and bless your words and proclamation of the gospel, and I pray that He will, but it is the testimony of a Christlike life, lived out among the people that will be your most effective witness.

BE AN EXAMPLE IN SPEECH.

The way you talk should reflect your relationship with Christ. Local believers are well aware of the conflict that sometimes exists among missionaries. They don't forget a harsh word of criticism or an impatient outburst of anger. You will struggle with exasperating circumstances. The traffic in most world-class cities is horrendous. You can sit in gridlock for hours in places like Bangkok and Manila where few drivers heed traffic regulations. Succumbing to road rage and losing your temper in impatience is not exactly a beneficial testimony. How are you going to react when you are taken advantage of, inconvenienced, or find you have been defrauded when presuming to help a person in need? Do your words reflect God's grace? Are they edifying?

Do they minister healing in expressions of forgiveness? They'd better, or you will find people see you no different than everyone else, and your testimony will be meaningless.

BE AN EXAMPLE IN CONDUCT.

God has called you from a variety of backgrounds—not only church-related vocations but from business, engineering, medical work, a flight controller, computer technician, and other professions. He has taken that diversity and is sending you to fill a variety of assignments. Many are going to do general evangelism, church planting, and strategy coordination; but others will be assisting volunteers and providing business support services. You will be serving as teachers, working in media and literature, sports evangelism, dentistry, and business platforms. But never think for a moment that to fill those job descriptions is the reason you are going. Yes, they represent strategic needs, but they just provide the rationale for you to be there and a channel through which you can reflect Christ in your behavior.

First Peter 2:12 says, "Keep your behavior excellent among the Gentiles [nations], so that in the thing in which they slander you as evildoers, they may on account of your good deeds, as they observe them, glorify God in the day of visitation." How do people in the culture where you are going view Americans and Christianity? Most likely it is by what they see in American movies. You will be perceived as immoral, wealthy, self-centered, and probably as an arrogant infidel. But what will they observe in your behavior? Because God is sending you, it means He is planning for that day of visitation when His Spirit will reveal Christ and move to bring them to Him that He might be glorified. Will they be prepared to receive Christ because of your behavior and conduct? Let's admit it. If Christ is Savior of the world and He dwells within you, then it should make a difference in how you live. If you are going to proclaim the potential of a changed life in Christ, then there should be evidence of that changed life in you and your conduct.

BE AN EXAMPLE IN LOVE.

Jesus said, "By this all men shall know that you are my disciples, if you love one another." Love is self-giving; it is others centered. And that is such a contrast with the world, that love itself is a testimony of God. In a recent edition of our video program for students called *The Task*, there is a testimony of a Russian university student from Novisibirsk in Siberia. She said her parents were scientists, and she was raised being able to articulate an apologetic for atheism. She said she had an answer for every religious argument. She said whenever she talked with the missionaries she felt, even though she could refute their premises, she was arguing against the truth. Later she became a believer and upon reflection says, "I really don't remember anything they taught me before I became a believer, but I remember how they loved me."

The world is hungry for love; it is longing for someone to care. And it is only love that makes possible the phenomenon of sacrifice. There is no other motive for turning your back on the American dream and leaving the comforts and security of your lifestyle here. Only when you are motivated by a love for God will you find no sacrifice is too great to show His love to a lost world. But that love must be a practical reality in giving yourself to those in need. It must be a consistent expression of selflessness in your relationship with your colleagues and others. It's an example the world is desperate to see.

BE AN EXAMPLE IN FAITH.

Though we cannot identify where many of you specifically are going to serve, you are going to places in Central Asia and the Turko-Persian world like Azerbaijan, Kazakstan, India, and Turkey. You are going to plant your lives in Vietnam, Cambodia, Myanmar, and Thailand. Others are going all across Africa, Europe, and Latin America to proclaim the gospel, plant churches, and extend the kingdom of God. Many of these places have been resistant to a Christian witness; you may not see immediate results, but you have faith that God's purpose will prevail.

Go with a confident faith so that when the opposition intensifies and trials persist, you will continue to believe in the strong name of Jesus and that His mighty hand will act to bring the people to saving faith in Christ. Don't be discouraged by opposition or indifference. Believe, as the psalmist declared, "All the ends of the earth will remember and turn to the LORD, and all the families of the nations will worship before Thee. For the kingdom is the LORD's and He rules over the nations" (Ps. 22:27–28). God's purpose will be fulfilled.

The missionary testimonies are prolific of those who labored for years without visible results only to see a mighty harvest emerge later. Some have given themselves for a lifetime without seeing a breakthrough, but they laid the foundation through which a subsequent generation would come to the Lord because they never lost faith in the power of God and His purpose.

Let those around you see you walking in faith, believing in God, and claiming His Word, even when all evidence is to the contrary.

BE AN EXAMPLE IN PURITY.

Finally Timothy is reminded to be an example in purity. Temptations will come. You are venturing into Satan's territory, and he will find every way he can to entice you to compromise your convictions, indulge in fleshly gratifications, and succumb to carnal temptations that destroy your witness. There have been those who have stumbled and fallen; they have forfeited their witness in failing to live a separated life of holiness and purity. The only way to walk in holiness is to maintain an intimate relationship with God that comes through a devoted time of prayer and Bible study each day. Don't neglect to nurture patterns and habits that are essential to maintain fellowship with Him. Walking with God in a way that will result in a pure and holy life will come not from a perfunctory discipline but from a heart that is desperate for Him and a desire to know Him in all of His fullness. It is Christ in you that is the hope of glory. Walk with Him and be an example in speech, conduct, love, faith, and purity that others may see Christ in you.

In a final admonition and challenge in verse 14, Paul says, "Do not neglect the spiritual gift within you, which was bestowed upon you through prophetic utterance with the laying on of hands by the [elders]." Even though this is an exciting time, and not without some emotion, if you are a typical group of new missionaries, you are probably experiencing a tinge of anxiety. Some of you have been in process toward missionary service for some time, confident of your call; but now that you have arrived at this time of appointment, it is natural that you would have some self-doubts about what you are getting into. You may wonder if you are really qualified, if you have what it takes. You've heard the expression, "Where God guides, He provides." It is not your ability but your availability. Because God has called you, He gifts you with all you need to fulfill His will. And tonight we are here to affirm your gifts and calling. Do not neglect all that God has given you which is of His Spirit. Jesus said, "You shall receive power when the Holy Spirit is come upon you, and you shall be my witnesses . . . to the uttermost ends of the earth." It is God who has called you. It is God who has gifted you. We affirm you and send you in the power of His Spirit.

19

ASSURED VICTORY IN SPIRITUAL WARFARE

Revelation 12:10–11

I recently sat in a restaurant on a mountaintop overlooking the city of Almaty in Central Asia. The snow-capped peaks of the Tienshan Mountains towered behind us. But as we ate barbecued skewers of goat shaslik, the spiritual darkness of Central Asia offset the beauty of a setting sun highlighting this massive capital city of Kazakhstan. I was completing a three-week trip through the Central Asian republics, a region that represents the black hole of lostness. On a scale of lostness and relative access to the gospel, Central Asia represents the center of the target. Less than one-tenth of one percent of the people have embraced a faith in Jesus Christ. Most have never heard of His love.

How could such a situation exist two thousand years after our Lord sent out His followers to disciple the nations? Many explanations could be presented, but it was evident to me that the kingdom of God is engaged in a spiritual warfare against an enemy that is intent on depriving God of His glory among the nations. Several days with our team seeking to impact the twelve million Uighurs in the Xinjiang Province of Western China and Kazakhstan, the fourteen million Kazaks, along with the Uzbeks, Kyrgyz, Tajiks, and 535 other people groups in this region convinced me that we, indeed, do not wrestle against flesh and blood but against powers, principalities, and rulers of darkness.

For generations our adversary has captured the hearts of these people with two of his most formidable weapons. Marxism has hardened their conscience in an atheistic ideology that would deny an inherent spiritual need, and Islam has perverted their understanding of God to a fatalistic cultural tradition that holds the people in bondage.

Our personnel sensed the ubiquitous presence of the adversary, not only in religious resistance to the message of hope they proclaimed but also in the constant, excessive bureaucracy of government red tape and corruption. They felt it with a family's witness being aborted when their son had to be medically evacuated. They felt it when an office was burglarized and our missionary assaulted. They are alert to the enemy seeking to discourage them when colleagues are imprisoned in the neighboring country of Afghanistan, when the gas is turned off for the winter because the destitute government cannot make payments, and when pastors of the emerging church are interrogated and tortured.

It is not only in Central Asia, but wherever you are going in the world, you are entering into Satan's territory. For, you see, where Christ is not known—where Jesus is not Lord—the peoples, the nations, and cultures are the domain of Satan. But let me alert you to the fact that it is easy to get a distorted view of reality. Satan cannot win. Jesus said, "All authority is given Me in heaven and earth," and any perception otherwise is simply an illusion. First John 3:8 tells us, "The Son of God appeared for this purpose, that He might destroy the works of the devil." Colossians 2:14–15 says that when our sins and accusations against us were nailed to the cross, Jesus disarmed the rulers and authorities and made a open spectacle of them. And God's Word reminds us that Satan and all his demonic following will be ultimately defeated and cast into outer darkness, and our Lord Jesus Christ shall be exalted among the nations.

But as a defeated foe, Satan is seeking vengeance. He is seeking to rob God of His glory and defer His kingdom being established among every tribe and people and tongue and nation. He tempts you and discourages you. He gets you to serve selfish interests and to hold onto your comforts and your desires in order to keep God from being glorified in your life. He is at work tonight, convincing many in attendance that God doesn't really need them on the mission field; they can pursue their own plans, stay close to Momma and Papa, avoid the risk and still faithfully serve God. He is using totalitarian governments, intensified persecution and any tactic possible to keep God's purpose of being glorified among the nations from being fulfilled.

Many who have gone as missionaries have had to overcome these kinds of temptations and pressures. The subtle and devious arguments of Satan keeping you from being obedient to God's will can be powerful. A commitment to go to the ends of the earth represents a victory, but the final battle has not been fought. Tonight we are sending you off to war. Let me tell you how you can be assured of victory. In Revelation 12:9–11 we read:

> And the great dragon was thrown down, the serpent of old who is called the devil and Satan, who deceives the whole world; he was thrown down to the earth, and his angels were thrown down with him. And I heard a loud voice in heaven, saying, "Now the salvation, and the power, and the kingdom of our God and the authority of His Christ have come, for the accuser of our brethren has been thrown down, who accuses them before our God day and night. And they overcame him because of the blood of the Lamb and because of the word of their testimony, and they did not love their life even to death."

We have a picture here of that final judgment when all of Satan's wickedness and deceit will be thrown down once and for all. But notice the testimony of those who overcame his accusations and temptations. These are those who walked in victory. How did they prevail in the spiritual battles of the kingdom and in their personal walk with the Lord?

THEY OVERCAME HIM BY THE BLOOD OF THE LAMB.

They overcame him by the blood of the Lamb. It wasn't their own efforts. It wasn't in their ability to walk in holiness and purity. It wasn't because they had been discipled and educated to the level that they could resist temptation, discouragement, and avoid succumbing to self-pity and a sense of worthlessness when the results they hoped for did not materialize. Their victory was in the blood of the Lamb who shed His blood on Calvary and purchased redemption by His mercy and grace. It was not in their own righteousness and strength but because they accepted the righteousness of Him who became sin on their behalf.

Remember, we are told, that the Son of God appeared that He might destroy the works of the devil, and this is what He did on the cross. Don't ever think there is any merit in your own ability or as a result of your commitment to serve as a missionary. It is only in Christ that you will overcome; everything you are is because His blood was shed for you.

THEY OVERCAME HIM BY THE WORD OF THEIR TESTIMONY.

Christ's death on the cross doesn't exempt us from trials. It doesn't provide us a default victory in the spiritual warfare you will encounter personally nor in your efforts to penetrate the strongholds of Satan with the gospel. We are told that they overcame him because of the word of their testimony. The Scripture tells us (Rom. 10:9–10) that with the heart man believes unto righteousness, but with the mouth confession is made unto salvation. What you believe, you confess. There is power in confessing openly and verbally your faith in Jesus Christ. When you were baptized, it was an open testimony of what you believed in your heart, that Jesus' death, burial, and resurrection was for your sins, and you were confessing that was what you believed personally in your heart.

There is power in confessing and speaking something that you believe. There is a power in verbalizing your testimony. Confessing God's promises will give you peace that passes all understanding when circumstances threaten and there is no rational basis for a peaceful spirit. Confessing the truth of God's Word will overcome discouragement and doubts, enable you to resist temptation, and keep your vision on the One who is sovereign over the nations and holds all things in the palm of His hand. One of the most valuable lessons I learned on the mission field was that praising God in all things, confessing that praise with my voice, was the practical key to walking in victory. As the prophet Habakkuk said (3:17–18):

> Though the fig tree should not blossom,
> And there be no fruit on the vines,
> Though the yield of the olive should fail,
> And the fields produce no food,
> Though the flock should be cut off from the fold,
> And there be no cattle in the stalls,
> Yet I will exult in the LORD,
> I will rejoice in the God of my salvation.

But notice the final thing we are told that enabled them to overcome was not just the blood of the Lamb and the word of their testimony.

THEY DID NOT LOVE THEIR LIFE, EVEN UNTO DEATH.

And what could Satan do with that? You see, everything Satan throws at us has to do with an appeal to our ego and self-centeredness. That's the nature of the flesh which is antithetical to the Spirit. Indulge in pleasure and selfish gratification. He is behind the attitudes expressed by "my rights, my opinion, my space, my time." That's the very thing that will rob God of His glory. Getting you to be concerned about your house and comforts, focused on entitlements and whether or not you get a just cost-of-living allowance are the things that erode the power of an effective witness. But when one is willing to lay it all on the altar, even to the point of not even holding on to one's life, the accuser cannot gain a foothold to defeat you.

Do you know why the church is exploding with New Testament vitality and growth in China—as many as thirty thousand new believers are coming to faith in Christ everyday? When one is receptive to a Christian witness, they are immediately told that they will possibly be arrested; they could be tortured or even lose their life for the decision to become a Christian. Having dealt with that before they are ever baptized, nothing can deter them in their witness and faithfulness. In Northern India, where a number of believers have been martyred, they are taught to say at the time of baptism if such a threat should come, "You do not take my life from me, but I give it to you in the name of Jesus Christ, that one day you too might know Him."

What can Satan do with that? Absolutely nothing! He is not capable of understanding the concept of sacrifice and is totally disarmed by a motive of love that would lead one to give of their life. Jesus said in Matthew 16:24, "If any man would come after Me, let him take up his cross daily and follow Me." Paul said, "I beseech you, brethren, by the mercies of God, that you present your bodies a living sacrifice, holy, acceptable unto God, which is your reasonable service (Rom. 12:1). That is the ultimate victory.

You go in the blood of the Lamb that was shed for the sins of the world. You go in the power of your testimony that you belong to Him who is Lord of lords and King of kings and has won the victory. You are here tonight being commissioned because you have said, "I will give my life to serve Him and make Him known." But that is a continual, conscious commitment as you go, that you will not love your own life, even unto death. And you, too, will overcome and rejoice to see the kingdoms of this world become the kingdoms of our Lord.

Chapter 20

DELIGHT IN THE LORD

Psalm 37:4–7

I have often shared with our staff a testimony of my pattern for many years of choosing an annual "life verse." We all probably have the life verses that have reflected the values of our life and foundation of our faith. One of mine has been Proverbs 3:5-6: "Trust in the LORD with all thine heart; and lean not unto thine own understanding. In all thy ways acknowledge him, and he shall direct thy paths." Another would be Matthew 6:33: "Seek ye first the kingdom of God, and his righteousness; and all these things shall be added unto you."

The idea of a verse for the year was something new for me when my daughter suggested it. She had been in a discipleship group in college. She was visiting us over the Christmas holidays and asked me if I had a verse for the new year. When I asked what she meant, she explained that God knows everything we are going to face in the coming year, the challenges we are going to encounter, and what we are going to need. She went on, "Isn't it neat to ask Him to give you a verse to claim that is relevant to all these needs?"

I began to seek God's leadership to identify a specific verse that He knew would keep me focused and to keep the trials and challenges I would face in perspective. Over the years it has been phenomenal how that annual life verse would be so relevant to the situations I would experience.

I didn't realize that I would face several life-changing decisions concerning the direction of my ministry and would desperately need to cling to God's leadership the year I was led to choose Isaiah 30:1-2, "Woe to the obstinate children, declares the Lord, who carry out plans that are not mine, who form an alliance but not by my Spirit, who go down to Egypt without consulting me." I did not realize the spiritual growth and intimacy with God that would come in a year of challenges, criticism, and doubts when I chose Psalm 91:1: "He who dwells in the secret place of the Most High shall abide under the shadow of the Almighty."

Now the point I want to make is not a challenge to choose yearly life verses, though that is a good idea and has been a blessing to me in helping me to be aware of God's providence in my walk with Him. Nor is my purpose to remind you of the sufficiency of God's Word and how important it is to read it, study it, and cling to it because it is true and must be the foundation of your life and ministry. You must believe it and live it as the unequivocal authority of all you believe and do. But I want to reflect back on that first suggestion to choose a verse for the year. It brought me to a passage of Scripture that needs to be applied to your life and ministry as you prepare to leave for the mission field.

DELIGHT IN THE LORD.

As I thought about my daughter's suggestion, I realized that God had been impressing me with Psalm 37:4. For some reason it would come to mind each morning as I would pray and often throughout the day. I responded and told her that I think God has given me this verse for the next year, "Delight thyself also in the LORD and He shall give thee the desires of thine heart." My daughter responded, "What are the desires of your heart?" It is a startling experience when your kids reach a level of maturity that they confront you with the challenge of accountability. When she went off to college, I was the one asking the questions, giving the instructions, holding her accountable. But it is thrilling when you see their spiritual growth and can begin to relate as peers in sharing spiritual insights and discussing the issues of life.

Her question was a challenge to me to begin thinking about what are the desires of my heart because God had promised I would have them, contingent on my delighting in Him. My initial thoughts were that I want to have more balance in my life and respite from the unceasing travel and administrative responsibilities. The real desire of my heart was to lose weight and to get in shape physically. As I meditated on it, I began to feel that those desires were pretty self-centered and that the desires of my heart should be focused on something more significant, such as the peoples of South and Southeast Asia coming to know the Lord. The passion of my life personally and in leading our missionaries in the area was to see a great harvest sweeping this largely unevangelized region. Those were the real desires of my heart.

So every morning I would start my devotional time reading or quoting that verse. It became the template of my prayers. All that I would ask for, all my petitions, all my desires were based on my love for the Lord, delighting in His faithfulness and His promises. But an interesting thing happened through that year. As I grew in worship and time with the Lord and became mindful of His abiding presence, a strange realization occurred. I discovered that when we truly delight in the Lord, the only desire of our heart is for Him! It is not for some self-serving gain to lose weight or even an effective evangelistic breakthrough. To delight in the Lord, to find abiding joy and peace that passes all understanding in His abiding presence, results in a desire to know Him even deeper and for a more intimate relationship with Him. All else pales in comparison. He will lead you in a desire and stronger commitment to personal discipline and practicing good health but only that He might be glorified. He does give a greater passion for reaching a lost world but only because you have such a desire and passion for Him.

COMMIT YOUR WAY TO THE LORD.

But notice what happens when your delight is in Him, and He is the desire of your heart.

We are instructed in the next verse, Psalm 37:5, "Commit your way to the LORD, trust also in Him, and He will do it."

Last year on a trip to Central Asia, I was thrilled to see how God was beginning to move in many places. In Kazakhstan, among the Azeris in Azerbaijan, the Kyrgyz, and other people groups, many were coming to the Lord, and churches were multiplying in places where, a few years ago, they had never heard the gospel. One of our single ladies, who had been assigned to a remote Muslim people group, was enthusiastically telling me how God had brought her into contact and given her favor with a "woman of peace." This person of influence had opened the door for a witness among her extended family and village and into other villages. As she described her heart for the people and her confidence in what God was doing, and the way she had so identified and bonded with this community and had devoted herself to them, I was deeply impressed. I continued to listen to testimony after testimony of how God was working in this one-way conversation; finally she paused, and I called her by name and said, "Would you be willing to share something with me? I don't want to embarrass you or put you on the spot, but I would like to know about your personal walk with the Lord. You are isolated with no missionary colleagues, no support group or church where you live; I sense you have a deep dependency on the Lord, and I would like to know about the pattern of your devotional time and prayer time. She dropped her head and didn't say anything immediately. I was uncomfortable and felt I had violated an intimate and personal area of her life. Then she looked at me and with tears in her eyes said, "I love Jesus so much. He is the total focus of my life and my reason for living. I often find myself up at 3:30 in the morning worshipping Him and pouring out my heart in intercession for these people to whom He has called me. The passion of my life is that they would know Him, and whatever it takes, I have given my life to Him."

You are going to face many decisions, not just about your place of service, where you live, and how you do your job and care for your family, but choices regarding lifestyle and how you manage your time. You will constantly be deciding the degree to which you devote time for yourself and how much you give yourself with abandon to the people to whom God has called you. You are not capable of making those decisions. Commit your way to the Lord. Trust Him, for He is the one who will do it and bring His will to pass. You are just the instrument, the channel that God has chosen to use for what He wants to do. Jesus said, "Apart from me you can do nothing." Trust Him not only to lead day by day, but trust Him for the power you need. Trust the promises of His word and realize, "It is not I, but Christ who lives within me" (Gal. 2:20).

REST IN THE LORD.

There is a third admonition that makes this all fit together and puts it into perspective. Not only are we to delight in the Lord, commit our way to the Lord, and trust in Him, Psalm 37:7 says, "Rest in the LORD and wait patiently for Him." If God is sovereign and all authority has been given to Him in heaven and earth, why do we get all out of sorts trying to make things happen according to our agenda and in our time frame? Why do we succumb to stress and feel we are a failure if we don't see immediate results?

Resting in the Lord doesn't mean being laid back and irresponsible. But as we devote ourselves to the task God has given us, we persevere and devote ourselves with a passion to what we know He wants done, confident that He will bless us and our efforts in His time. We can't discern what He is doing behind the scenes and how He may be working in the hearts of people, but we continue faithful and steadfast, knowing that window of response and harvest will come because God's desire is to be exalted among the nations. We are told in 2 Peter 3:9 that God is "not willing that any should perish, but that all should come to repentance."

I'll never forget a missionary serving in a difficult assignment and yet to see any results saying, "We had to realize that God did not call us to success or personal fulfillment, but to obedience." That's the attitude that will enable God to use you; that's what it means to be obedient and rest in Him. We do extensive research on the factors that result in the resignation of missionaries. Our attrition rates are not high and, in fact, are among the lowest of any mission agency. It is interesting that the majority of those who leave active service express that they would not choose to resign, but personal and family needs and other circumstances make it necessary for them to return to the States. Yet everywhere I travel overseas there are those missionaries, I am impressed, that are so devoted to what God has called them to do that absolutely nothing would pull them away and cause them to come home. They don't get frustrated and discouraged when results are not forthcoming. They are not deterred when tragedy comes into their lives or opportunities emerge that would give them more recognition and acclaim or a more comfortable lifestyle back in America. Another translation of this verse translates "patiently" as "longingly"; they rest in the Lord, confident of His power and providence, and they wait or hope longingly for Him to produce the results of their efforts.

Many of you are going to China, Central Asia, and to the Middle East, places God is penetrating with the gospel for the first time. Others will fill a variety of assignments in places like Spain and Germany, Nepal, Zambia and Tanzania or Chile, Peru, and Bolivia. You have visions and desires of what you hope to see God accomplish. You go in confidence there will be results because of your faith in Him, the One who called you. I encourage you to follow this simple pattern as a key to success, not necessarily evangelistic success or personal fulfillment but success in all God wants you to be in Him. Delight yourself in the Lord; let the foremost passion and focus of your life be Him and His lordship. Make your life a reflection of unceasing worship and desire for His glory. Commit your way to Him. Trust Him, and then rest in Him and wait patiently and longingly for whatever He is seeking to do in your life and through your ministry. And He will give you the desires of your heart; He will bring it to pass.

21

A Calling Compelled by Passion

2 Corinthians 5:14; Acts 4:20; Jeremiah 20:9

There is a diversity of backgrounds and a variety of divine impressions that gives one a sense of God's call to international missions. For some this is the result of a pilgrimage that actually began as a child being nurtured in a Christian home with a heart for missions. Most were in a church that helped them to understand that God had a special plan and purpose for their life, and they pursued God's will with a heart that was compliant; obedience was a foregone conclusion wherever God would lead.

Others would never have dreamed of one day being appointed a missionary. Missionaries were those super pious people who had lost all rational sense of acceptable behavior. Even if one wanted to do something significant in helping to reach a lost world, they thought they could never measure up, or the course of their life had followed too many diversions of carnal living and self-serving pursuits. Yet God reached down and grabbed their heart, tapped them on the shoulder, and said, "I've got a place for you; yes, I can use even you." And here you are, having fulfilled all the qualifications, having satisfied all the criteria, and having passed scrutiny of staff and trustees, to stand called of God and prepared to give your life for the sake of reaching a lost world.

Many struggle with that concept of a call of God, and it is something difficult to explain. We have no problem believing that God calls us to salvation. We readily understand that we are called to live a holy life, to be witnesses for Jesus Christ and reflect other characteristics of the Christian life. But we have succumbed to the myth that to go as a missionary is a unique, special calling for a select few. Never mind that multitudes are dying around the world because they have never had anyone to tell them about Jesus.

Never mind that God's Word tells us He is not willing that any should perish but that all should come to repentance. Many others have a heart for missions; they go on volunteer mission trips, pray for missionaries, and give generously to missions; but they have embraced the idea that one is not called to missions unless they see a burning bush or have a Damascus Road experience. Our tendency is to presume we can choose to be doctors, lawyers, teachers, pursue our aspirations for a business career and be in the center of God's will without any distinct directive or calling of God, but to be a missionary requires a mystical, abnormal encounter with God. Your testimonies, and that of many other missionaries, have indicated otherwise.

There does seem to be several common elements in your call to missions. One of these is obviously your awareness of the needs of a lost world. Perhaps you participated in a short-term volunteer trip and were overwhelmed by the lostness you encountered in a foreign country. It would be difficult to watch the images on daily newscasts and not be moved by the suffering and hopelessness of much of our world, especially when you know that Jesus is the answer. Some of you had begun to comprehend the reality of unreached people groups and 1.7 billion people who had no access to the gospel and have not yet even heard of Jesus. Their lostness and eternal destiny separated from God very likely had something to do with your call to give of your life and do something about it.

Many expressed a sense of obligation to be obedient to the Great Commission. As you grew in submission to the lordship of Christ and the desire to do His will, that mandate of our Lord to disciple the nations became a personal call, and you could not say "No." However, you are not being appointed as missionaries simply because of the needs of a lost world or out of a sense of obligation—an attitude of somebody's got to do it! And it is not a response to the need or a sense of obligation that will be enough to keep you on the mission field through times of difficulty and hardship. That will not enable you to persevere through cross-cultural adjustments, language study, and subsequent discouragements. There must be a compulsion that comes from your calling as a passion of your life.

IT IS A PASSION COMPELLED BY THE LOVE OF CHRIST.

Paul said in 2 Corinthians 5:14 that the love of Christ constrains us. It is the love expressed in John 3:16 that compelled God to give His only begotten Son. It is the love for a lost world that drove Jesus to the cross. And it is only when you are compelled by that kind of love within you that you will give your life to the people to whom God has called you. It is not a natural love that you can generate or decide to have, but it comes from the reality of Jesus Christ living within you. Your heart and life are simply a vessel or channel of the passionate love He has for a lost world.

I must admit there were times in Indonesia that I didn't feel a lot of love for the people. There were times when the congested crowds in the market became an inconvenience. The constant flow of beggars and con men to our door became an irritation. When the kids on the street would yell slanderous remarks about us as foreigners, my self-centered nature that had not been fully crucified would cause me to feel anger and resentment. But when you cease to love those whom God has chosen to love through you, you cease to give of yourself and the passion grows dim.

Ted and Frances York are cluster leaders of a group of unreached peoples in West Africa. They recently wrote, "Here in West Africa we cannot escape seeing the deception and lostness that comes to those who have chosen to rely on African traditional religions or Islam. But rather than driving us to despair, it reminds us to consider how God feels about the lost and why He has called us to show His love through Jesus Christ. As followers of Christ, we have received such abundant love ourselves. It is that love that compels us to reach out to the lost peoples of Africa."

IT IS A PASSION COMPELLED BY KNOWING CHRIST.

Your calling must not only be based on a passion compelled by the love of Christ; it is also compelled by your personal experience of knowing Jesus. Each of you came to a point in your life of being confronted with your own lostness and had a personal experience of trusting Jesus Christ as your Savior. That redemptive experience resulted in Christ's coming to dwell within your life, and it transformed your purpose for living. What was it that compelled the early disciples to ignore the religious and legal authorities that ordered them not to speak or teach in the name of Jesus? They said in Acts 4:20, "We cannot stop speaking what we have seen and heard!" It was because they had had an experience of knowing Jesus and walking with Him. Their lives had been impacted by His compassion and ministry. They had witnessed manifestations of His power and authority, and they were never the same.

People often ask me about my own call to missions. I can recall many impressions and experiences that could be interpreted as a call to missions, but I invariably find myself all the way back to my salvation experience as a ten-year-old boy. I was raised in church and knew all the Bible stories. I knew that I ought to join the church and be baptized but had not yet been motivated to make that decision. At a Billy Graham crusade, as I listened to the message, for the first time I came to the deep conviction and under-standing that I was a sinner, separated from God. Without any reticence whatsoever, I readily walked the aisle and without a doubt received Jesus into my heart. There was such a sense of joy that my relationship had been made right with God for all eternity, I can remember thinking, *I wish all the people in the world could know Jesus.* I wanted everyone to find what I had found in that moment of trusting Jesus as my Savior, and I believe God planted in my heart at that moment something that He would nurture into a call to missions. It was an understanding that there was the potential in my heart of going some-where and telling people who had never heard the gospel about what Jesus had done in my life and what He could do for them. The passion of your call must be driven by your personal experience of knowing Jesus.

IT IS A PASSION COMPELLED BY THE CALL OF CHRIST.

Not only do you go compelled by the love of Christ and your personal experience of knowing Christ but also by His calling within you. Jeremiah was discouraged. He had not found a response among the people, just as many of you will find as you go to distant places where people are resistant to the gospel. You, too, will get discouraged and be ready to give up. You will question your call and entertain thoughts of coming home. But Jeremiah remembered the word of the Lord saying, "Before I formed you in the womb I knew you, and before you were born I consecrated you; I have appointed you a prophet to the nations," (Jer. 1:5). People were laughing at him and rejecting his message. He said in Jeremiah 20:9, "If I say, 'I will not remember Him or speak anymore in His name,' then in my heart it becomes like a burning fire shut up in my bones; and I am weary of holding it in, and I cannot endure it."

Why are you being appointed as missionaries? Why are you being sent to strange places all over the world and to people groups and cultures you have never heard of? It is because, like Jeremiah, before you were even born, God knew you and had a plan and purpose for your life to carry the gospel to the nations. You have described it in different ways, and God has used a variety of circumstances to communicate that call, but it is that compulsion of His call that takes you overseas. It is that burning conviction within your heart that God has called you, a conviction that cannot be restrained, that will keep you there.

So you go, not just because the needs are great or reluctantly in response to a command. You go because of a passion, compelled by the love of Christ, compelled by your experience of knowing Jesus and compelled by His calling within you. As you go, may you have the passion that David expressed for building the temple. In Psalm 132:3–5 he said, "Surely I will not enter my house, nor lie on my bed; I will not give sleep to my eyes, or slumber to my eyelids; until I find a place for the Lord, a dwelling place for the Mighty One of Jacob." He was not willing to indulge in personal comforts until he had provided a dwelling place for God in the midst of His people. That must be the passion that compels you. It is passion to find a dwelling place for God in a lost world and among the peoples to whom He has called you.

22

PHILIP AND THE ETHIOPIAN EUNUCH

Acts 8:25–38

G od is moving in these troubled and chaotic times to open the hearts of people around the world to His redemptive love. It is important that you give yourself fully to the task as you join not only more than five thousand missionary colleagues but also multitudes of national coworkers around the world. You are joining God at work in places such as China, India, Russia, and Kazakhstan. You have the privilege of being on the cutting edge as God penetrates the Muslim world in Northern Africa and the Middle East. You will be participating in a growing harvest in Mexico, Brazil, West Africa, and Western Europe. In all of our strategic planning and visionary projections, we never would have anticipated the opportunities you will encounter today as you obey His call and give your life to reach a lost world.

I have read the account of Philip and the Ethiopian eunuch many times, but as I read this story in Acts 8:25–38 recently, I was impressed with three things that need to characterize you and your task on the mission field. Philip followed in submission wherever God led. He was faithful to proclaim God's truth. And he led others to obedient discipleship.

Many of you, like Philip, are laymen. He was not one of the apostles, and many of you did not come out of the pastorate, ordained for the ministry. Among this group being appointed are teachers, businessmen, a physical therapist, a sports broadcaster, a banker, computer analyst, salesman, retail manager, and other vocational backgrounds. But like Philip, the passion of your life is not to pursue personal ambitions and success but to share the good news of the gospel with a lost world. Whether you have been a pastor, a pastor's wife, served on a church staff, or lived out your faith in the secular world, God has called you to put past roles on the shelf and follow Him.

Philip had joined some of the apostles in a revival taking place in Samaria. The gospel had begun to explode out of its limited Jewish context, and Gentiles began to come to faith in Christ. There was a mighty move of God's Spirit in Samaria, and Philip was among those being used of God to proclaim Christ to the people; miracles occurred, and multitudes were coming to faith. But strangely, right in the middle of this wonderful ingathering, God removed Philip to an isolated, desert place. There were no crowds flocking to hear the gospel; in fact, there were no people there at all, but God had a purpose in where He placed him. Note three things that enabled God to use Philip.

HE WAS SUBMISSIVE TO GOD'S LEADERSHIP.

It didn't make a lot of sense from the standpoint of conventional wisdom for God to pull Philip out of a place that was seeing such responsiveness to the gospel, and sometimes we don't understand why God places us where he does. But His heart and desire is to see all peoples come to know Him and worship Him. He may do some strange things and lead in unusual ways to get us in the place that His purpose can be fulfilled. Yes, He was pleased that the Samaritans were now embracing faith in Christ, but His purpose was for other peoples, including those of Africa, to have the opportunity of knowing Him. So in His providence and timing, He placed Philip on that road to Gaza at the time an influential Ethiopian was passing by.

In verse 26 we read, "An angel of the Lord spoke to Philip saying, 'Arise and go south to the road that descends from Jerusalem to Gaza' . . . and he arose and went." Philip did not question the instructions; he did not analyze the unreasonableness of what he had been told. He was simply obedient. And in verse 29, "[When] the Spirit said to Philip, 'Go up and join this chariot,'" Philip obeyed. You need to be constantly sensitive to what God is saying and where He is leading. Too many missionaries get locked into a narrow perception of God's calling and fail to realize God's call is to follow. Obedience means being sensitive to where He wants us at any given time. Many have forfeited being a part of something God is doing because they never move beyond their own understanding of God's will.

This summer, while attending a gathering of all our missionaries in Mexico, I had a chance to fellowship with Charles and Jan Collins. They had had a very fruitful career of service in Guatemala but in 1995 strangely felt led to move across the border into Southern Mexico to accept an assignment in Chiapas. They really didn't understand why God would lead them to make that change, but six months later the Zappatista revolt broke out, and Chiapas was inundated with tens of thousands of Indian refugees. Not only were the Collins in place to coordinate relief ministries; dozens of churches were started through their witness as refugees returned to their villages.

At a recent retirement recognition week, I asked a group of emeritus missionaries how many had completed their missionary service in the place to which they were appointed. In that large group only two raised their hands. You have responded to a personnel request and been matched with a job description and are headed for a place of assignment, and we expect you to fulfill that assignment faithfully. But don't be surprised if someday God taps you on the shoulder and through a strange, inexplicable impression says, "I've got another place for you." He will use colleagues and leadership to enlarge your vision and to recognize that your experience and gifting has served to prepare you for somewhere else God is at work.

God's heart is for the whole world. Just as in His providence He began to penetrate the peoples of Africa through the Ethiopian eunuch and Philip's obedience, God is engaging new unreached people groups through missionaries that are moving to the edge of lostness where people have never had access to the gospel. Who is He calling and using? He uses those who do not give priority to their own comforts and conveniences, those who are submissive to His leadership and are willing to endure isolation and sacrifice. You will experience nostalgia about your American lifestyle and may even recall that you could reach many more people through your church-related ministry here, just as Philip did in Samaria. That may be so, but people who never have an opportunity to hear the gospel would never hear except for your willingness to go.

HE PROCLAIMED THE TRUTH OF GOD'S WORD.

Verse 35 is so significant and captures the heart of your missionary task. "And Philip opened his mouth, and beginning from this Scripture he preached Jesus to him." This is why God has called you to plant your lives in a foreign culture, to go through the rigors of learning another language, and to leave your family and friends. It is not about a job description that needs to be filled—that is just what God is using to get you where He wants you. Whatever your task, assignment, and ministry, never forget the purpose for being there is to lift up Jesus Christ and make Him known through a bold, positive witness. Go with unwavering confidence that the Word of God is inspired and indwelt by God's Spirit and will bring revelation and conviction regarding God's truth. As you encounter obstacles, opposition, and skepticism, wield the sword of the Spirit in confronting people with the claims of Christ.

It is amazing how you will sense God going before you. Philip did not have to initiate a witness; God was already at work, speaking to a spiritually thirsty heart. He just had to be available. But he had to be prepared to explain God's truth. All over the world we are hearing reports of people whom God has prepared, just waiting for someone to come and explain how they can know God. As you initiate work among an unreached people group or urban area of Asia or Latin America, expect God to reveal a "man of peace," a person of influence that will open doors of access and witness. Expect to encounter hearts that are hungry among people living in despair, in bondage to superstition, going through empty rituals in their religious traditions. And God has given you a tool; it's simply a story, a story of His love and the hope that can be found in Jesus Christ. As Paul wrote to Timothy (2 Tim. 4:2), "Preach the word; always be ready in season and out."

HE LED TO A COMMITMENT OF OBEDIENCE.

Philip's witness was not a passive one for whatever might come of it in God's timing. He led to a decision. He drew in the net. He persuaded the Ethiopian to confess Jesus Christ and follow Him in baptism. Why did the Ethiopian eunuch ask to be baptized? It was because Philip had presented the total picture of what it meant to follow Christ in obedience. People need to hear what Jesus has done for them but also to be challenged to receive it in a commitment of faith. After all, the mandate of the Great Commission is to make disciples. Christ died that people might be saved. Because of the redemption provided by His death and resurrection, the Scripture says (Rom. 10:13) that whosoever calls on the name of the Lord shall be saved. But we are then confronted with the question, "How can they call on Him of whom they have not believed; and how can they believe on Him of whom they have not heard, and how can they hear without a preacher"—someone to proclaim the truth. But don't stop with sharing the good news. Don't leave them hanging in the lurch. With persuasive passion plead for that step of repentance and faith and confessing Christ as Lord. For you must model what you want them to replicate.

There are remarkable reports of church growth sweeping China in spite of opposition, restrictions, and persecution. One of our representatives was instructing a group of house church pastors in scriptural baptism.

He told them to ask the new believers three questions. One, do you believe Jesus is the Son of God and died on the cross for your sins? Two, are you trusting Jesus Christ as your own personal Savior? Three, are you committing your life to live for Christ as Lord of your life? If the answer is "yes" to all three questions, then you should baptize them. But the house church pastors said, "There is a fourth question you need to ask to be sure their faith is genuine. You should ask, 'When the authorities come to your home, threaten your family, put you in prison and take away all that you have, will you still follow Christ?' If they answer 'yes,' then they should be baptized."

These new believers, when they pray to receive Jesus Christ, are immediately taught to share their faith and lead someone else to Christ. Then they are taught how to train their new convert to lead others to Christ. Then they are taught how to start a church among those confessing Christ and immediately taught to train others to start churches. The Ethiopian eunuch was receptive to the Word of God, he made a decision to believe, and he was obedient as a new disciple to follow Christ in baptism. But he needed someone to guide and mentor him in what to do. Why is God leading you to plant your life in an incarnational witness among people who are lost? They could read the truth in Bibles and tracts that are distributed. They might even hear the gospel on the radio or through a media presentation, but they need someone to show the way, a flesh-and-blood witness living out their faith in a way that can be observed and imitated.

As Paul said in Colossians 1:6, "All over the world the gospel is multiplying and bearing fruit." And you have the privilege, like Philip, of getting in on what God is doing. So be submissive to God's leadership and willing to follow wherever He leads. Stay focused on sharing and proclaiming the truth of God's Word, and make disciples by teaching and modeling obedience.

23

FOLLOWING WHEREVER GOD
LEADS

Joshua 1:16

L ast year I was asked to speak to a group of personnel staff from about 120
mission groups associated with the Evangelical Fellowship of Mission
Agencies. I had been asked to speak on the topic "Sending Out Missionaries
in a Dangerous and Chaotic World." You would recognize that this is certainly a relevant topic in our contemporary world. We live in a volatile world
where Americans are not especially appreciated, and a Christian witness is
despised. Yet God is calling you to go into that world to share the gospel of
Jesus Christ, and here you are tonight, undeterred by the risks and dangers,
being commissioned, literally, to the ends of the earth. In fact, many of you
are going to places that cannot be identified publicly because missionaries
are not welcome; but you recognize that Jesus is the answer for the turmoil,
suffering, and hopelessness throughout the world; and you are willing to be
obedient to a higher authority that has told us to go into all the world and
make disciples.

Just last week I received an e-mail report from one of our missionaries in
the Middle East—not exactly a safe and secure location these days—who was
in a group like you being appointed as a missionary a little more than a year
ago. In his reflections he said:

> I cannot believe that it has been a whole year. And what a year
> it has been. It has been one of the greatest years of my ministry
> and life. I never imagined how fulfilling and fun it would be to live

overseas. Simply living in another culture has forever changed our outlook on life. We have grown so much in our understanding of the world and people. I did not dream that in our first year overseas we would have the depth of friendships we have here.

As great as life has been from a personal standpoint, it fails in comparison to what our Lord has done. We came here fully expecting our Lord to do great things but did not have any idea we would see Him work in such a powerful way in our very first year on the field.

God is at work throughout the world in unprecedented ways. We are seeing almost an exponential growth in baptisms, new churches being planted, and unreached people groups hearing the gospel. There are movements to Christ in isolated places throughout the Muslim world for the first time. As Paul said in Colossians 1:6 that all over the world the gospel is multiplying and bearing fruit. And that is why you are here tonight. Your call is not just an isolated, personal experience. The timing in which you are being sent is not just a coincidence. You are being appointed tonight because in God's providence He is bringing together your gifts, experience, and calling to a specific place where He is at work in the midst of violence, chaos, confusion, and social upheaval in the world.

I have thought that what is happening, and your call, is not unlike the children of Israel as Joshua assumed leadership upon the death of Moses. In the first chapter of Joshua, we find them preparing to cross the Jordan River to possess the promised land. That is not unlike our preparing to send you across the oceans to claim the nations for our Lord Jesus Christ. Joshua had given them a number of instructions. He told them to be strong and courageous. He assured them that God would be with them and would not fail or forsake them. He reminded them to do all that they had been told in the book of the law and to meditate on it day and night. All of this is very relevant for you today in the twenty-first century. But I want you to focus on the people's response in Joshua 1:16. The people responded and said, "All that you have commanded us we will do, and wherever you send us we will go." Forgive me for extrapolating an application and ad-libbing to this simple declaration—something you have probably never heard a preacher do—but there are four things I want to emphasize as we send you out to disciple the nations.

THERE IS A COMMAND TO BE OBEYED.

If there is any verse of Scripture a good Southern Baptist knows, next to John 3:16, it is the Great Commission of our Lord in Matthew 28:19–20. Just as He prepared to ascend to the Father, having finished His earthly ministry and provided redemption for a lost world, Jesus gathered His followers on that mountainside in Galilee and with passion and urgency commanded them to go into all the world and make disciples of all nations, baptizing them in the name of the Father, the Son and the Holy Spirit. And tonight, you are here in obedience to that command. It is tragic that many have resisted ever accepting that mandate of our Lord personally. Churches have diluted it to make it apply to whatever they do in witness and ministry, ignoring the fact that the grammatical structure of the imperative verb demands an object. And the object that Jesus clearly stated was to be discipled is "the nations— *panta ta ethne*" which are the peoples of the world. Others have said, "I will be obedient by praying and giving to support missionaries," and certainly that is needed, but ignoring the fact that Jesus said, "Go!"

We are deeply indebted and grateful for those who serve our country with devotion in the military. We have been especially aware of their sacrifice and commitment with the recent deployment to Iraq and Afghanistan. The basic foundation of military training is discipline and unquestioned obedience to the command of one's officer. When orders came for a unit to go to Iraq, it wasn't accompanied by an "if you please" or "if you don't mind." Everyone knew there was the possibility they would not return, but that fact was irrelevant. There was a task to be done, an order had been issued and there was a command to be obeyed. It would have been unthinkable, and, in fact, would have subjected one to court martial if they dared to disobey their orders.

The previous generation of the children of Israel had been disobedient, but now they said, "All that you have commanded us we will do." God has made it clear in your call that the Great Commission applies to you, and you are going in obedience to His command.

THERE IS A COMMITMENT TO BE MADE.

Not only is there a command to be obeyed; there is also a commitment to be made. It is not enough that you have come to this point of saying, "God has called me, and I am willing to go as a missionary." It is not enough to say, "I am being obedient to the Great Commission and going to places like Bangladesh, or Moscow, China, Kazakhstan, Morocco, and Mozambique, and that takes care of my commitment. The people of Israel added, "And wherever you send us we will go." A couple of months ago we held our annual retirement recognition for all those missionaries who had retired during the previous year. There were seventy-four emeritus missionaries, some of whom had served for more than forty years. They had given themselves to a lifetime of service in almost every region of the world. During one of our sessions I asked how many of them were living in the same place and assignment upon retirement as when they were appointed years ago. Only two of them raised their hands.

God calls us to a relationship of trust; He calls us to a commitment to follow by faith. Some of you will never get your visa to your country of assignment. Others will arrive and find war and ethnic violence erupting that will necessitate evacuation; changing government regulations, or personal health concerns, will result in a transfer of fields for others. Does that contradict God's will? No. It may simply be the circumstances that God uses to get you where He really wants you, and the country of your focus tonight is just an intermediary step. Don't you want to be where God is at work? Well, there is a commitment to be made, and it is not to a specific country, location, or assignment as much as it is a commitment to the lordship of Christ and His leadership.

I recall a missionary family that had been appointed to an unreached people group in a restricted country. They were unable to secure a visa and had to take an interim assignment in another location while they awaited their work permit. They were able to go in and out of their assigned field on a short-term basis but had to assume other assignments while they waited. Finally after eighteen months their visa was granted. They had lived in fifteen different places in five different countries over that year and a half; it was not a very convenient lifestyle for a family with three small children. With their visa now in hand and prepared to plant their lives in a place where people were yet to hear the gospel, they said, "We never knew where we would be from one month to the next over this last year and a half, but one thing God has taught us is that He calls, not so much to a place as to Himself."

When you answer that call, it really doesn't matter where you are. When you respond to the lordship of Christ, you no longer hold on to your comfort and security or to your own plans. There is a commitment to be made. But not only is there a command to be obeyed, and a commitment to be made that says, like the children of Israel, "Wherever you send us, we will go"; there is also a cost to be paid.

THERE IS A COST TO BE PAID.

You have already been prepared through the appointment process to understand that you aren't going to the mission field with the expectation of an affluent and comfortable lifestyle. If you serve faithfully throughout your career with the International Mission Board, I can guarantee you will be cared for and supported, but I can also guarantee there is no possibility of your children getting into a legal squabble over how to divide a wealthy inheritance upon your death!

I recall hearing about our first missionary family assigned to Chad a few years ago arriving in the country and finding the temperature 120 degrees with no electricity for fans or air conditioning. Another missionary in West Africa shared with me that he planned to get his wife a flush toilet for Christmas. He then acknowledged that there was no running water and the toilet would have to be filled with a bucket by hand, but it would still be quite a luxury. Prior to traveling through that part of the world, I had read a United Nations report that eight of the top ten countries in the world with the worst quality of life were in West Africa. The missionaries there often talked about getting malaria—not whether or not they got it but when they last had it and what they used to treat it. It was accepted that it went with the territory.

In the late 1980s the government of Indonesia declared that foreign missionaries would be limited to only ten years of service, and those who had been there longer would have to leave. Many families, some of whom had planted their lives there for twenty and thirty years lost their visa. Clarence Griffin, however, recognized there was an alternative to leaving, and that was to apply for Indonesian citizenship. It was quite a cost to consider giving up the security and benefits of one's American citizenship, but he said, "This is where God has called me, and whatever the cost, I must be obedient." You will find that it is difficult not being with your family for significant events such as graduations, weddings, the birth of a new niece or nephew, but there is a cost to be paid!

THERE IS A COMPROMISE TO EVADE.

Finally, there is a compromise to evade. I remember talking to a group of missionary candidates and encouraging them to consider an assignment to the Philippines. It was a time of communist guerilla insurgency, and Americans were being targeted for kidnapping and threatened with assassination. Yet it was also a time of harvest as the social turmoil throughout the country was turning the hearts of people to the Lord. One of the candidates responded,

"I know God has called me, and we are committed to going to the mission field, but I don't think God would have us to go to a place where our health and safety would be at risk." Not many places would ever hear the gospel if that were the attitude we took regarding God's call. Would we dare compromise the call of God and be unwilling to take the risk in being obedient to the One who told us to take up our cross and follow Him?

Many people say they would be willing to answer God's call and serve Him in the ministry as long as they can do so in the States. They say that they will pastor a church, they will be faithful to witness and serve the Lord as long as they can do it in a place near to family and friends, or where their children can have the convenience of educational and social outlets, but don't ask them to consider going to the ends of the earth.

When God called Moses at the burning bush, he responded with excuses. He tried to compromise with God, claiming, "I can't speak, the people will not follow me, let someone else go." And we read in Exodus 3:14, "The Lord was angry with Moses" (sic).

God has called you, and you have said, "All that the Lord has commanded us, we will do, and wherever you send us we will go." There is a command to be obeyed, a commitment to be made, a cost to be paid, and a compromise to evade.

24

OPPORTUNITIES AND ADVERSARIES

1 Corinthians 16:9

Most Southern Baptists have had the opportunity to meet and interact with a number of missionaries. You have heard their testimonies and are not unacquainted with some of the challenges they face. You have heard testimonies of those who have been privileged to see a phenomenal response, both on traditional mission fields as well as among previously unreached people groups, such as in China. But this is not without encountering obstacles and struggles.

Those of you being appointed as missionaries will face these same experiences. A verse that appropriately reflects this is 1 Corinthians 16:9. Paul is writing from Ephesus, expressing his desire to come to Corinth as well as to visit Macedonia. But he says he is going to remain in Ephesus, "for a wide door for effective service has opened to me." He could not leave because there was such a response to the gospel. But notice he adds a subsequent observation, "and there are many adversaries." It is important for you to realize that the two go together. Satan is not just going to roll over and ignore places where the kingdom of God is being extended nor can the one who attacks the powers of darkness with the light of the gospel expect to be exempt from opposition. There are only two points I want to make. First, God is moving in a time of harvest and response to the gospel that is unprecedented around the world. And second, never has the opposition to evangelizing a lost world been so intense.

GOD IS PRESENTING AN OPEN DOOR OF RESPONSE AND OPPORTUNITY.

Last year missionaries, working with Baptist partners around the world, reported a 24 percent increase in new believers baptized, exceeding 500,000 for the first time in the history of Southern Baptist missions. There were more than twenty thousand new churches started and thirty-eight thousand additional missions and preaching points where the gospel was being proclaimed. It is estimated that thirty thousand new believers are coming to Christ everyday in China. Church planting movements are multiplying in the most unlikely places such as Cambodia, Azerbaijan, Mozambique, Ethiopia, Algeria, India, and Latin America. In the past it was quite easy to identify the places where there was an open door for service. We used to refer to them as the big seven—Brazil, Mexico, Nigeria, Kenya, the Philippines, Korea, and India. But now we can't even identify the places where many of you are going because God has opened the door of opportunity all over the world.

I recently received an e-mail from one of our strategy associates in South Asia. He had focused on an area where a handful of churches had grown to over nine hundred among the Kui people in the last ten years. This memo shared what they were discovering is happening among other neighboring people groups. There were no churches among the Mohanta people six years ago, but a survey has revealed there are now 150 Baptist churches, 207 outreach groups, and more than one thousand other communities where the gospel is being shared. The Ho people had no churches two years ago but now have sixty-nine Baptist churches and 116 outreach groups meeting for worship, witness, and Bible study. These are just a sample of reports we are getting from all over the world. Truly an effective door of opportunity has opened for you.

But note that Paul was already there when he discovered the door of service opened to him. He did not get the news of a sudden response to the gospel in Ephesus while off on one of his journeys and then divert his plans and go rushing to Ephesus. He was there in obedience to God's leadership when God began to work. It was kind of like Esther, who found herself in the palace of the king. She had no idea what God was going to do, but God placed her there; and when He needed someone to intervene for His people, He had an intercessor in place.

Soon after I became president of the International Mission Board and growing numbers were being appointed, it occurred to me that we are not appointing any nonresidential missionaries. This was an assignment that had been pioneered by the IMB to initiate outreach strategies among restricted people groups where missionaries could not gain a presence. This innovative approach to deployment had seemed to be effective, so I asked one of our administrators leading this initiative why we were not appointing nonresidential missionaries. He explained that as we sent out NRMs and strategies began to be initiated, invariably the door would open to a creative access assignment and an opportunity to establish a presence among the people group, so we no longer had to rely on a nonresidential approach. He said, "It seemed that God was just waiting for us to be obedient to the Great Commission, and when someone took responsibility for discipling a nation or people group, God would work to break down the barriers and open the door!"

Several years ago Charles and Jan Collins felt led to transfer from their long-term assignment in Guatemala, across the border into Southern Mexico. They were strangely drawn to a place called Chiapas where there was no Baptist witness. A few months after they had gotten settled, the Zapatista revolt broke out, and tens of thousands of refugees from the indigenous peoples were swept into Chiapas. The Collins were able to mobilize Mexican Baptists and volunteers from the States to minister, and doors of opportunity for witness opened resulting in many churches being started, all because they were obedient to follow God's will and plant their lives where He was leading them.

God is already at work where many of you are going, but others of you are accepting the challenge to go to the last frontier. Some are joining colleagues on historic fields that have not yet seen a breakthrough or movement to God. Never doubt that God is sending you there. Yours is a unique calling. Go in obedience and to persevere. Learn the language, identify with the people, faithfully share God's love and the claims of Christ, and you can look forward to that day when you can say with Paul, "I am going to remain here for a wide door for effective service has opened to me."

BUT THERE ARE ALSO MANY ADVERSARIES.

First John 5:19 says, "We are of God, and the whole world lies in the power of the evil one." You see, where Christ is not known, where the gospel has not been proclaimed, the nations, peoples, and cultures are in darkness and under the domination of the prince of the power of the air. This opposition will come in the form of religious barriers and resistance. Just this week word came of a volunteer group in Romania that was run out of town by a mob organized by the Orthodox priest. It will come in the form of government restrictions that are designed to prohibit freedom to proclaim a Christian witness. The adversary may be manifested in persecution of local believers and harassment of you and your efforts as a foreigner. House church pastors continue to be arrested in China. Church buildings are being destroyed in Central Asia.

But the greatest adversary you may encounter may be within your own heart. The enemy would want you to feel sorry for yourself in your isolation and deprived of the basic amenities that you have taken for granted here in America. You will be tempted to succumb to discouragement. Satan will deter your effectively seizing that window of opportunity by creating interpersonal conflict with your missionary colleagues and national coworkers. And it is not unlikely that you would even be subjected to moral temptations that would compromise your witness and effectiveness. Satan will do whatever it takes to keep the kingdom of God from being extended and God being glorified and exalted among the nations.

When you don't experience immediate success, he will create self-doubts regarding your calling. As you struggle with those initial cross-cultural adjustments and are immersed in the plodding task of language learning when the words and sounds just don't come, Satan will tell you to give up; go back to the States where you can be surrounded by family and friends, and enjoy the recognition and success you deserve. This is the time to heed Paul's advice in Ephesians 6:10–13:

> Be strong in the Lord, and in the strength of His might. Put on the full armor of God, that you may be able to stand firm against the schemes of the devil. For our struggle is not against flesh and blood but against the rulers, against the powers, against the world forces of this darkness, against the spiritual forces of wickedness in the heavenly places. Therefore, take up the full armor of God, that you may be able to resist in the evil day, and having done everything, to stand firm.

OVERCOMING THE ADVERSARY AND SEIZING THE OPPORTUNITY.

As we send you out, I want to assure you that you will find an open door of opportunity for witness and effective service. Each of you are being appointed to fill a strategic assignment to join God where He is at work. But also, you will encounter many adversaries. What should be your anticipated response? Paul seems to sum it up in 1 Corinthians 16:13–14: "Be on the alert, stand firm in the faith, act like men, be strong. Let all that you do be done in love."

1. Jesus was constantly reminding His disciples to be vigilant, to be sober and alert, because He was aware that the enemy was unceasing in his efforts to defeat us, divert us, and discourage us. First Peter 5:8 tells us, "Be of sober spirit, be on the alert. Your adversary, the devil, prowls about like a roaring lion, seeking someone to devour."

2. Second, we are reminded to stand firm in the faith, believing God, claiming His promises when all evidence is to the contrary. Never lose the perspective of God's sovereignty and providence in your life and the place to which He has called you. First John 5:4 says, "This is the victory that has overcome the world—our faith."

3. Then we are told to act like men and be strong. There is no place for wimps in the task to which you have been called. The Marine Corps has a recruitment appeal that says, "We need a few good men." Service in the Marines is nothing compared to the warfare to which you have been called—from the halls of Montezuma to the shores of Tripoli, go forth and take our world for Jesus Christ. Hear God saying, as He did to Joshua (1:9), "Be strong and courageous! Do not tremble or be dismayed, for the LORD your God is with you wherever you go."

4. And finally, let all that you do be done in love. Why is that the key to victory? Because it will enable you to die to self and give yourself totally to the people to whom God has called you. As Paul said in 2 Corinthians 5:14, "The love of Christ constrains me." Allow His love to be poured out through you, until you love the people and recognize Jesus gave His life that they might be saved. When you go with such a love and passion for God, your heart will be broken by the multitudes that do not know Him. And furthermore, Satan, the adversary, does not understand love; he does not even comprehend it. He is totally self-centered and the only power and enticement of his temptations is self-serving. So when you act in love and give of yourself, he is totally disarmed; for there is nothing he can do with that.

So God is placing before you as you go throughout the world an effective and open door of opportunity, but there will be adversaries. Be on the alert, stand firm in the faith, be strong and courageous, and let everything that you do be done in love.

25

WHATEVER IT'S GOING TO TAKE

1 Corinthians 9

There has never been such a response to God's call to take the gospel to the ends of the earth. The number of missionary candidates continues to increase, and the International Mission Board continues to send out more new missionaries than ever before in our history. What is amazing is that they are going into a world that is filled with conflict and risks. Many of you are going to use your skills and training to plant your lives in places restricted to a missionary witness. You are going to places not only opposed to a Christian witness but where Americans are hated and despised. How is it that you would be willing to give your life in such a time of economic uncertainty, global tensions, rampant ethnic warfare, and unprecedented suffering? It is because you realize that Jesus is the answer, and if the peoples of the world are ever going to know of God's love and His redemptive grace that can give them hope in the midst of darkness and despair, someone must go and tell them.

Why are we seeing record numbers responding to God's call to missionary service and thousands of Southern Baptists rallying to participate in short-term volunteer projects? A silly little slogan has evolved in recent years among our missionaries as we have focused our vision on bringing all the peoples of the world to saving faith in Jesus Christ. It is "wigtake." When a missionary says "wigtake" in response to a challenging assignment, it is a kind of shorthand for "whatever it's going to take." It's an expression of total abandonment for the cause of Christ.

This is what God called Abraham to do when He told him to leave his home and family in order for all nations to be blessed. When Jesus went to the cross, it was because God had said, "Whatever it takes." You have had to deal with that in your life personally and have probably responded much as Jesus did as He prayed in the garden of Gethsemane and said, "Not My will but Thine be done." You have come to the point of turning your back on successful and fulfilling ministries here in the US. Some of you have put your profession, your vocation, your life dreams of success and an affluent lifestyle on the shelf in order to be obedient to God's call. Paul came to that point of whatever it's going to take when he said that he would be willing to become accursed if his people, Israel, could be saved.

I want to direct your attention to several aspects of Paul's testimony in 1 Corinthians, chapter 9, that I believe may help you to understand a "wigtake" commitment and the key to your potential effectiveness as we send you out all over the world.

An Incarnational Calling

In verses 19 and 22 Paul says, "For though I am free from all men, I have made myself a slave to all, that I might win the more. . . . To the weak I became weak, that I might win the weak; I have become all things to all men, that I may by all means save some." Paul was willing to identify with those to whom God had called him. And that is why you are being sent to Africa, Asia, and the places of your assignment. As you serve among impoverished people, suffering deprivation, where their only concern and agenda is survival, God is saying to come alongside them, identify with them, show a caring and loving concern they have never seen before. Sure, you can live in the affluent suburbs with businessmen, diplomats, and other expatriates; shop at the international supermarket; and if trouble threatens, you always have your American passport and can evacuate to the safety and security of America. But what kind of witness does that give you among people who don't enjoy those privileges.

I have often told of the first-term experiences of Brian and Vicki Barlow, assigned to Liberia. They were in the country less than a year when the tribal conflicts escalated to the point they had to leave, losing all their household and personal belongings. They moved across the border into Guinea only to have the war spread, forcing a subsequent evacuation. They accepted an interim assignment as manager of the Baptist camp in Togo when the government was overthrown in a political coup and the country thrown into turmoil. Thousands of Baptists fled to the camp for refuge, overwhelming the facilities with the lack of adequate food and water. After a year things had settled down in Liberia, and they were able to return, only for the war to flare up again. Returning to the states, I heard them reflecting on their experiences and say, "Isn't it amazing what God allows you to go through in order to identify with the people to whom He called you and earn credibility for sharing a Christian witness."

Jim and Betty McKinley recently retired after more than thirty years of service in Bangladesh. Jim is known and respected all over the country. His Christian witness is respected in that Muslim country because when all others had left, he and his family stayed through the war for independence in 1971. The local people who had no other option know about the McKinleys hiding under mattresses in their hallway while Pakistani planes bombed and strafed their city.

Paul's passion was that people would be saved, but he understood that it required him to go to any extent to identify with them that he might live out Christ's love. It will not be your preaching and words of persuasion that will draw people to Jesus but living out the reality of your faith in flesh and blood, allowing them to see the victory you have in Him.

How do you do that? Paul realized he was in bondage to no one; he had been set free, but he willingly made himself a servant that he might win others. You will not impress anyone regarding the claims of Christ if you go in pride, isolating yourself from the masses that become only an inconvenience and irritation. Go with a servant heart. Love the people and give yourself to them no matter what the cost. One couple, completing their first term in a very difficult assignment without much success, reflected, "When we got here, we had to realize God had not called us to success and personal fulfillment but to obedience." God has called you to an incarnational witness; do whatever it takes to live out your calling incarnationally.

AN INHERENT COMPULSION

In verse 16 Paul said, "For if I preach the gospel, I have nothing to boast of, for I am under compulsion; for woe is me if I do not preach the gospel." Your testimonies have reflected a diversity of factors that led you to sense and understand God's call to missions. For some it was the need of a lost world that you encountered on a volunteer mission trip or began to comprehend as you saw the turmoil and conflict overseas on daily newscasts. For others, in a time of spiritual growth and your walk with the Lord, the imperative of the Great Commission began to become personal and you felt an obligation to be the one to go. As valid as those impressions are, let me say that the needs of a lost world or an obligation to be obedient to our Lord's command are not sufficient to result in a sustained and effective witness. There must be a driving, inherent compulsion that comes from your personal relationship with Jesus Christ that will allow you to do nothing else.

J. E. Conant, in his book on evangelism, said, "The Great Commission is sufficient authority to send us after the lost, but it is not sufficient motivation; for it is not the authority of an external command but the impulse of an indwelling presence that sends us after the lost." Let me remind you that you are not just going to fill a job request, to teach in a seminary, to provide business support services, engage in humanitarian relief projects, even to plant churches but to proclaim the gospel of Jesus Christ. That's nothing to take pride in, but it is something you have to do, you cannot help but do, because of the intense compulsion that drives you to share Christ.

AN INTENSE CONSECRATION

In verse 12 Paul had declared, "We endure all things, that we may cause no hindrance to the gospel of Christ." Do you know the greatest hindrance to getting the gospel to all the peoples of the world? It is not religious opposition or government restrictions. It is one's own reluctance to go all the way in consecration and surrender to do whatever it takes. At this point you should be so pumped that you are ready to charge hell with a water pistol, but Satan knows our vulnerability. He knows where to attack and create discouragement and compromise. Many of you have already had to work through the hindrance of parents and family who are not supportive and would have persuaded you to turn your back on God's call; they would encourage you to be content with serving Him here in the States. You will struggle with a location where you can enjoy fellowship with colleagues, shopping conveniences, and your children can have social opportunities with other Americans, rather than going to the edge where people need to know Christ. You will discover that you have subconsciously drawn a bottom line beyond which you're unwilling to go, and that will hinder getting the gospel to all people.

Last year on a trip to Africa, I visited Larry and Terry Singletary in northern Uganda. I had not realized they had responded to an assignment to which I often referred as representing the challenge of penetrating the last frontier. The job request had said, "In this assignment there will be no running water or electricity. There are no nearby medical facilities. At night you are likely to hear gunfire among warring tribal groups. The Muslim influence among the animistic people in this location restricts an open Christian witness, but it is an opportunity to bring the gospel to people who are lost." That realistically described the place where the Singletarys lived.

During my visit their son showed me a plastic bag of AK47 shells he had picked up in their front yard after a recent battle between two Karamonjong tribes living on each side of them. Later I read about their jeep being ambushed on the road, and one of the bullets grazed the arm of their daughter. In reflection on that dangerous event, the little girl had said, "They just need Jesus."

You can hinder the spread of the gospel by withdrawing or, like many others, not going at all. You can hinder the gospel by succumbing to fear or limiting how far you are willing to go in a sacrificial lifestyle. But the consecration that influences others to receive the gospel is one that is willing to endure all things.

AN INTENTIONAL COMMITMENT

Paul said in verses 26–27, "Therefore I run in such a way, as not without aim; I box in such a way as not beating the air; but I buffet my body and make it my slave, lest possibly, after I have preached to others, I myself should be disqualified."

I have always been intrigued that Paul, of all people, would be concerned about being disqualified—he who had planted churches and evangelized the known world. But even Paul realized that if he did not stay focused on God's call and purpose for his life, unless he disciplined his life to walk in holiness and avoid being distracted and diverted to secondary and trivial matters, even he could come to the point of no longer being useful to God. This verse has always been an encouragement to me to stay focused with an intentional commitment on God's calling. I don't want to be disqualified from whatever it is that God desires to do through me.

Some have been disqualified from joining God in what He is doing around the world and being used of Him because they became distracted by pride and selfish gratification that led to interpersonal conflicts or moral failure. Some took their eyes off Jesus, His all-sufficient grace, and the joy of walking in faithful obedience, and came to the point they were unwilling to make the sacrifice and to give of themselves with a servant heart. Others, simply in the busyness and demands they encountered from day to day, began to neglect their time with the Lord and that intimate time of prayer and Bible study that is so essential for effectiveness, and they became disqualified. Oh, it was not anything sudden; it was gradual as their lives became dry spiritually, passion for the lost began to diminish; they began to succumb to self-pity, loneliness, and long for the fellowship of family and a comfortable lifestyle in America; and they became disqualified.

Paul pretty well covered the ground of what it takes for an effective ministry overseas. If you are going to be a part of "wigtake," doing whatever it's going to take to reach a lost world, you will need to go with an incarnational calling, an inherent compulsion, an intense consecration, and an intentional commitment.

26

YOU HAVE NOT PASSED
THIS WAY BEFORE

Joshua 3:3–7

While reading from the book of Joshua, I was impressed by a passage that I believe has remarkable relevancy for those being appointed as missionaries. In chapter 3, verse 3, Joshua instructed the people, "When you see the ark of the covenant of the LORD your God with the Levitical priests carrying it, then you shall set out from your place and go after it."

The ark represented God's presence among His people. The children of Israel were now committed in faith to be obedient to God's purpose and leadership. After forty years in the wilderness, they were ready to cross the Jordan River and possess the land God had prepared for them. So Joshua was saying when you see God moving, go with Him. When God leads, set out from your place and follow.

It is that kind of conviction and experience that has brought you not only to a willingness but a commitment to go overseas to serve the Lord. Your place has been in locations such as Georgia, Tennessee, Missouri, Colorado, or Virginia; but you sense God moving in other parts of the world in a way that has something to do with where you should be as you follow Him. Your place has been in a pastorate, teaching school somewhere, or as a student in seminary; yet you have felt God saying, "Leave your place and follow Me." Many of you would have been content to continue fulfilling the roles you have enjoyed here in the States, to keep your comfortable home and the attractive social environment for your children. But you have heard God say that it is time to set out from your place and "follow Me."

This was a bold, new experience for the children of Israel, just as it is for you. Joshua says in the next verse, "For you have not passed this way before." They were familiar with their wilderness surroundings and had experienced His sufficient provisions, but now they were venturing into new territory, both geographically and spiritually. They had become accustomed to God's supply of manna and protection from their enemies while preparing them and equipping them in the wilderness. But now they would be treading on unfamiliar ground. They would encounter a new lifestyle and have to enter into battle against the pagan tribes that inhabited the land in order to fulfill God's purpose.

As you come to this time of missionary appointment, you are well aware that you have not passed this way before. Most of you have had experience overseas, some even in the country to which you are returning; but you went out before planning to come back. Whether for a two-year Journeyman or ISC assignment or a short-term volunteer project, you were exposed to the needs of a lost world; you came to understand what it meant to relate cross-culturally; you experienced God's grace providing your needs, but I assure you that you have not passed this way before. God has called you now to plant your lives overseas and make a new country and culture your home. As you anticipate that challenge, I want to call several things to your attention that parallel the experience of the children of Israel.

YOU MUST BE CONSECRATED AND COMMITTED TO HOLINESS.

In verse 5, Joshua said to the people, "Consecrate yourselves, for tomorrow the LORD will do wonders among you." You can go to the place to which God is leading with the assurance that He will do wonders among you, for you go in the power of God. As you go to Ethiopia, Kenya, Tanzania, Malawi, or South Africa, you can be assured that God is moving in the midst of suffering and political turmoil to bring people to Christ. As you go to Bulgaria, Hungary, the Ukraine, and China, you will find God drawing people to Himself who have so long been deprived of the good news of the gospel. God is moving in an unprecedented harvest in Latin America, enabling the gospel to take root in Asian cultures that have previously been resistant and opening doors for outreach among unevangelized people groups throughout the world.

But if you expect to be a channel of God's power, if you expect to see God do wonders among you and through you, then as Joshua admonished the children of Israel, you must consecrate yourselves. It is amazing that some people miss the wonders of what God is doing because they have never paid the price in commitment and holiness to be entrusted with God's power. Certainly you have come to a significant level of consecration to say, "I'll respond to God's call. I'll go overseas. I will become a missionary." But being commissioned by the International Mission Board and crossing the waters gives no assurance that the Lord will do wonders among you. I could wish that it did, for we would represent a mighty force of spiritual power of more than five thousand missionaries impacting a lost world and claiming the nations for God as Israel claimed the land of Canaan. But you must realize that God is leading you to a deeper level of consecration. You cannot presume that you have arrived in your walk with the Lord and a depth of surrender that will unleash the power of God in your ministry.

To be consecrated means to be set apart. There is a discipline and holiness that God expects of those who desire His anointing. He does not entrust His wonder-working Spirit to those who hold on to the pride of self-sufficiency or to those who compromise with standards of the world. Unfortunately there have been those who have forfeited their effectiveness and settled for mediocrity instead of seeing God work wonders in a new land because they never paid the price in a consecrated life of holiness and commitment.

YOU SHOULD GO WITH THE ASSURANCE THAT GOD GOES WITH YOU.

Second, as you are obedient to leave your place to go where God is leading and consecrate yourself to Him, you have assurance that the presence of God accompanies you. You do not go alone. In verse 7 the Lord said to Joshua, "This day I will begin to exalt you in the sight of all Israel, that they may know that just as I have been with Moses, I will be with you." God would not have told Israel to follow the ark and move across the Jordan without the assurance that He would go with them.

There will be times when you question whether or not God is present. There will be times when you feel forsaken. I must confess there were times when I felt God had let me down and was not keeping His end of the bargain. In times of dryness, fruitlessness, frustration, and self-pity I would find myself thinking, *Lord, I have committed my all to You and am following by faith the best I know how. Why aren't You doing Your part and honoring me with results? Why are my family and I being subjected to trials and difficulties?* But He was always there working in His way, according to His divine providence and timing. People will note something different about you as you allow Christ to be manifested through you because that Christlike spirit and demeanor represent such a contrast with the darkness and hopelessness in which they live. He would not be saying, "Move from your place and go," if He did not go with you.

GOD IS LORD OF ALL THE EARTH AND GOES BEFORE YOU.

Then Joshua assures them that not only will God go with them; He goes before them and will dispossess the pagan tribes in the land of Canaan. Joshua 3:11 says, "Behold, the ark of the covenant of the Lord of all the earth is crossing over ahead of you into the Jordan." Don't miss the implication of that. The Lord of all the earth is crossing over ahead of you. As you are obedient to follow the Lord, His presence not only accompanies you, but He goes ahead of you.

Jesus, who called you and sends you to make disciples of all nations, says that "all authority is given Me in heaven and earth." "Are not the nations and the kings of the earth mine?" as He said through the psalmist. He told Joshua, "Yes, the Canaanites, Hittites, and Jebusites are there, but I will assuredly dispossess them before you, for I am Lord of the universe; I am King of kings. I have authority to do whatever I desire." And just as it was His desire for Israel to possess the promised land, so is it His desire that you disciple the nations to which He sends you. Some of you will see Islamic people come to the knowledge of the gospel for the first time, and they will be dispossessed of their centuries of religious heritage as they embrace faith in Jesus Christ. Some of you will witness and see the power of God move among those in irreligious societies as they enter into the kingdom of God. Never question His providence, His power, His lordship to bring the nations to repentance and the fact that He precedes you to prepare the way for your witness to dispossess those in bondage and darkness from a hopeless spiritual destiny.

YOUR OBEDIENCE WILL OVERCOME THE OBSTACLES YOU ENCOUNTER.

Israel was ready to consecrate themselves and follow God's leadership. They were assured of His presence. They were assured He went before them to possess the land. But there was a problem to crossing over and following Him. The Jordan River was at flood stage. There was an obstacle to going where God said go and doing what God said to do. But the people ignored the obstacle; and when they stepped into the Jordan, the waters rolled back in a heap, and all Israel crossed over on dry ground.

Some of you look on the process you have been through in moving toward missionary appointment as one in which many obstacles have been overcome, and certainly that would be the case. But it has been nothing like the obstacles you will encounter from this point on as you pack your belongings, as your family experiences dislocation, and as you go through an extended time of transition. Some of you will encounter opposition from your family; some will encounter visa problems and travel complications. You are likely to arrive on your field and find obstacles in providing adequate living accommodations. Transportation in congested cities will be a problem, not to mention communication barriers and relationships that challenge your threshold of patience and tolerance.

So what do you do when these obstacles arise? Exactly what Israel did—you step into the waters in obedience and watch God roll back the obstacles and provide His abundant grace to fulfill the task to which He has called you.

You are facing a new experience. Even though you may have been overseas and think you know something of the cross-cultural challenges you face, you have not been this way before. Like Israel you are now fortified by faith and prepared to be obedient to His call. Consecrate yourselves to walk in holiness with the Lord. Go with assurance that He not only goes with you; He goes before you preparing the way, stirring the hearts of people, convicting of sin, creating a spiritual hunger that you can claim the land and the people for Jesus Christ. And never lose heart in the face of obstacles and discouragements, for God will roll them back as you remain obedient and steadfast in your call to follow Him.

27

UNCONDITIONAL DISCIPLESHIP

Luke 9:57–62

Missionaries are those who have felt a specific call of God and have testified of a personal response of obedience to that call. It is a calling to a unique place of service overseas to which one responds because of a conviction that Jesus is Lord and has a rightful claim upon one's life. It is His prerogative to lead one wherever He would desire him or her to serve.

Those being commissioned should be excited about the uncertain future they face, for God would not have called them to a place unless He was at work there and, even now, had a plan for bringing the people of that country or people group into a saving relationship with Him. Missionaries are going to fill a specific assignment because, even before they knew the mission field would be their destiny, God was preparing them, stimulating certain gifts and interests and providing the experience needed to carry out His mission.

Many others have committed their lives to serving Christ and are being used in ministry and witness, some in full-time, church-related vocations, and others as dedicated laymen and women. They, too, have responded to God's calling, but some have the privilege of leaving family and friends and planting their lives cross-culturally in countries abroad. What they will be doing will not be altogether different from what they have done here, but I want to point out the implications of following Jesus in obedience to places where missionaries are being called today, places such as Benin and Togo in Africa, Japan, Taiwan, and Hong Kong in East Asia. Many are going to countries in Latin America and others to countries and people groups in Indochina, Central Asia, and Eastern Europe.

Jesus not only called the twelve but was constantly calling others to be His disciples and to follow Him. In the ninth chapter of Luke, He tells about three individuals, two at their own initiative, who offered to follow and serve Him. In response, Jesus made quite clear the implications of those who would presume, as you are doing, to be His disciple and to follow Him wherever He leads. Verse 57 gives us the context: "And as they were going along the road, someone said to Him, 'I will follow You wherever You go.'"

TO FOLLOW AS JESUS' DISCIPLE REQUIRES A NEW LIFESTYLE.

In reply Jesus explained, "The foxes have holes, and the birds of the air have nests, but the Son of Man has nowhere to lay His head," (v. 58). I hope you realize that God has called you to give up some of the comforts to which you have been accustomed. I am often amazed how often candidates express concern about the kind of house they will live in or whether or not their children will have an American school to attend, as if their commitment were qualified by being guaranteed the comforts and amenities they enjoyed here.

Bill Moseley, from the Sunshine State of Florida, after years in the idyllic climate of South Brazil, felt led to go to Siberia last year. Can you imagine the adjustment to snow on the ground nine months of the year and no more than six hours of light each day through the winter? Can you imagine being the first missionaries to go into Chad? Jim and Sharon McPherson went there and found the temperature 120 degrees with no electricity for cooling or fans. A pioneer missionary in Azerbaijan told me when I was in Central Asia that he would never take bread for granted again after standing in lines for hours to get a few loaves when it was available. A couple appointed last year to Eastern Europe wrote me a note of appreciation and a request for prayer upon their arrival. They said that they thought they were prepared for the austere lifestyle they would encounter only to find they were still enslaved to a disgusting materialistic attitude, feeling sorry for themselves as they fantasized about shopping malls, grocery stores, and diet Coke.

As you go to the thronging cities of Asia and Latin America, you will not have the space and privacy so valued by Americans. As you identify with African villagers, they will not comprehend your resentment for their constant intrusion into your family life and claims upon your time. As you strive to impact an unreached people group, you will find that it demands identifying with their lifestyle and immersing yourself in their society in order for them to understand the incarnational expression of your faith. The calling to follow Jesus requires a new lifestyle. It entails a willingness to sacrifice and forego all the entitlements and comforts you may presume to have.

TO FOLLOW AS JESUS' DISCIPLE DEMANDS A NEW ALLEGIANCE.

Jesus invited one of those in the crowd to follow Him, but the potential disciple replied, "Permit me first to go and bury my father" (v. 59). Jesus seemed to have a harsh reply for this "wannabe" follower, not even permitting him to bury his deceased father. But commentators tell us that the man's father had likely not yet died; he was expressing the cultural custom of an obligation to one's parents as long as they lived. Though he was willing to follow Jesus, he had other obligations that were a priority.

Likewise, Jesus has called you to leave your family in order to be obedient to His calling. It is not because you do not love them and honor them, but Jesus has called you to a higher allegiance, and that family bond will transcend the distances separating you. Some of you have very close family ties and will have difficulty not being present for significant birthdays, anniversaries, the birth of a niece or nephew, or the funeral of a grandparent. It will seem like a long time until furlough, and many new missionaries think International Mission Board policies are cruel because they are not allowed to fly back to the States for every meaningful event.

Jesus is not advocating disrespect for family but is emphasizing that the lordship of Christ and following Him obediently supersedes earthly relationships. It always grieved me to have a person responsive to my witness overseas say something like, "I really believe what you are saying about Jesus is true, and I would like to become a Christian, but I cannot dishonor the religion of my parents." This was not uncommon among the Chinese of Singapore or Buddhists of Thailand. In some cases the parents had already died, but the children had promised them that they would never change their religion. How tragic that one would reject eternal life and continue to live under condemnation for sin because they were unwilling to accept a new allegiance. But also, how tragic that many reject the joy and abundant life of following Christ completely because they are unwilling to make the commitment you are making tonight.

If your parents and family are also committed to Christ and supportive of your missionary service, you are indeed blessed because many do not have that support. Some of you in this group are here with a heavy heart because of parents who do not understand why you would be doing what you are doing. They are angry because you are depriving them of the joy of being with their grandchildren as they grow up. I remember my in-laws saying, "You and Bobbye go on to Indonesia if you have to, just leave the kids here!" But families need to understand that God's grace is sufficient for them, too. God's call to a son or daughter, or brother or sister, is a call for a family to commit to a new and deeper allegiance to Christ and pledge their support and prayers. Your family will be blessed as they experience vicariously the victories of sharing Christ with a lost world.

To follow as Jesus' disciple provides a new purpose.

Jesus also declared that what you are doing results in a new life purpose. In verse 60 He said, "As for you, go and proclaim everywhere the kingdom of God." Certainly your assignment is not radically different from what you have already been doing. Many of you have been teachers or preachers or homemakers. Some of you have business skills that God is leading you to use overseas. Many of you have already served a significant short-term period of service overseas. You have all become adept at sharing Christ, or you would not have qualified for missionary appointment. But the scope of your witness has been rather limited in a west Texas town or south Georgia where there are many churches.

As we have heard your testimonies and rejoiced in the places you are going, you are literally going to proclaim everywhere the kingdom of God. You will be amazed to encounter people who have never before heard of Jesus Christ. I can assure you that is the greatest thrill in the world—to be able to introduce someone to Jesus who has never heard of Him before. Although many of you will be serving where people are aware of Christianity, they have never truly comprehended the reality of the gospel.

Don't ever be diverted from the purpose for which Jesus has called you. You will be busy in your assignment. Sometimes survival and providing for your family is a time-consuming task, but the reason you have been called to distant, far-away places is for the purpose of proclaiming the kingdom.

To follow as Jesus' disciple results in a new future.

Finally Jesus makes clear that following Him means facing a new future. He said in verse 62, "No one, after putting his hand to the plow and looking back, is fit for the kingdom of God." You will be tempted to look back, even in the next few weeks as you pack your crates and have to part with belongings that are precious to your family and leaving a nice comfortable suburban home for who knows what. When you go through those emotional farewells of hugs and kisses at the airport and as you struggle through cultural adjustments and language learning, you will be tempted to dream about how comfortable and wonderful life was here. When results are not readily forthcoming and you seem to hit a brick wall, in frustration you will remember how wonderful it was to stand in the pulpit of your church, loved and appreci-ated by your congregation. When you face dangers, as some do every day in Liberia, Gaza, or Tajikistan, or when your children are burning with fever or suffering infections, you will entertain thoughts of throwing in the towel and going home—we have all been there.

But Jesus has chosen you as those who are fit for the kingdom—those who have what it takes to persevere and go all the way. You are here tonight being commissioned because you have been willing to burn your bridges behind you. You go out, like Abraham and others, in that roll call of faith in the eleventh chapter of Hebrews, confident of a higher calling and a better hope. Do not look back; do not hold on to former things. You have a new future that contains an outpouring of God's grace and power as you have not yet known it.

You cannot fully understand the implications of appointment to mis-sionary service. God has impressed you with the needs of a lost world, and you realize the potential within your life of doing something about it. God has impressed upon you a specific call, and you have responded in obedience. You are making a faith commitment to follow Jesus, and that means (1) a new lifestyle, (2) a new allegiance, (3) a new purpose, and (4) a new future. May God bless you as you go.

28

TRUSTING GOD'S PROVIDENCE

Acts 2:21–24

Missionary appointment is a very significant occasion as it represents a pivotal point between the past and the future. Though you have walked with the Lord and given evidence of your faith and a commitment to serve Him, your appointment represents a new direction that launches your life and witness into a strange cross-cultural setting. In the midst of joy and excitement of coming to this point in your pilgrimage of following God, it is not unlikely that there would be an element of anxiety and sense of inadequacy as you face a new lifestyle in an environment unlike what you have known here in the States.

Some will be serving in Eastern Europe where people long deprived of the gospel are responding at a phenomenal rate; some are joining the harvest reapers in Africa and Latin America while some are going to plant the seed of the gospel for the first time and develop strategies for impacting the "last frontier" among new people groups. Whether in massive cities that are overwhelming in their need or the desolate outback of Central Asia, your stateside experience, education, and personal competencies will do little good apart from the anointing of God.

You have responded to God's call because of a desire to be obedient to His will wherever that might be. God used the needs of a lost world to impress upon you that His place of service was not in the comfortable environment of America but overseas. Most of you testified that it was not just the need but also an awareness that God was at work in Nigeria, Tanzania, Romania, the Philippines, and other countries where you are going.

In the second chapter of Acts, the promise of Jesus had just been realized with the outpouring of the Holy Spirit upon the apostles and believers. For more than three years, they had lived and traveled with Jesus, listened to His teachings, seen the miracles He performed, and observed a unique kingdom lifestyle. Now He was gone, returned to the Father, and the task was theirs. In the gospel we get the instructions, but now in Acts we begin to perceive a practical manual of how the new church, that body of believers, was to touch the whole world with the message of salvation and a living faith. Peter puts things in perspective in his message in verses 21–24. The dynamic of the gospel message and implications of what Jesus had done are expressed when he said, "And it shall come to pass that whoever calls on the name of the LORD shall be saved."

Then he explains how this could be; it was because of what God did through Jesus. "Men of Israel listen to these words: Jesus of Nazareth, a Man attested to you by God with miracles and wonders and signs which God performed through Him in your midst, just as you yourselves know—this Man, being delivered by the predetermined plan and foreknowledge of God, you nailed to the cross by the hands of godless men and put Him to death. And God raised Him up again, putting an end to the agony of death, since it was impossible for Him to be held in its power."

We would not deny the uniqueness of Jesus and His divinity, but notice the providence of God in His life and everything that happened to Him. (1) It was God that affirmed the ministry of Jesus; the miracles, wonders, and signs were performed by God through Him. (2) Jesus died on the cross; but note, He was delivered up by the determined purpose and foreknowledge of God. (3) And of course it was God that raised Him up from the dead.

Don't miss the point of who was in control directing the drama. It was God that wrote the script, chose the actors, and planned the plot! Jesus was simply the obedient Son, submissive to the Father's will. Do you recall how often Jesus said, "The words I speak are given me by the Father. The works that I do are the works of the Father"? It was the providence of God demonstrating His power through Jesus in His life and ministry, His death and resurrection.

One of the most important things you can do as you go to the mission field is to keep in perspective the providence of God in your life, His sovereignty over the universe and your life. He is on His throne, controlling the destiny of the nations by His predetermined will and foreknowledge. Psalm 33:10 says, "The LORD nullifies the counsel of the nations; He frustrates the plans of the peoples."

He has called you to participate in His plans and chosen you as an obedient child to go where He is sending you and to make your life available as a channel of His power. *Providence* comes from a Latin word, *pro-video*. *Video* means "to see," and *pro* means "to see beforehand." God knows what is going to happen as you go to Macao and Uganda and Brazil and other countries. He is already planning to use the circumstances and events that will occur in your life to fulfill His purpose.

TRUST GOD'S PROVIDENCE TO WORK THROUGH YOU AS A DEMONSTRATION OF HIS POWER.

Whatever you do is dependent on God working through you, just as He worked through Jesus to perform mighty works and proclaim the kingdom. You will be much more effective because of your seminary training, pastoral or professional experience, and growth in discipleship; but never think for a moment that you will accomplish anything apart from the power and presence of God. We are exhorted by Jesus in John 15 to "abide in Me . . . for apart from me you can do nothing."

I recently talked with John Langston who has just returned for furlough from India where he has served as an agriculturist in Orissa. John had been a journeyman in the Philippines; and as he was moving toward appointment, we asked him to go to India. Since missionary visas were not being granted for India, he asked how he would be able to serve there. We replied that we didn't know but felt that God would provide a way. While on a survey trip following his appointment, John met the officials at a government agricultural university; upon discovering he was interested in coming to India, they asked him if he would teach at the university part-time if they would sponsor his visa! John said, "OK, Lord, you got me here; now what do I do?" He started an agricultural training project among the Kui people in the Khond Hills and later with the help of the media consultant for the area launched a daily radio program with seven to eight minutes of agricultural information and seven to eight minutes of sharing the gospel. Since it was the only radio broadcast in the Kui language, word quickly spread throughout the villages, and everyone tuned in to the broadcast. The churches in the area formed listener groups and saw that there was at least one radio in each village. After six months it was reported eight thousand people were gathering in over two hundred villages in these listener groups. Upon John's arrival in the US at the end of the year, he said five thousand new believers had been baptized and eighty new churches started in the last two years. John Langston didn't do that; he would never claim credit, but he was there, obedient to go to that lonely, isolated assignment, and God worked through him.

TRUST GOD'S PROVIDENCE IN TIMES OF TRIAL AND AFFLICTION TO ACCOMPLISH HIS PURPOSE.

However, the providence of God doesn't assure that everything will go well and you will necessarily experience victory and success. It didn't seem victorious when Jesus was nailed to a cross. It didn't appear that God was in control when His ministry came to an abrupt end with rejection and suffering. Some of you will suffer; the providence of God doesn't make you immune to tragedy any more than it did for Job. In the last month we have been saddened by the news of the death of three missionaries, two from illness and another in an automobile accident. Three others have been wounded in armed robberies and hijacking. Others have lost their visas and had to transfer from the place where they had planted their lives, or the family was suddenly displaced by evacuation when war and violence erupted. But they were not forsaken; God had not abdicated His throne.

As Paul reflected in 2 Corinthians 4:8–9, "We are hard-pressed on every side, yet not crushed; we are perplexed, but not in despair; persecuted, but not forsaken; struck down, but not destroyed." Never lose sight that God is in control, no matter what you experience; even when you suffer, He is working to accomplish His purpose in and through you.

TRUST GOD'S PROVIDENCE TO DRAW PEOPLE TO CHRIST.

Just as God raised Jesus from the dead, He will raise up a people who are dead in trespasses and sin, people who are in bondage to pagan cultures, wandering in the hopelessness of ignorance and superstition because you go and allow Him to work through you. Romans 9:26 expresses the resurrection miracle among a people who heard the gospel for the first time—"And it shall be that in the place where it is said to them, 'you are not My people,' there they shall be called the sons of the living God."

As it was God who worked in the life and ministry of Jesus, God will work through you. As God was in control and planned the suffering and death of Jesus on the cross, He will work through the suffering and trials that He allows to come into your life. And as it was impossible for the grave to hold Jesus, it will be impossible for the spiritual darkness to hold the people to which you go as God will raise them up to know Him because of His power to work through your witness and ministry.

In this message of Peter in Acts 2, he looks for an example of someone who saw the providence of God in its fullness, and he found David. In the next two verses (2:25–26) he says, "I was always beholding the Lord in my presence; for He is at my right hand, that I may not be shaken. Therefore my heart was glad and my tongue exulted; moreover, my flesh also will abide in hope." David's testimony kept the providence of God in perspective.

1. He always saw the Lord before Him. Keep your eyes on the Lord; don't let your vision be diverted. Keep Him always before you.

2. Then he says that the Lord is "at my right hand," therefore he will not be shaken. One who is at the right hand of the throne is the one who is delegated with the power and authority of the king. The disciples coveted the position. Jesus was seated at the right hand of the Father. We talk about someone being our "right-hand man." David says the Lord is at his right hand. Isn't that amazing! God goes with you as your right-hand man. There is nothing you cannot do with Him beside you. Jesus said, "All power has been given unto me in heaven and in earth," and Jesus, in all His power and authority, is your right-hand man. No wonder David says I cannot be shaken.

3. Because David understood the providence of God, he said, "My heart was glad and my tongue exulted or rejoiced." You will find an amazing key to practical victory and practicing the presence of Christ is through praising Him in all things.

4. Finally, David says that he "will abide in hope." Whether there is any evidence for optimism or not, hope and vision cannot be destroyed because your hope, your confidence, your security are in God.

In conclusion, notice the result of seeing and understanding the providence and power of God that was revealed through the life, the death, and the resurrection of Jesus. It was the convicting proclamation of the gospel. In verses 36–37 Peter declared, "'Therefore let all the house of Israel know for certain that God has made Him both Lord and Christ—this Jesus whom you crucified.' Now when they heard this, they were pierced to the heart, and said to Peter and the rest of the apostles, 'Brethren, what shall we do?'"

I pray that your conviction, confidence, and awareness of God's providence will enable you to boldly lift up and proclaim Jesus Christ so that His power would draw people to Him. And it would not be simply a theological truth but a practical reality that "whosoever shall call upon the name of the Lord shall be saved." Therefore, keep your eyes on Jesus, remember He is at your right hand, praise Him in all things, and abide in hope.

29

DRAWING ALL MEN TO JESUS

John 12:19, 21, 32

As you prepare to go to the mission field and still face a time of orientation, language learning, and cross-cultural adjustments, there are many areas of which you are aware of the need for growth and development. One of the most important is to nurture your walk with the Lord, for your effectiveness will be directly proportional to the time you spend with the Lord in prayer and feeding on His Word.

A number of years ago, I developed a pattern of reading a psalm each morning and a chapter from the Gospels before praying. I would come back to a more systematic, intensive Bible study, but the Psalms seemed to create in my heart an attitude of praise, and reading from the Gospels gave a sense of reality to the presence of Jesus. It is not my purpose to speak to your devotional life, but I share that simply to say that in reading from chapter 12 of the Gospel of John recently, I was impressed by three comments that seem to characterize what you will face and experience overseas.

THE WHOLE WORLD SEEMS TO BE RESPONDING TO THE GOSPEL!

In John 12:19, as the crowds were praising Jesus on the occasion of His triumphal entry into Jerusalem, the scribes and religious leaders exclaimed, "Look, the whole world has gone after Him!"

God has called you to the mission field overseas at a time of unprecedented harvest when it seems that the whole world is responding to follow Jesus. Mission historians have pointed out that more has been accomplished in the last two hundred years in global evangelization since William Carey went to India than in all two thousand years of Christian history. Furthermore, there has been more accomplished in the last fifty years since World War II than in all the last two hundred years and more advance in fulfilling the Great Commission and reaching the nations in the years since the Berlin Wall fell than in the last forty years. God is moving on every continent toward the fulfillment of Habakkuk's prophecy that "the earth will be filled with the knowledge of the glory of the LORD as the waters cover the sea" (Hab. 2:14).

Since 1988 we have seen the number of Baptist churches overseas grow from 17,000 to almost 100,000 at the end of 2004. Ten years ago baptisms on Southern Baptist mission fields had reached 300,000, but last year the number of baptisms exceeded 600,000. For several years missionaries around the world have collectively been reporting a thousand new believers a day being baptized. Researchers indicate that the number of baptized, born-again believers is growing three times faster than population growth. Two countries with the greatest harvest in a recent annual report were Albania and a field in Central Asia that cannot be publicly identified due to sensitive security issues related to our work there. Swaziland, Togo, Uganda, and Mozambique led Africa in the highest baptism rates while Honduras, the Dominican Republic, and Venezuela in Latin America baptized one new believer for every six members.

Brazil reported fifty thousand baptisms and Nigeria forty-two thousand; 627 new churches were started in Nigeria alone in spite of economic and political turmoil. A Journeyman teacher in China reported witnessing fourteen hundred new believers baptized in one day in December a year ago. One of our agriculturists reported five thousand baptisms and eighty new churches started in the remote area of India where he was working. An American evangelist saw thirty-two thousand professions of faith during a crusade in the Ukraine. A year ago there were more than six thousand believers baptized and over three hundred new churches started in countries and people groups where people had no access to the gospel and had never heard of Jesus just a few years ago.

As Paul said in Colossians 1:6, "All over the world the gospel is multiplying and bearing fruit." The Pharisees were disturbed that all the people in Jerusalem seemed to be welcoming Jesus as the Messiah and proclaiming His praise; they did not realize that their reactionary overstatement was a prophetic word that would one day be fulfilled. And this could be that time. Barriers are crumbling, doors are opening, and the global harvest is accelerating at a time God is calling you to join that harvest.

THE WHOLE WORLD IS SEEKING FOR WHAT ONLY JESUS CAN PROVIDE.

A couple of verses later, in John 12:21, we read of some Greeks—foreigners, Gentiles—who came to Philip and said, "Sir, we would see Jesus." The reality of the world today is that people desire to see Jesus. Oh, they don't necessarily know that it is Jesus they are seeking, but as the tribal animist in Benin or the Congo carefully arranges his fetishes and places a sacrifice in a sacred place to appease the evil spirits, he is seeking for the salvation that only Jesus can bring. As the Hindu bows before grotesque idols, a Buddhist anticipates endless cycles of reincarnation, or a Chinese prays to his ancestors, they are seeking the assurance of eternal life found only in Jesus. During the month of Ramadan on the Muslim calendar, one billion Muslims are fasting all across North Africa, the Middle East, and Central Asia, and literally around the world; at no other time do they seek and pray so diligently for religious truth that supersedes the fatalistic hopelessness of their faith. Each year we hear testimonies of how Jesus reveals Himself as the one they are seeking through dreams and visions or other revelations.

A teacher in China told about a student who came to her at the end of the semester and said, "All of my life I have been told there is no God. My parents told me there is no God. My school taught me there is no God; my government said there is no God, but in my heart I knew there had to be a God. I have never had anyone to show Him to me until you came." There is that emptiness within every human soul that is never satisfied, is never complete until one is reconciled with his Creator and Redeemer, through Jesus Christ.

Why has God called you to places like Brazil and Israel, Indonesia and Zimbabwe, and Mexico? Because all over the world people in their poverty and suffering, in their emptiness and sin, are crying out, "We would see Jesus." We want to know the Prince of Peace. We want a Savior that can atone for our sins. We want our life of darkness to be illuminated by the Light of the world. But the only chance of their meeting Jesus is for you to go in obedience to God's call—for you to be a mediator like Philip and introduce them to the Savior. You see, there is dwelling within you the person of Jesus Christ waiting to be revealed to a lost world. He goes with you and empowers you. That is why I don't want you to miss the significance of the third expression in John 12.

THE WHOLE WORLD CAN POTENTIALLY BE SAVED WHEN JESUS IS LIFTED UP.

These two observations—an unprecedented harvest throughout the world and a world yearning to know Jesus—are brought into focus by an amazing claim by Jesus Himself in John 12:32, "And I, if I be lifted up, . . . will draw all men unto me."

Isn't that astounding! When we think that what Jesus said applies to one billion Muslims, 900 million Hindus, 1.7 billion people in unreached people groups who have not yet had a gospel witness, the multitudes across Eastern Europe and the Communist world so long deprived of the freedom of religion. Jesus said, "I will draw all men unto me!" Jesus was clearly referring to His death on the cross. He was lifted up from the earth and died for the sins of the world in order that all men night be reconciled to God. But still many are lost. He was lifted up to heaven that we would be empowered by the Holy Spirit to be His witnesses to the uttermost ends of the earth. But still many are lost. It is not enough that Jesus was lifted up on the cross and not enough that He was lifted up to heaven. We must lift Him up before a lost world if they are to be drawn unto Him.

Romans 10:13 says, "Whosoever calls on the name of the LORD shall be saved." But the Scripture goes on to say, "But how can they call on Him of whom they have not believed? And how shall they that believe on Him of whom they have not heard? And how shall they hear without a preacher?" Someone has to tell them, to proclaim the gospel that they might know when Jesus was lifted up on the cross it was for their sins!

When we first arrived in Indonesia as missionaries many years ago, we busied ourselves with all those ministries and activities in which missionaries engage in an effort to build relationships and create a forum for witness, but there was little response. People were largely indifferent to us and our ministry, sometimes even antagonistic. We were isolated and lonely, feeling that God had let us down. My frustration grew to discouragement and despondency, and I found myself on my face crying out to God, "Why have you brought us here?" During that time of fasting and seeking the Lord, I found myself reading the book of Acts, and it occurred to me that all these uneducated and untrained disciples did was lift up Jesus in a bold, positive witness. I realized that is why God had called me to Indonesia; it was not because of my education and abilities and clever strategies but simply to lift Him up in a bold, positive witness. I am still amazed at Muslims who began to come to Christ, even though they would be rejected by their family, ridiculed by their community, lose their jobs, sometimes their lives threatened. Why would they turn their backs on their society, family, culture, and religion to embrace the Christian faith? Because Jesus said, "If I be lifted up, I will draw all men unto me."

So we are sending you out into an unprecedented harvest when it seems the whole world is going after Him. We are sending you out to touch a world who would see Jesus, and we are sending you out to lift Him up that all the world might be drawn unto Him. But there is another message here in John 12 for others here tonight as well. Why are only these few being appointed when there are so many needs and God is at work all over the world? They are so few among a lost world, so few to fill the hundreds of personnel needs around the globe while so many remain here at home, never considering the possibility of God's call to missionary service? Have you come to the point of surrender like each of these who relinquished the right to their own life and submitted it to the lordship of Jesus Christ? Another verse in John 12— verse 9—tells us, "And many came, not for Jesus' sake only!"

There may be those here tonight that, like the Greeks, are still seeking Jesus. You have never yielded your life to Him and trusted Him as your personal Lord and Savior. These missionaries are going overseas to tell people in Africa and China and Eastern Europe that if people there will believe on the Lord Jesus Christ they can be saved. But you can be saved right here tonight, by simply praying a prayer with sincerity and saying, "God, I know that I am a sinner; I believe that Jesus Christ came and died on the cross for my sins. I am sorry and want to turn away from my sin; I trust Jesus to save me. I want to give my life to live for Him."

But most of you here tonight are Christians. You have trusted Jesus as your Savior and may be attending a church faithfully, but can you say what you are doing with your life is for Jesus' sake and Jesus' sake alone? Probably not. Many simply choose their own vocation and course of life without ever considering God's will. But tonight God is speaking to you. There is an awakening in your heart, realizing that God could use you on the mission field. Why would only four couples respond last year to more than 150 personnel requests for Russia? Because there are many living not for Jesus' sake but for themselves. Why would more than two thousand people groups today still not have the opportunity to know Jesus? Why hasn't someone taken the gospel to them? Why would 95 percent of the preachers stay in America among 5 percent of the world's population, when only 5 percent would respond to God's call to reach the ends of the earth? Could it be because many, perhaps you, have never yielded to the lordship of Jesus Christ and to live for His sake alone?

30

FOR SUCH A TIME AS THIS

Esther 4:14

When Jesus began His ministry, He announced that the kingdom of God was at hand and sent His disciples out to proclaim that kingdom. He said that the gospel of the kingdom would be preached in the whole world as a witness to every nation before the end would come. Throughout the Scripture we read of that coming kingdom where God would reign and every knee would bow and every tongue confess that Jesus is Lord to the glory of God the Father!

That vision of the kingdom was born in the heart of God even before the foundation of the world. The Old Testament patriarchs and prophets were privileged to share in that vision as they foresaw a Messiah who would one day come and reconcile a lost world to Himself. That kingdom came when Jesus left the glories of heaven and humbled Himself as a servant in the form of man and died on the cross that the power of sin might be destroyed. He arose from the tomb, as we just celebrated on Easter Day, and lives to bring redemption to the nations!

Those of you being appointed as missionaries need to recognize that you have been called to a kingdom purpose. You are not being appointed just to go overseas and do evangelistic work or train pastors. You are not being appointed just because there was a need for a business manager or strategy coordinators in a foreign country. You are not being appointed because we needed more personnel to carry out the International Mission Board's strategy. You are being commissioned to join God in a kingdom purpose that is bigger than your mission in Spain or Uruguay or South Africa. It is bigger than the International Mission Board and Southern Baptists.

You are joining a movement that supersedes human plans and denominational programs. It is a movement that is eternal, directed by the Lord of the universe, and will culminate in His reign over the nations as Lord of lords and King of kings.

The book of Esther portrays a drama not unlike that in which you are participating today. You are familiar with the setting as the Jews were in captivity in Babylon and how Esther had come to be chosen as queen. You remember that King Xerxes had been manipulated by Haman to issue a decree that the Jews should be exterminated. Esther's uncle, Mordecai, had become aware of the plot and recognized that God had placed Esther in a unique position at this special time to intercede on behalf of the Jews and provide for their deliverance. That familiar verse in Esther 4:14 puts her life and the challenge she faced in perspective when Mordecai said, "But who knows but that you have come into the kingdom for such a time as this."

GOD HAS CALLED YOU TO A SPECIFIC PLACE FOR A KINGDOM PURPOSE.

I would like to draw some parallels to the experience of Esther and say that you have come into the kingdom "for such a time as this!" First, God has called you to the place you are going for a kingdom purpose. Esther did not have any idea what she would face and how God would use her when she was chosen to be a part of the royal community of the king. She was simply obedient to go and be where God had placed her.

God is extending His kingdom in places where His lordship and rule have not been known. Some of you are going to serve through educational channels in China, chosen because of a unique equipping that you bring to the kingdom. It is impossible to know the extent to which the kingdom of God is being extended in China. Some say there are as many as seventy-five to 100 million believers in that country where religious freedom is still restricted. But God is sovereign over rulers and authorities and principalities. I heard a missionary to Hong Kong recently say, "People are anticipating the sovereignty of Hong Kong changing in 1997 when China takes over, but God will continue to be sovereign over the nations; He will not relinquish His throne just because the government changes."

God has called you to be a part of that kingdom purpose, just as He commissioned those first disciples to go out to the cities and villages of Galilee and Judea to proclaim the kingdom. He has called you into His kingdom as it is beginning to impact those isolated countries of Mali and Burkina Faso where Islam has merged with animistic traditions to keep the people in darkness and spiritual bondage. He has called you to His kingdom purpose in Macedonia, Southern Africa, and Indochina where the people have known little of the peace that God's reign can bring to their hearts and society.

GOD HAS CALLED YOU AT A SPECIFIC TIME FOR HIS KINGDOM PURPOSE.

Not only has God called you to the specific place where you are going, but the timing in which He has called is equally significant—"for such a time as this!" Never have we seen such unprecedented opportunities for evangelizing a lost world as right now. Never, since New Testament days, have we seen such an evangelistic harvest taking place. It was just a few years ago that the International Mission Board reported 100,000 baptisms, and now for the last four years more than a quarter of a million baptisms have been reported annually. The number of evangelical believers is growing three times the population growth rate throughout the world.

We could never have anticipated the kind of opportunity "at such a time as this" that God is providing in Eastern Europe where generations have been deprived of the gospel. As we move toward the close of the twentieth century and into a new millennium, doors are opening for the gospel of the kingdom to be preached in every nation. Who would have thought that we would be commissioning personnel to go to Romania, Morocco, Vietnam, and all across the Muslim world and former communist strongholds? What must God be planning to do because you go where He is placing you at this time in His kingdom purpose?

When Esther was chosen as queen and came into the kingdom, there was not yet a threat to the Jewish people. That would come later. But because God knew what would happen, He used other circumstances to have Esther in place at the proper time.

In the early 1990s Cambodia was still under a communist government that restricted religious freedom and open proclamation of the gospel. But the country was destitute after the genocide that had decimated society and desperate for rehabilitation and social work. Some missionaries with those skills were found who were willing to take the risk of going into this environment, not knowing what God might do and how He might use their presence. In two years twenty-four house churches had come into existence in the capital city of Penom Phen; two years later a Baptist convention was formed with forty organized churches, and after a few years those churches had multiplied to more than three hundred throughout the country. We can't know in advance how

God may fulfill His kingdom purpose; we can only answer the call wherever He sends us in His timing that we might be positioned to be used according to His providence and plan.

THE PLACE AND TIMING OF GOD'S CALL ALWAYS CONFORMS WITH HIS PURPOSE.

Where you are going and when you are going is for such a time as this, but also there is a purpose for your going. God had placed Esther in a unique position that she "might plead for the people." It was God's plan to save the Jews, but there had to be someone to intercede before the king, to make supplication and plead for them. Esther 4:8 says of Mordecai that he instructed "her to go in to the king to make supplication to him and plead before him for her people."

It is God's desire that repentance and forgiveness of sins be preached among all nations that He might bring to salvation and deliverance those who would be saved, but someone must go and share the good news. Romans 10:13 tells us, "Whosoever shall call upon the name of the Lord shall be saved." But then we are confronted with the question of how can they call on Him if they have not believed, and how can they believe on Him of whom they have not heard. How can they hear unless someone is sent and pleads on their behalf with the news of God's deliverance and salvation?

Jeff Pearson, with his wife Margie, went to Ethiopia as an engineer to install a water project during the drought of the 1980s in which thousands of people were dying. They were able to tap into the springs in the bottom of the canyon and devise a system to bring water to the villages in the highlands. But in doing so they also brought the water of life through their witness, and now there are churches multiplying throughout the Bulga District where they lived and served.

Dr. Chris Austin, with a Ph.D. in public health, and his wife Karen went to the Gambia, a destitute country in West Africa to provide sanitation and other improvements to the village. They were quite successful in these projects, but Chris put their ministry in perspective at a recent health-care workshop when he said, "We may have succeeded in our projects to improve the health and welfare of the people, but healthy in hell doesn't count for much. We are failures until these people know Jesus as their Savior. We are there to present the claims of Christ and plead with them to be saved."

You may be going to fill assignments in recreation and youth work, to guide construction projects and serve as business managers, but don't ever lose the focus on your kingdom purpose to plead for the salvation of the people through sharing the message of salvation in Jesus Christ.

THE CALLING FOR SUCH A TIME AS THIS ENTAILS RISK.

Finally, I would want you to be aware that there is a risk in your going. There is a cost in being called into the kingdom for such a time as this. Esther recognized this when she went into the court of the king contrary to the law and said, "If I perish, I perish." But she knew there was no other alternative through which her people might be saved.

It is unlikely that you will experience martyrdom, but some have. Missionaries today are serving in many dangerous situations. The world is deteriorating into anarchy as social structures are breaking down and ethnic violence is escalating. Just last week we had to evacuate our missionaries from Liberia. In the last year three missionaries have been wounded in armed robberies and carjacking. Several in active service have died in automobile accidents, plane crashes, or illnesses. Others have been imprisoned or deported by hostile governments, antagonistic to a Christian witness. Obedience to God's call does not exempt us from tragedy or nullify the risk. Yet none of those who suffered would have chosen any alternative but to fulfill God's calling in order to share the gospel where He had placed them.

I have been told that one of the reasons the church is growing so rapidly in China is because new believers have to reconcile themselves to the fact that they might die or be imprisoned for their faith. Having faced that possibility and decided to go with Christ, there is no threat or anything that can deter them in their witness. Esther was worthy of God's kingdom and found herself used to deliver a nation because she was willing to take the risk. That decision and comment of Esther foreshadowed the deliberate action of our Savior who left the glories of heaven to die. There was no other choice for Jesus except to say, "If I perish, I perish." What Jesus did, and what you are being called to do, was ironically reflected in the words of Caiaphas the high priest when he said, "It is expedient for one man to die for the people than the whole nation should perish."

It was necessary for Esther to take the risk of dying lest the whole nation perish, and it is necessary for you to take that risk lest the nation to which He has called you—Malaysia, Portugal, Germany, Nigeria, or the Philippines—should perish without the message of salvation and deliverance through Jesus Christ. Jesus called on anyone who would come after Him "to take up your cross and die to self." Esther was able to take this bold courageous step of faith and be used of God because she had already died to self.

You have been called into the kingdom for such a time as this. It is a call to count the cost and consider the risk and die to self. It is a call to plead for the people to be saved as you bring the message of salvation. It is a call to extend the kingdom of God and allow Him to work at this unique time in history in bringing a lost world to Jesus Christ.

31

VICTORY THROUGH PRAISE

2 Chronicles 20

Whether going to be a part of an accelerating harvest in Africa, Latin America, and Eastern Europe or to fill in the gaps in our Christian witness where people for so long have been denied the privilege of hearing the gospel, it is an exciting time to be following God's call to the mission field. Many are currently going to sensitive, restrictive places that cannot even be identified publicly in the Middle East and Central Asia because God has opened the door, and you have been obedient to His call.

Although record numbers of new missionaries are being commissioned by the International Mission Board, the numbers are still small and the laborers so few, relative to a lost world. More of God's people need to recognize the potential in their lives of joining those going to share Christ with a lost world. Some of you are schoolteachers, businessmen, accountants, an agriculturist, or a doctor; others may be a pastor, minister on a church staff, a seminary or college student, but there is a place in God's mission. Whether or not one hears God's call is contingent on catching a vision of what God is doing and, in submission to the lordship of Jesus Christ, saying, "I am willing to go and trust God to use me to share the light of His love with a world in darkness."

Many have a closed mind to the possibility of missionary service. Some say, "I'm willing to serve you, to be faithful to my church, to witness in my community, anything but go overseas as a missionary." They stop short of full and total surrender to God's will because they are overwhelmed by the idea of living in a cross-cultural situation, having to learn to communicate in another language, and facing the prospects of giving up their comfortable home and lifestyle to identify with masses of impoverished people.

Some of you have been there on volunteer trips or short-term assignments, but let me alert you that you are going to be overwhelmed by the masses, the poverty, the lostness, and the challenge of finding the handle to impact them with the gospel. When my wife and I were appointed to Indonesia in 1970, the largest Muslim nation in the world, we arrived at our assignment in East Java to find we were the only missionaries among five and a half million people. We could drive four hours in any direction before reaching another missionary family. Most of these people were Madurese, one of the largest, resistant, fanatical, antagonistic unreached people groups in the world.

We felt like Jehoshaphat, the king of Judah, when the armies of Moab and the Ammonites were coming to attack. He gathered Judah and prayed in 2 Chronicles 20: "A great multitude is coming against us" (v. 2). "We have no power against this great multitude . . . nor do we know what to do" (v. 12). That is exactly how we felt.

YOU WILL BE OVERWHELMED BY A MULTITUDE OF PEOPLE AND PROBLEMS.

Some of you are going to the Muslim world and will encounter one of the most formidable barriers to reaching the last frontier of an evangelized world. On a recent trip to Uzebekistan, I was told that two thousand new mosques have been built or renovated in the last three years in that Islamic republic. Last month I traveled in India and went to Hardiwar on the Ganges River where the Kumbh Mela festival was going on. Millions of Hindu pilgrims will gather during this three-months festival to bathe in the Ganges River in their belief they will receive cleansing of their sins. A letter from a missionary in Mexico City indicated the population is projected to reach twenty-eight million in a few years. If you crammed all the people of Texas and Oklahoma combined into your city, you would not begin to have that many people. Some of you are being assigned to unreached people groups such as the Jula, the Fulbe, and Toura in West Africa, and though many of the two thousand plus unreached people groups are being targeted, most of the 1.7 billion people represented by these people groups have not yet been effectively engaged and impacted by evangelism strategies.

How does one missionary get a handle on the task? What are you among such a vast multitude? However, it is not just the masses of people and the lostness of a world without Christ, but you will be entering into Satan's territory. First John 5:19 says, "We know that we are of God, but the whole world lies in the power of the evil one." A culture, a country, or people group where Christ is not known—where the gospel has not taken root—is the kingdom of Satan, ruled by the powers of darkness. That power may come against you in the form of restrictive government policies that forbid you to witness; they may withdraw your visa and work permit and threaten to deport you. You will experience hardship through the reversal of economic conditions such as that which recently swept Southeast Asia. It may be through ethnic violence and war that has resulted in evacuation such as has occurred in Rwanda, Albania, Angola, and Liberia in recent years. Satan will do everything he can to defeat you, divert you, and diminish your effectiveness. It may be the sickness of your children, discouragement in your work, or just illusions of the comfortable lifestyle you left behind in America, but be prepared for it—you will encounter opposition. You will find yourself praying like Jehoshaphat, "O God, we have no power against this great multitude that is coming against us; nor do we know what to do, but our eyes are upon You."

RECOGNIZE THAT THE BATTLE IS THE LORD'S—KEEP YOUR EYES ON HIM.

I want you to notice how God answered this prayer. In verse 15 we read, "Thus says the LORD to you: 'Do not be afraid nor dismayed because of this great multitude, for the battle is not yours, but God's.'" Then He tells them (v. 17), "You will not need to fight in this battle. Position yourselves, stand still and see the salvation of the LORD, who is with you. . . . Do not fear or be dismayed; tomorrow go out against them, for the LORD is with you." You are familiar with this passage and know that God told Jehoshaphat to appoint those who would go before the army singing praise to the Lord. Verse 22 tells us, "Now when they began to sing and to praise, the Lord set ambushes against the people of Ammon, Moab, and Mount Seir . . . and they were defeated."

Never forget that the most powerful weapon in your arsenal is a song of praise in your heart and on your lips. You will be going through an intense time of orientation before departure for the field and upon your arrival overseas in an effort to equip you for all the skills you are going to need as a missionary. Most of you have had seminary courses to prepare you for ministry, and all of that is needed and is valuable; but more than anything else, the thing that will assure you of victory is a constant relationship of walking with the Lord in praise. The Bible tells us that God's ultimate purpose is not what He calls us to do but that we would "be to the praise of His glory" (Eph. 1:12). Psalm 22 tells us that God resides in the praises of His people. Isaiah 43 says, "Everyone who is called by My Name, and whom I have created for My glory will declare My praise." Israel realized in Psalm 106 the purpose of their salvation when they sang, "Save us, 0 LORD our God, and gather us from among the nations, to give thanks to Thy holy name, and glory in Thy praise."

It is an attitude of praise, a heart of praise, an expression of praise that is essential to your relationship with God; and that will sustain you in times of trial. Praise will release God's power for victory over the opposition you will encounter. Remember, "the battle is not yours, but God's." How can you not be afraid or dismayed when the multitudes come against you? It is by relinquishing the battle to God through praise.

Notice first of all when Jehoshaphat encountered this great multitude coming against him, he sought the Lord and acknowledged His sovereignty and power. In 2 Chronicles 20:6 he reminded God, "O LORD God of our fathers, are You not God in heaven, and do You not rule over all the kingdoms of the nations, and in Your hand is there not power and might, so that no one is able to withstand You?"

You are going to find yourself in the kind of situations where you come to the end of yourself and your ability and exclaim, "O Lord, this great problem has come against us; we are overwhelmed and do not know what to do." But like Jehoshaphat, keep your eyes on the Lord and be reminded that He is sovereign over the nations. His power is over the kingdoms so that no one is able to stand against Him or prevail against His divine purpose. And how do you appropriate that power, access His presence, affirm His providence and accept His promises? It is through praise.

APPROPRIATE CONSTANT VICTORY THROUGH PRAISING THE LORD.

While serving in Indonesia, we lived in a remote area of East Java. Whenever we had to travel for meetings or personal R&R to other parts of the island, we would always try to leave very early in the morning as the narrow broken-paved highway would become congested and the heat and dust oppressive. If we waited until later in the day, the trip would take at least a couple of hours longer. One particular morning we had planned to drive to Surabaya, and everything began to unravel. The helper that was to stay and guard our house did not show up; word came that someone in our pastor's family was in the hospital, and we had to go minister to them. There were other interruptions and delays, and by the time we finally got away, my patience had worn thin; to say I was irritated that our plans had gone awry and we had been delayed and inconvenienced would be to put it mildly.

Then to top it off, we had a flat tire before getting out of town. We would have to change the tire and get it repaired. Getting dirty and greasy meant I would have to go home and clean up, delaying us further. As I was tightening the final lug bolts, my four-year-old son who had been watching me out the window said, "Praise the Lord; we had a flat tire."

Well, the last thing I felt like doing was praising the Lord. Why did he say that? It had become the practice in our family, anytime anything went wrong, to praise the Lord. This was because praising the Lord takes our focus off the circumstances and puts it on the Lord. We used to sing a little chorus that expressed what we discovered as the key to practicing the presence of Christ and walking in victory:

> *It's amazing what praising will do; hallelujah, hallelujah.*
> *It's amazing what praising will do, hallelujah!*

When you praise God and give thanks regardless of the situation, (1) your heart and thoughts become focused on God rather than your circumstances; (2) when your attention is focused on God, you become aware of His presence (remember, He resides in the praises of His people); and (3) when you become aware of His presence, the lordship of Jesus Christ is able to take control, not only of the situation and the problem, but He also takes control of your heart and attitude to bring peace and trust that comes from confidence in Him.

Paul reminds us in Philippians 4:6–7, "Be anxious for nothing, but in everything by prayer and supplication, with thanksgiving, let your requests be made known to God; and the peace of God, which surpasses all understanding, will guard your hearts and minds through Christ Jesus." The key is praise and thanksgiving; Christ will put a guard around your heart and set an ambush to defeat the enemy.

Whenever a need arises and things start to overwhelm us and we lose control, we usually work harder, become stressed out and filled with anxiety. But remember, you don't need to fight this battle; do not fear nor be dismayed. When opposition comes, stand still and see the salvation of the Lord. You have heard the expression, "Don't just stand there; do something!" Well, what I am saying is when opposition comes and you are overwhelmed, "Don't do something, but stand there!" Don't fret and try to work it out; stand there, praising the Lord, and watch the victory He will bring!

The psalmist says again in Psalm 34, "I will bless the LORD at all times; His praise shall continually be in my mouth. . . . Oh, magnify the LORD with me, and let us exalt His name together." Hebrews 13:15 exhorts us, "Through

Him then, let us continually offer up a sacrifice of praise to God, that is, the fruit of lips that give thanks to His name."

God's ultimate purpose for you is to praise Him and all you do to be to the praise of His glory. Praise and thanksgiving is the key to a consistent walk and relationship with the Lord. It will remind you of His sovereignty and power and sustain you through times of trial and opposition. Praising God in all things will keep you focused on His glory and will keep you from taking personal pride in any results of your ministry. And when the multitudes of people or problems come against you, it is the key to victory.

32

PAUL'S FOOLISH DECISIONS

Philippians 1:12–14

Most of us would share the consensus opinion that the apostle Paul was the first, the foremost, and probably the greatest international missionary that ever lived. He set the standard for cross-cultural missions. He was the prototype for evangelism and church planting. It was Paul that saw the gospel applicable beyond its original narrow Jewish context. It was Paul that wrote to those in Rome that he was coming to preach the gospel to them and going on to Spain. He said, "I have been called to the regions beyond."

He represented the ideal model for preparation for the task in theological education and taking the time for spiritual development in isolation and retreat. He was the orator who was able to present the gospel with wisdom and relevance in skilled apologetics before Jew and Gentile, Greek philosophers, and pagan idol worshippers. He was a precursor to those of you going to sow in unevangelized fields, to reap where the harvest is plentiful, and those of you going to the edge of the last frontier. He was an example of one who was committed to completing the task, from saturation sowing to discipleship training. He said in Romans 15:19, "From Jerusalem and . . . as far as Illyricum I have fully preached the gospel of Christ."

But Paul made some very foolish decisions in his life and ministry, and I want to point those out to you tonight, with the hope that you can learn from them as well.

HE TURNED HIS BACK ON THE REPUTATION OF A SUCCESSFUL MINISTRY TO GO TO THE GENTILES.

As the New Testament church began to emerge, Paul was quickly received and recognized as an effective and reputable leader among the church at Antioch and, after some initial skepticism and reticence, by the believers in Jerusalem. He had one of those thrilling, one-of-a-kind, high profile testimonies of a former persecutor who had come to the faith, a Jewish Pharisee among Pharisees who was now a believer. He could have become the prominent leader of the early church in Jerusalem, been at the forefront of the harvest that was sweeping Jews into the kingdom and gained an unimaginable reputation for himself, if he had not had such a passion for the Gentiles.

How foolish to give all of that up to traipse about over wilderness and desert, attacked by wild animals, shipwrecked, subjected to hunger and deprivation, to be misunderstood, stoned, beaten and imprisoned when he could have stayed in Jerusalem and Antioch and enjoyed a comfortable and successful pastorate!

Many people would consider you equally foolish. Some of you have family that just cannot understand why you would leave a successful career and an affluent lifestyle. Your church has provided well for you and reminded you how much you are needed here in America. But something compels you, like Paul, to turn your back on all the advantages of staying in your comfort zone in order to carry the gospel to those Christ died to save and are still waiting for someone to proclaim to them that God loves the whole world.

There were many discouraging times in Indonesia when I thought of the alternatives. In times of loneliness and isolation, during seasons of unresponsiveness that seemed unfruitful, feeling under-appreciated, that no one cared, I thought of college and seminary classmates who were enjoying successful pastorates, preaching in evangelism conferences, and elected to positions of leadership. I could have stayed at home and baptized more in a year than I did my entire first term, but God reminded me the Madurese in East Java and multitudes of Muslims in Indonesia would never have a chance to be saved if I had not been obedient to God's call. May you be so foolish, as Paul, to understand it is not about you, your success, and your fulfillment but God's priority of reaching the nations.

HE COULD NEVER SETTLE DOWN AND FOCUS
ON A PLACE OF SERVICE.

Paul was also foolish because he could never stick with his sense of God's leadership. As he set out on his second missionary journey, he felt that God was leading him to Bithynia. If he had had any real conviction about God's will, he would have stuck it out, in spite of the closed doors. He blamed it on the Holy Spirit in being forbidden to go where he said God had led him. Instead of following through and persevering, he found himself in Troas wondering, *What in the world does God want me here for?* He received the Macedonian vision, swept across Europe planting churches, and that's ultimately why you and I are here today.

God has revealed His will for you, and you have responded in obedience. That's why you are going to places like Budapest, Bashkortostan, Kyrgyzstan, Morocco, and cities in China. But never forget that God's will is dynamic. It is not a once and for all call, and that's it. That's why He demands that we walk by faith, develop a relationship of trust, and in submissiveness follow His lordship. God has the right to direct your life anywhere and at anytime. I asked a group of emeritus missionaries how many of them, when they retired, were serving in the same location and assignment in which they began their missionary career, and only a handful raised their hands.

My own daughter and son-in-law left six months ago for where they felt confident God was leading them to serve in Central Asia. After six weeks their platform was rejected, and they were deported. After a few weeks in a neutral country, they accepted an interim assignment in another Central Asian republic, still wondering where God wanted them. Now the ideal assignment has opened in the third country in six months which uniquely fits their gifts and calling. Visas and ministry permits have been granted, and God has miraculously brought in others to join the team. That possibility did not even exist when they went to the field, but now they express greater excitement and confidence than they ever did about their original assignment. During all that upheaval and uncertainty, we wrote them that wherever they end up, it will not be God's second best. Paul recognized God was sovereign over the nations and Lord over his life. Some would think it was foolish when Paul didn't stick with what he felt was God's will, but a change of plans didn't upset him because he knew God was working through the circumstances to get him where He wanted him to be.

HE WAS ALWAYS GETTING IN TROUBLE BECAUSE OF RASH ACTIONS.

Paul was always getting in trouble because he acted rashly instead of playing it safe. If he had not cast out the demon in Philippi, he would not have been put in prison. He should have backed off and played it safe, been a little more tolerant, and not gotten so carried away when he encountered spiritual warfare. Paul was always getting himself in trouble. He was stoned in Lystra and had to escape over the wall in Damascus. He was imprisoned in Philippi and created a citywide riot in Ephesus. Everywhere he went there was either a riot or revival and sometimes both.

Now I would advise you to be wise and use discretion when you encounter opposition, but never back off from standing firm on the Word of God. You are venturing into Satan's territory. Be prepared for God to manifest His presence through power encounters, and when God moves in a pagan environment, there will be consequences. There are risks involved, but your greatest security is faithfulness in seizing every opportunity to declare that Jesus is Lord.

When one of our creative access personnel was assigned to a closed country, his strategy coordinator warned him that he could be arrested for preaching the gospel. He said, "Don't forget why you are here, why you are taking this risk; if you are ever arrested for witnessing or preaching the gospel, just be sure it's true." Paul said in 1 Corinthians 15: "What profit is it if I fight wild beasts at Ephesus from human motives?" He was declaring that the gospel is worth the risk, and you can trust God with the consequences.

HE FOOLISHLY APPEALED TO CAESAR WHEN HE COULD HAVE BEEN FREED.

Finally, Paul was foolish in his decision to appeal to Caesar; for had he not made that rash appeal, he probably could have gone free. After hearing Paul's testimony, King Agrippa said to King Festus in Acts 26:32, "This man is doing nothing worthy of death or imprisonment. He might have been set free if he had not appealed to Caesar." This was probably the most foolish decision of all. If he had just let the legal process play out, he may have eventually been cleared, but stupid Paul had to go and appeal to Caesar! He might have been freed and continued his missionary journeys. No, probably not. It is more likely he would have been lynched by a Jewish court and his ministry ended prematurely. Instead, he could write from that Roman prison (Phil. 1:12–13), "Now I want you to know, brethren, that my circumstances have turned out for the greater progress of the gospel, so that my imprison-ment in the cause of Christ has become well-known throughout the whole praetorian guard and to everyone else."

God is able to use what may appear to be foolish decisions, contrary to conventional wisdom, to advance His kingdom. He has called you to take risks and trust Him. He has called you to leave your comfort zone and face rejection and humiliation. Realize that when God is in control, your circum-stances will turn out for the progress of the gospel. Don't forfeit the oppor-tunity God will give you by holding on to your comfort zone, locking Him into your own plans, and failing to recognize unconventional opportunities to make Him known to a lost world.

I had the privilege of participating in a retirement recognition service for Tom and Gloria Thurman in Camden, Alabama. They were retiring after thirty-four years of service in Bangladesh. Gloria's sister, Martha, was giv-ing a testimony about what it was like having missionaries for relatives. She said she quickly discovered they make foolish decisions. For example, when Bangladesh was going through a war for independence and they were spend-ing nights cowering underneath mattresses in the hallway during the bomb-ing of their city, they should have come home, but they didn't. When their sons were born with respiratory infections, they should have come home, but they didn't. When they spent their first twelve years in that Muslim country without seeing any response and tidal waves swept the country killing hun-dreds of thousands of people, they should have come home, but they didn't. When Gloria contracted leprosy and Tom was stabbed in a robbery, they should have come home, but they didn't. They didn't make very good deci-sions. They stayed and, because they did, eventually saw over 120 churches started in the Gopalgonj district where they served.

Thank you for making the foolish and irrational decision to give your life to carry the gospel to the ends of the earth, to leave your comfort zone and the security of family and friends. Thank you for your willingness to carry your children to a distant land, to plant your lives in a strange culture, to learn another language, and to take the risk that others may have the opportunity of knowing your Lord. May He bless you, as He did Paul, with His guidance, protection, a fulfilling ministry, and fruitful witness. Paul's decisions were not foolish, and neither is yours.

33

CALLED BY GOD'S GRACE

Romans 15:15–16

I find it unavoidable to keep coming back to the apostle Paul as an example and prototype for one's role as a missionary. His testimony and passionate commitment to cross-cultural witness reflect an admonition and charge that is still appropriate to our role and calling today. Though many Jewish believers had become followers of Jesus Christ, there were still many who had not come to faith in the Messiah who had suffered and died for their sins. Paul had such a deep burden for his people that he said in Romans 9:3 he would be willing to be accursed and eternally condemned himself if it would result in their salvation. But when God was ready for the gospel to break out of that narrow Jewish context and be proclaimed to the rest of the world, it was Paul that God chose. He, more than the other apostles who had laid the foundation and launched the kingdom, saw the gospel as applicable to other cultures and peoples. He understood that the atoning death of Christ on the cross was to provide redemption for the whole world.

Paul went to Cyprus, Asia, and Bythinia. When the door was closed, he responded to the Macedonian vision and swept across Europe planting churches. He said he had been called to the "regions beyond." You, too, are leaving your hometown and American culture where people are lost. It is not because you do not care or are unconcerned. Many of you have a burden for lost family members, yet unsaved neighbors and friends to whom you have faithfully witnessed have not responded. But God will not allow you to stay in your "Jerusalem." The gospel has been planted here; there are others carrying on the witness. The calling of your life is to go to "the regions beyond" where people have not had an opportunity to hear, understand, and respond to the gospel. So here you are tonight being commissioned to go to China, Indonesia, Russia, Mozambique, Mexico, and other places that represent the uttermost ends of the earth. Listen to Paul's testimony in Romans 15:15b–16: "Because of the grace that was given me from God, to be a minister of Christ Jesus to the Gentiles, ministering as a priest the gospel of God, that my offering of the Gentiles might become acceptable, sanctified by the Holy Spirit." I want you to note three things Paul observes about his calling. He defines it as a role, a responsibility, and a result.

YOUR CALLING IS A ROLE RECEIVED BY GOD'S GRACE.

Paul's calling was not something he personally chose to do; in fact, he often declared how unworthy he was to be a minister of the gospel. In another passage he confessed to being the least of the apostles, unworthy to be called an apostle. But Christ had appeared to him and called him. He promised to empower him and use him. And Paul discovered that interesting paradox of the Christian life, that in weakness we are strong; in our own sense of inadequacy, we become dependent on God's all-sufficient grace.

You did not simply decide being a missionary would be a neat vocation or an opportunity to travel and see the world. You weren't motivated by prospects for financial gain and an affluent lifestyle. In fact, there are a lot of people, possibly including your family, that just don't understand why you would do such a thing. You know you will face hardship and even danger. What is it that compels you to go? It is a deep conviction that God has called you. He has given you the privilege of taking the gospel to people who are lost. It is not out of a sense of obligation—somebody's got to do it—but recognition that God has chosen you as an unlikely earthen vessel to be the channel through which His love is declared and lived out. It is not because you have such a spectacular résumé and stunning personality. It is certainly not because of your academic achievements or success here in the States. We have read your bio data and know, as you do, you are here being appointed tonight only because of God's grace who reached down and tapped you on the shoulder and said, "I've got a place for you." For some of you it came on a short-term, volunteer mission trip in which you saw a people without Christ, and God led you to recognize the potential in your life for going and telling them about Jesus. Others just came to a point of dedication and submission to the lordship of Christ in which the desire to do His will superseded all other concerns, and you were willing to put your personal plans on the shelf in recognition of God's grace in choosing you to go as a missionary and be a minister of the gospel.

As the media responded to the tragic death of our missionaries in recent months, they usually ask, "Why do you send missionaries to dangerous places where their lives would be at risk?" They just don't get it, do they? They never ask why journalists go to dangerous places, just so they could tell us bad news of what's happening around the world. They don't question our military forces placing their lives in danger for the purpose of warfare and destruction of life when their commander in chief demands it in a desire to remove threats and bring about peace. But that is not the solution to the needs of our world. The answer is someone, chosen by God's grace, to share a message of God's love and hope to those in despair, hopeless, and lost. You go as a minister of the gospel because the gospel is the power of God unto salvation. You go to give your lives because God gave His when Jesus came and died on the cross. You are the fortunate ones. You are the privileged ones. You are the ones that will be blessed and rewarded because of God's grace that has chosen and appointed you to be a minister of the gospel where it is needed so desperately.

YOUR CALLING IS A RESPONSIBILITY TO BE A PRIEST OF THE GOSPEL.

A priest is typically understood to be a mediator between God and man. We know that each individual has direct access to God and is not dependent on another human filling a priestly office in order to know God and commune with God. But what about those who do not know of God and have never heard of our high priest, Jesus Christ, who came to remove the barrier of sin that we might be reconciled to God? Even before the creation of the world, God designed a plan of redemption to save us from our sin. He sent Jesus, the sinless Son of God, to die on the cross for the sins of the world. He paid the penalty of death for the sin that separates us from Him. He provided a way to be saved and reconciled to God by simply believing and trusting what God has done for us. It is not something we deserve or can earn through our own works but something we can receive only by faith. But how can people believe it if they do not know what God has done for them? This is where your responsibility and calling come in!

A strategy coordinator in China was telling me recently about her people group in a remote, isolated area. They had had little access to education or the outside world; they were illiterate, worshipping rocks and trees. They had a rich, oral tradition and passed on their culture through stories. While visiting in a village one night, she asked an elderly man to tell her the very oldest story about their people. He said, "One time a long, long time ago our people knew the true and living God, the most high God who was above all other gods. But our people did something bad, we don't know what it was, and they haven't been able to know this God ever since." They were waiting for someone to come and function as a priest to introduce them to Jesus Christ and bring them back to the knowledge of God.

Some years ago John Witte, a missionary in East Africa, told about his witness among the Boran people of Kenya. Using chronological storying of the Bible, they came to understand the nature of God and His holiness; they also came to understand their sinfulness and separation from God. Before he came to the story of Jesus, John asked them one day how they, as sinful men, could know and relate to a holy God. After discussing the question among themselves, they said, "We must have someone to represent us and be a mediator with God." It was a perfect setup to tell them of the mediator between God and man, Jesus Christ the righteous, who became sin that we might become the righteousness of God in Him.

Just as Jesus was our great high priest to bring us to God, God calls you to a priestly function to bring people to Jesus Christ by declaring the gospel to those who are lost. All over the world people are perishing, not because they have rejected Jesus Christ; it is not because they do not recognize their need for salvation but because no one has ever told them. No one has ever gone to introduce them to the way, the truth, and the life. And that's what God is calling you to do. Regardless of your job assignment and task, you are going to plant your lives among people who are lost because of their need for the gospel. You are the one that is standing in the gap between them and a Christless eternity. You are the one that will introduce them to Jesus who will reconcile them to God.

YOUR CALLING IS TO RESULT IN THE NATIONS BECOMING AN OFFERING TO GOD.

Everyone of us should contemplate the question of what we will have to offer to God when we stand before Him and give an account of our life. Paul's ministry and calling were for the purpose of one day presenting the Gentiles, those who were not Jews and were not the people of God, as an offering to Him. He envisioned that day when those considered pagans and outcasts and sinners would be sanctified by the Holy Spirit and acceptable to God. The Scripture tells us that that is God's desire and purpose. As the psalmist expressed it (Ps. 22:27), "All the ends of the earth will remember and turn to the LORD, and all the families of the nations will worship Him, for He is the LORD and He rules over the nations." Jesus came and died

(Luke 24:47), "that repentance and remission of sins would be preached in His name among all nations, beginning in Jerusalem." And one day there will be those from every tribe, people, and tongue and nation gathered around the throne of God, worshipping the Lamb. Many of them will be there because you go in response to God's call.

I remember going with R. T. Buckley and a group of Bangladeshi co-workers to a remote people group called the Tippera. R. T. was encouraging these Bangladeshi evangelists to be faithful and diligent in reaching these and other unreached people groups with the gospel. He graphically described what it would be like in heaven when they encountered a short Tippera man with dark skin, matted hair, and mud between his toes included among the multitude around the throne because they were willing to go into those villages and pay the price for getting the gospel to those who had never heard.

Just two days ago I gathered with friends and family and missionary co-workers for the funeral of Bill Hyde. Although we grieved his death, it was a time of celebration of his life and ministry. For almost twenty-five years he had given his life with a passion to reach the peoples of the Southern Philippines. He pushed to the edge, traveling to remote tribal areas in the mountains, penetrating rebel Muslim areas. As one colleague testified, "There was no place that Bill felt was out of reach of the Holy Spirit and his truck filled with a load of national pastors and laymen." He had just organized church planting seminars in which over four thousand workers were trained. They had formed almost a thousand church planting teams to start churches in the next six months. Bill's life and passion to reach the lost was a model and example to those with whom he worked. His death strengthened the resolve of these coworkers to press forward with the task. People ask why he would serve in a dangerous place. Bill Hyde discovered there was a cause worth living for, and worth dying for. And as we reflected at the funeral, as Bill was welcomed into the eternal glory of his heavenly reward, his offering at the throne of God will be people of the Toboli and the Maguindanao who have gained eternal life because he was faithful in his calling.

Paul envisioned the nations, those lost and in darkness, being saved and sanctified by God's Holy Spirit, and becoming the people of God. He was driven by the vision that the result of his ministry would be to present the nations as an offering to God. And this will be the result of your ministry. Because you go, you will be able to present the peoples of Africa, Latin America, Europe, and Asia—multitudes of unreached people groups—as an offering to God.

You are here tonight being commissioned for a special and unique role. You have been called and equipped for this role by God's grace. We send you out with a responsibility to be a priest of the gospel among those who are lost. And you go compelled by the vision of the peoples to whom you go, those who have yet to become a part of His kingdom, will one day be your offering before the throne of God.

34

CHOSEN AND ANOINTED

Isaiah 42:6–9

It is evident that God calls in many diverse ways. For some it is a growing awareness of the needs of a lost world and of unreached people groups that made you willing to say, "Here am I; send me." Others grew in a profound new relationship with God in which you recognized His lordship and were willing to relinquish the direction of your life from one that you chose and determined to now follow Him by faith. Whatever God has done in your life to bring you to this point, it divinely coincides with what God is doing in the world.

We continue to hear of a miraculous evangelistic harvest in China and stirring throughout the Muslim world as a result of the chaos, war, and political and social upheaval in that part of the world. Responsiveness is accelerating across Latin America, Africa, and Asia; and unreached people groups are systematically being engaged with the gospel for the first time. In Isaiah 42:9 God says, "Behold, the former things have come to pass, now I declare new things; before they spring forth I proclaim them to you." Then He proceeds to say that His praise will be sung from the end of the earth. Those who go down to the sea and dwell on the islands will lift their voices; inhabitants in the tops of the mountains will shout for joy. The coastlands will declare His praise; the wilderness, or unreached people groups, and those in the cities will lift their voice in giving glory to the Lord.

That pretty well describes the places you are going—to the island nations of Southeast Asia and the Caribbean, to the coastlands, the cities of Latin America, Asia, and Eastern Europe. You are going to the unreached people groups, lost in the wilderness. Isn't it exciting to think that you may be called for such a time as this, that you would be going out when God chooses to fulfill this prophecy of the ends of the earth singing His praise? That is a distinct possibility, but I want you to note what God says about His people, those who will see this come to pass, for these things should be true of you.

YOU ARE CHOSEN OF GOD.

Scholars disagree on when Isaiah is speaking of the nation of Israel and when he is referring to a Messianic prophecy when he speaks of God's servant. In Isaiah 42:1 he says, "Behold, My Servant, whom I uphold; My chosen one in whom My soul delights. I have put my Spirit upon Him." This may refer to Jesus or the nation of Israel, but I believe it refers to you as well. God has chosen you as His servant. He delights in you and is pleased to anoint you with His Spirit. If your appointment as a missionary is simply the result of a personal life choice, you have done an excellent job of misleading our staff and board, for the bottom line of each one being sent out by the IMB is the conviction that you are called of God. He delights in you not because you are so worthy and qualified; in fact, I have reviewed your bio data, and it is evident that you are nothing but a trophy of God's grace. It is not because of your excellent qualifications, commendatory experience, or supposed holiness of life. God delights in you because of your willingness to yield your life in conformity to His will. It is because you are willing to lay your life on the altar of self-sacrifice and go as a servant to identify with the suffering and hopelessness throughout the world. He delights in you because you have turned your back on the materialism and values of this world, a comfortable lifestyle, and success to walk in obedience with Him.

And because He has chosen you and delights in you, He has put His Spirit upon you. Of course the Holy Spirit came to indwell in your life when you were born again and trusted Jesus Christ as your Savior. But there is an anointing of power that accompanies His calling. Acts 1:8 tells us that we receive the Holy Spirit for one primary purpose, and that is to be empowered for witness where we live and to the ends of the earth. Yes, the Holy Spirit works in our lives to build character and conform us to the image of Christ, but it is for the purpose of being a witness for Jesus Christ to a lost world. Yes, the Holy Spirit gives us gifts for the completion and equipping of the body of Christ, but it is so that the church can fulfill God's mission and be His instrument of witness. At this point you probably have a little anxiety about what you are going to encounter in your cross-cultural adjustments and whether or not you will be adequate for the challenges you will face. But let me remind you that God doesn't call the qualified; He qualifies the called. His Spirit goes with you and indwells you to empower you to serve Him and fulfill His will.

GOD HAS APPOINTED YOU AS A COVENANT TO THE PEOPLE.

"I will appoint you as a covenant to the people, as a light to the nations, to open blind eyes, to bring out prisoners from the dungeon, and those who dwell in darkness from the prison" (vv. 6–7). These verses are packed with several powerful promises. First of all, God has appointed you as a covenant to the people. Each one of you is focused on an assignment to a people group or population segment. You may be going to a particular city that can't be named because of security precautions. Some are being appointed as strategy coordinators to direct the efforts to plant the gospel among those where there are no churches and among people where God continues to be deprived of their worship and praise. Did you realize that you represent God's covenant with these people? The Bible is prolific with promises and prophecies in which God will bless the nations. He assures us that each one of them will be eventually touched by the gospel and represented around His throne in heaven. You are the channel through which God will fulfill that covenant.

Jesus claimed to be the light of the world, but God has called you to be the one to share that light with the nations. You have the privilege of being the one to represent Him and His promise of redemption to your people group. There is no greater thrill than to share the gospel with those who are hearing it for the first time. I was struck by one of you who wrote in your testimony that when you realized your church-related ministry was in a church-saturated area of the south in which you were actually competing with other churches to reach those in the community, you became nauseated as you thought of those who had no churches, no opportunity whatsoever to hear the gospel even once and living in darkness.

In proclaiming the light of the gospel, you will find it is the power of God unto salvation. Eyes that are blind to the truth will be opened, and those imprisoned by bondage to sin will be set free. You are going to people that are resistant to the gospel. They think their own cultural and religious traditions represent the truth, but the Scripture tells us that the god of this world has blinded their eyes lest they should believe and turn again and be saved. You are going into Satan's territory where he has had dominion and authority to deceive and delude the people and cultures because he is an adversary opposed to the extension of God's kingdom and anything that would bring glory to God. I was disillusioned when I arrived in Indonesia and found people to be indifferent, and even antagonistic, to my witness until I realized the scope of spiritual warfare in which I was engaged. But God has empowered you and called you to be His witness and in doing so to open blind eyes to the truth that people might be delivered from bondage.

Paul recognized this as he expressed his testimony before King Agrippa. In Acts 26 he said that Jesus had appointed him as a minister and witness to the Gentiles "to open their eyes so that they may turn from darkness to light and from the power of Satan to God." Whatever your assignment and job description, that is why you are going. You are to be a witness and minister of Jesus Christ, but through the power of your witness and message of the gospel to open eyes that have been blinded to the truth that they might turn from darkness to light and be delivered from the power of Satan, the prison of sin, to God.

GOD WILL HOLD YOU BY THE HAND AND WATCH OVER YOU.

In verse 6 we read, "I am the LORD, I have called you in righteousness, I will also hold you by the hand and watch over you." As you go to be the instrument of God's covenant with the people, God will not only watch over you, but He will hold you by the hand. I want you to lock into a mental image tonight. Many of you have small children, in fact, altogether you have a lot of small children! Some of them are getting older, but you can remember when they were small. You had to watch them constantly to be sure they were safe, didn't wander out in the street as they were playing in the yard, or didn't pick up the scissors or anything dangerous that might bring them harm. When you went anywhere, you held them by the hand. Visiting with my grandchildren this summer was a wonderful experience. Anytime we went anywhere, my strong-willed, two-year-old granddaughter did not always want to hold my hand; "Miss Independent" felt big enough to do it by herself, but that wasn't an option when we were on a busy street or crowded shopping mall. I held her firmly by the hand, even against her objections, because I loved her and wanted to protect her; it wasn't out of a selfish desire to control and dominate, but it was for her welfare and best interest.

You don't go alone, but someone who loves you deeply and cares for you goes with you. Parents and family, it is hard to release your children to go to strange places on the other side of the world, to be separated from your grandchildren, and to read headlines of turmoil and conflict in those countries. But you need to know that someone who loves them even more than you goes with them. It doesn't guarantee that they will be exempt from illness and accidents, from threats and danger, but the God who called them is the all-powerful, omnipresent Lord of the universe. As the psalmist declared (Ps. 139:5, 7–10), "Thou hast enclosed me behind and before, and laid Thy hand upon me. . . . Where can I go from Thy Spirit? Or where can I flee from Thy presence? If I ascend to heaven, Thou art there; If I make my bed in Sheol, . . . take the wings of the dawn, if I dwell in the remotest part of the sea, even there Thy hand will lead me, and Thy right hand will lay hold of me." As you go in obedience, you go with a hedge of protection, undergirded by God's love. As you face decisions, you will find He is faithful to guide you and lead you as you look to Him. One of my favorite life verses is Proverbs 3:5–6, "Trust in the LORD with all your heart, and lean not on your own understanding; in all your ways acknowledge Him, and He shall direct your paths."

You can go with that assurance because He said, as Isaiah reminds us in verse 8, "I am the Lord, . . . I will not give My glory to another." He is God and His desire to be worshipped and praised among the nations is for the sake of His glory. It is not about you and your success. It is not about your being able to report impressive statistics and to take pride in what you are able to accomplish, for He will not share His glory. You go as a servant, and as you go to serve in obedience and in humility for His glory, His Spirit goes with you and anoints you as a light to the nations.

We are truly seeing new things that God is bringing forth throughout the world. Baptisms have surpassed half a million for the first time. Last year IMB personnel engaged 192 new people groups previously identified as unreached. That cannot be attributed to International Mission Board strategies and long-range plans; it is the power and providence of God doing a new thing that all the ends of the earth will sing His praise. These new missionaries have the privilege of joining God in His mission and being a part of all that He is doing to reach the nations, the coastlands, the cities, the islands, and peoples that will one day be gathered around the throne, praising our Lord, but what about you?

35

REVEALING THE MYSTERY
OF THE GOSPEL

1 Corinthians 2:7–8

I would assume there is no question about why you are being appointed as a missionary and preparing to go with your family to a strange place on the other side of the world. You may be going to fill diverse assignments and roles, but the primary reason you are going is to proclaim the gospel and share Jesus Christ with the people where you are being assigned. You can go with confidence that the gospel is the power of God unto salvation for all who believe. Jesus said in John 12:32, "And I, if I be lifted up from the earth, will draw all men to Myself." He was lifted up on the cross to die for the sins of the whole world. He was lifted up from the earth and returned to the Father so that we would receive the power of the Holy Spirit to be His witnesses. And as we lift Him up in a bold, positive witness, people will be saved.

Even in Muslim cultures I discovered that principle to be true. It is valid whether you are going to Ecuador, to Spain, to Moscow, to Cairo, the Ukraine, Indonesia, or China. It is true whether you are seeking to reach Buddhists, Muslims, Hindus, or African animists. Wherever Jesus Christ is lifted up in a bold, positive witness, people will be saved. Maybe not all of them, but it is the nature of the gospel message, indwelt of God's Holy Spirit to draw people to Jesus. That message speaks to a heart that is empty, hopeless, and in despair, searching to know the way of truth, yearning for that which will bring salvation and peace to one's heart. One of our personnel in Northern Africa said, "We have discovered the principle that where you sow abundantly, you reap abundantly; where you sow sparingly, you reap sparingly.

The only reason we haven't had a more abundant harvest throughout the Muslim world is that we haven't found the way to sow more abundantly." He was affirming the gospel itself is the power of God for salvation.

TO MOST OF THE PEOPLE IN THE WORLD THE GOSPEL IS A MYSTERY.

You could stay right here in the United States and serve the Lord; in fact, there is no shortage of lost people all around us here. So why are you going to these faraway places? It is all about lostness. Yes, people here are lost, and we would never diminish the value of one lost soul being won to faith in Jesus Christ, but here people have heard of Jesus. Churches and Christians may not be diligent to declare the gospel, but there would be few who do not have access to a Bible and knowledge of the way of salvation. That is not true for most of the people of our world. Researchers tell us that 1.6 billion people live in places that are isolated culturally and geographically from any Christian witness and have not yet even heard the name of Jesus. Twice that number live in places where there may be a nearby church or even a missionary, but they themselves have never been personally touched by a witness and heard the good news of the gospel.

The Bible describes these people as lost, alienated from God and without hope. In fact, the apostle Paul uses an interesting term for the gospel with reference to those who have never heard it. He refers to it as a "mystery." In Ephesians 1:9 he says, "He made known to us the mystery of His will," and goes on to describe God's plan of redemption through Jesus Christ. In Ephesians 3, verses 3–5, Paul testifies, "That by revelation there was made known to me the mystery . . . which in other generations was not made known to the sons of men, as it has now been revealed to His holy apostles and prophets in the Spirit." God's plan of redemption was not known and understood in past generations; God gave the prophets a glimpse of it, but it is the Holy Spirit that fully revealed it to Paul and other apostles. In Ephesians 6:19 he appealed for prayer "that utterance may be given to me in the opening of my mouth, to make known with boldness the mystery of the gospel." Now that would be an appropriate request for you to make of your family and prayer supporters! You need boldness to make the mystery of the gospel known. What did Paul mean when he referred to the gospel as a "mystery?" He did not mean that it was something strange and mysterious like you might encounter on Halloween night, but the word "mystery" in the Greek simply means that which is unknown; it is veiled or unrevealed.

THE GOSPEL IS A MYSTERY BECAUSE IT HAS NEVER BEEN REVEALED.

Once again, in 1 Corinthians 2:7–8, we find Paul referring to the gospel as a mystery. This is one of the most tragic passages in the entire Bible. Paul says, "But we speak God's wisdom in a mystery, the hidden wisdom, which God predestined before the ages to our glory; the wisdom which none of the rulers of this age has understood; for if they had understood it, they would not have crucified the Lord of glory." How tragic; how utterly tragic! Had they understood it, they would not have crucified the Lord of glory. If they had known who Jesus was, if they had understood the wisdom of God that had predestined a Savior to come, they would not have rejected Him. Now we know Christ had to be crucified and to die on the cross for our sins, but that does not diminish the tragedy of those who rejected Him because they did not know; they did not understand, and they crucified the Lord of glory.

That is what you will encounter as you go to many of the people groups to whom you are being assigned. You are going to a world in which the gospel is a mystery. You will find people following their own cultural religious beliefs, or perhaps have reverted to self-serving humanism. Is this because they find it so fulfilling and satisfying and assuring? No! It is because they don't know anything else. No one has ever revealed the mystery and told them the good news of God's love and that Jesus came to save. Do you realize how fortunate you are to have lived in a country with freedom of religion, where there are churches proclaiming the gospel. Maybe it was because of Christian parents, or a friend who cared enough to share with you about the claims of Christ; that knowledge enabled God's Spirit to bring understanding and conviction to your heart. The mystery was unveiled, and you understood that Jesus had died for you. You trusted Jesus as your Savior, and your life has never been the same. In fact, that was such a life-changing experience that you are compelled to go and make that mystery known to others who don't have the opportunity you have had. First Corinthians 4:1 says we are stewards of the mystery of God.

Many of you are going to the Muslim world where God seems to be bringing down strongholds and barriers. You will find people deeply devoted to the ritualistic expression of their religious faith; they know Jesus as a prophet, but the gospel is still a mystery. Those of you going to the Buddhist world of Asia are likely to attend a funeral and observe saffron-robed monks encircling the casket chanting, "Dead, never to arise; gone, never to return; asleep, never to awaken." And your heart will cry out, "If they had only known." But the tragedy is that they did not know; the gospel was a mystery, and it was too late. Someone in our communication office circulates an e-mail briefing of news summaries and global events each day. Sometime ago I remember being impressed with the tragic events that occurred on one day. Several thousand died in a flood and tidal wave in Bangladesh, eighty were massacred in an Algerian village, hundreds died in an earthquake in Central Asia, a truck went off the road into a ravine in Peru killing twenty-four people. The thought occurred to me that all of these people probably went straight to hell, never having had the opportunity to hear and respond to the gospel. Even as I speak, every three seconds someone in an unreached people group will die and enter a Christless eternity in hell, not because they rejected Christ, not because they did not want the salvation He alone provides, but because they lived a lifetime and died in a place where the gospel remained a mystery.

YOU ARE TO UNVEIL AND REVEAL THE MYSTERY OF THE GOSPEL.

Never lose the focus of why you are being sent out as a missionary, why God called you, and why Southern Baptists are committed to support you. It is that you might unveil that mystery, proclaim the gospel, and lift up a Savior who died on the cross for the whole world.

You have said, "I'll go; I'll leave the comfort and security of America, a fulfilling ministry or promising career, to share Christ with a lost world." You have recognized that God could use you in spite of the challenge of learning a new language and awkwardness of trying to relate cross-culturally. You may be going as a teacher, a doctor, in business support services; or you may be a preacher or church planter; but it is important to realize it is not about your assignment but about making Jesus Christ known in order to reveal the mystery of the gospel. You have realized that God did not put a geographic restriction on your understanding of God's call. Many of you are going to China where we are seeing a harvest unprecedented in Christian history, yet one billion people have not yet heard the gospel; it remains a mystery. There are forty cities there with more than a million people that do not yet have a Christian witness. There are more than two thousand unreached people groups, like the Tuareg and Baktiari, to whom the gospel is still a mystery because no one has been willing to go. But God has called you.

There may be some here tonight for whom the gospel is still a mystery, right here in America. You have been in church, may even be a church member, but have never had a life-changing experience of knowing Jesus Christ. You can't understand why anyone would leave their home and family to go as a missionary, why they would be compelled by the desire to share Jesus, because you have never trusted Him as your personal Savior. You may know all about Jesus, but until you come to Him in repentance and faith, the reality of the gospel will remain a mystery.

But most of us here do know Jesus. We love our church, are nurtured by gathering regularly for fellowship and worship and one day will don our robes of white and prepare to enter our eternal glory. It will be a wonderful time of celebration and rejoicing. But across a great chasm will be a multitude of people with bowed heads and sad countenances who are entering an eternity of torment in hell. I believe they will look across that chasm on the day of judgment with a look that will say in astonishment, "You knew, but you never came and told us, and we never had an opportunity to know and believe."

But sadder still will be the eyes of our Lord, in one of those paradoxes of the Christian faith. Even as He welcomes us with joy into His eternal kingdom, His eyes will reflect a heart that is broken for the multitudes for whom He died that never knew what He did for them and never had the opportunity to be saved. I believe His eyes will meet ours, much as they did Peter's on that night of denial, and without a word that look will communicate, "I told you to go; I promised you my power and assured you of my grace. But you chose to stay at home, hold on to the comfort and security of your American lifestyle, follow your own plans, and these never knew of my love; to them the gospel remained a mystery."

God has called us to make known the mystery of the gospel. That's why you are going to the ends of the earth. Go, determined to proclaim the gospel, reveal the Savior, and dispel the mystery of redemption that God has provided for a lost world.

36

THE FRAGRANCE OF CHRIST

2 Corinthians 2:14–16

Whether the process by which God brought you to the point of offering yourself for missionary service was a long and circuitous journey, or a fairly recent experience in which God turned your life around, you are being appointed with a unique but common call to missions. You became aware of a lost world in darkness and recognized the potential within your life of sharing Christ and doing something about it. Some of you are older and have had to put your own plans and vocation on the shelf in order to be obedient to God's call, while others have most of your adult life before you to give in service overseas.

Now you are looking forward to moving to a particular field of assignment and getting on with the task, and the International Mission Board will be doing everything we can to equip you for an effective ministry cross-culturally. You will get linguistic training in preparation for learning another language. You will study your host culture and learn all about its religion and social mores. You will anticipate living among people who are different; they look different, dress different, talk different, act different. You can be prepared for the sights and sounds you will encounter, but unfortunately there is no way we can prepare you for the smells!

You will ride a crowded bus with people who don't know what a bath is. Some of you will live in a neighborhood with no proper sanitation, and the drainage ditch in front of your house may be the community toilet. In India I led worship in homes plastered with cow dung where the family and cattle all live together. The smell of spicy foods will attack your nostrils with a revolting odor that will make you wonder how anyone could entertain the thought of eating such an offensive concoction. In Southeast Asia one of the greatest culinary enigmas is the durian, a large thorny fruit that is prohibited on any form of public transportation. Its odor has variously been described as rotting meat or onions stored in an outhouse! To select one in the market it is necessary to choose between gross, grosser, and grossest. Actually, it is one of the most delicious delicacies you could ever eat, but most foreigners never discover the joys of this unique fruit because they are unable to get beyond the smell.

Many volunteer teams have returned home with stories, pictures, and reports of the mission field but unable to adequately communicate the smells they encountered. But it is not my intention to reflect negatively on some of the less attractive features of Third-World cultures. In fact, you will quickly adjust to some of the smells and other aspects that are initially offensive, and they will become a part of what makes the locations where you live seem like home. The point I want to make is that you are being commissioned, not simply to fulfill a task, not simply to go and proclaim a message, but you are being sent to add a new smell to the people and culture where you are called. That doesn't mean a presence characterized by Right Guard, Dial soap or Estee Lauder perfume; but you are going in order to be the fragrance of Christ. In 2 Corinthians 2:14–15 Paul exclaims, "Now thanks be to God who always leads us in triumph in Christ, and through us diffuses the fragrance of His knowledge in every place. For we are to God the fragrance of Christ among those who are being saved and among those who are perishing."

BEING THE FRAGRANCE OF CHRIST WILL DRAW PEOPLE TO HIM.

This is a beautiful metaphor for what will happen as you plant your life as an incarnational witness among those who are lost. There will be a beautiful contrast as you reflect the joy of knowing the Lord, an abiding peace that supersedes the trials and challenges you will experience, victory and assurance in the salvation you have and proclaim in Jesus Christ. What a contrast in a society filled with fear, superstition, and anxiety. Among people in darkness with no hope, your very presence will be like fragrant perfume that fills a room as you proclaim the good news of salvation.

That fragrance, which represents the presence of Christ in your life, comes through even more than the words you speak or the messages you preach. It will permeate your neighborhood as people see the reality of

Christ in you. One of our missionary personnel who moved into a slum neighborhood in a restricted Muslim country so demonstrated the compassion of Christ in the way he related to the community, always available to help in time of need, showing respect and building friendships, that he was invited to sit in on the village council. When the village elders introduced him to outsiders they would explain, "He is an American, but he is one of us; yes, he is a Christian, but he is a good man."

For many the testimony of your life will bring credibility to your message, and that will be such good news for those in darkness and despair that it will be like a sweet fragrance to which they will respond. For others, however, the very contrast of your life of holiness and moral character in the Holy Spirit will affirm the falsehood and perversion of other religions that hold people in bondage to sin; your life will be a testimony of their condemnation without Christ.

BEING THE FRAGRANCE OF CHRIST MEANS WALKING IN VICTORY AND TRIUMPH.

Verse 16 concludes with the question, "And who is sufficient for these things?" You would readily acknowledge, "Not I," for you recognize your own inadequacy. You are not going to Bosnia, Uzbekistan, China, Tanzania, and Brazil because of your own ability to make a difference; but, as Paul explains, it is from God! And it is in that confidence that Paul erupts into an exclamation of praise in verse 14, "Now thanks be to God who always leads us in triumph in Christ."

I heard one of our African-American pastors teach a conference audience a litany regularly practiced at his church. He would say, "God is good," and the congregation would respond spontaneously, "All the time." If he, at any time, would say, "All the time," and pause, the congregation would respond, "God is good."

God is in the business of victory—all the time! He is not sending you overseas to just spin your wheels in frustration or to fail. He is King of kings and Lord of lords. He is Creator and Sovereign of the universe. Before Jesus told us to go into all the world and disciple the nations, He prefaced that command with the claim that all power had been given unto Him in heaven and earth. You will not triumph because of the most skilled mission methodology; you will not be assured of victory in your witness because of your educational credentials or successful ministry experience but only because you are in Christ.

BEING THE FRAGRANCE OF CHRIST WILL OPEN DOORS TO THE GOSPEL.

Finally, look back to verse 12 where Paul puts this passage in context. He says, "Furthermore when I came to Troas to preach Christ's gospel, and a door was opened to me by the Lord." Some of you are going to places that are closed to the gospel. The government does not welcome missionaries, Christians are restricted and monitored, and the people would be characterized as resistant to the gospel. But you are going anyway through a platform that God has designed in order to establish an incarnational presence. You might be prohibited from witnessing and preaching openly, but no one or no power on earth can keep you from being the fragrance of Christ as you reflect Him in your daily relationships and activities.

But notice when the door was opened to Paul in Troas; it was when he came to preach the gospel. We don't wait for the door to open. We don't delay until we get an invitation. We cannot tarry until all the laws and official papers are in order. We have been commanded to go into all the world and preach the gospel to every creature, and the door will not open until we go in obedience. That's what opens the door—someone going to share the gospel.

It has been amazing to see the advance of the gospel in closed and restricted countries. Formerly we had settled into a paradigm of doing missions only where we could send missionaries, and half the world was cut off from the gospel. Through a subsidiary part of our organization, Cooperative Services International, we began to assign nonresidential missionaries to restricted countries and people groups. When I became president five years ago, it occurred to me that we were no longer appointing nonresidential missionaries as a prominent and distinct category of assignment. When I inquired as to the reason, it was shown how, time after time, once we assigned missionaries to an inaccessible people group, and a strategy began to evolve, invariably the barriers would crumble; and the doors would open to creative access personnel. We no longer had to rely on nonresidential personnel; God was just waiting on our obedience.

A missionary in West Africa found this to be true and exclaimed, "To me the gospel is no longer a message; it is something that is happening." Be assured that as you go, because you go to proclaim the gospel, the Lord will open the door.

All over the world there is the smell of death. Not only in the bombing sites in Nairobi and Dar Es Salaam, and in the genocide and massacres in Albania, Bosnia, and Rwanda, but wherever people have not come to saving faith in Jesus Christ. Where people are bowing down before Hindu idols in India, or across the Muslim world where multitudes declare their allegiance to Mohammed, or in a Latin American city where the typical Catholic ritual is just empty formalism and superstition, there is the odor of death, an eternal, spiritual death because of the condemnation of sin. God is sending you to bring the aroma of Christ to a lost world? Allow your life to bring a fragrance of hope in the midst of the stench of death? As you go forth in obedience to proclaim the gospel, live it out in your relationships, lifestyle, attitudes, and behavior; and your life will be a fragrant aroma drawing people to Christ, bringing triumph and victory to your life and will enable God to open the door among a people He died to save and is seeking to draw to Himself.

37

THE MASTER'S INSTRUCTIONS
FOR MISSION

Luke 10:1–17

As we have heard your testimonies of God's call and envision the places you are going to serve and share the message of God's redemptive love, several biblical precedents come to mind. We might think of Abraham who left his home and family in obedience to God's call, just as many of you are doing, so that the nations might be blessed. We recall Jonah, called to go to that great city of Nineveh, just as some of you who are going to great cities of Asia and Latin America. Also, like Jonah, some of you resisted until God has now brought you into submission to His will.

The apostle Paul would be a prototype for all of you. He saw the gospel beyond the context of the Jewish culture and responded to God's call to "the regions beyond," just as some of you are going to nations and people groups which have never before had an opportunity to hear the gospel. But the biblical parallel to which I want to call to your attention is that of Jesus sending out the seventy in Luke 10. In the previous chapter we read of Jesus sending out the Twelve, but here the Scripture says that "after this the Lord appointed seventy others also and sent them two and two ahead of Him" (Luke 10:1).

I have always had the perception that the twelve disciples had been those like pastors and evangelists that are called to full-time Christian service, but the seventy were the laymen and other believers who are also called to be His witnesses. I would not want us to miss that point. Many missionaries do not come from a background of pastoring and church staff but have been businessmen and women, accountants, teachers, medical practitioners, lawyers, and building contractors; and you are sent out like the seventy. I don't have the time to review this entire passage, but I do want to point out several observations and instructions that Jesus gave to those sent out as they have relevance to your mission calling.

YOU ARE BEING SENT TO INTRODUCE PEOPLE TO JESUS.

In verse 1 we are told that they were sent "into every city and place where He Himself was about to go." Don't neglect anyone in sharing the gospel. Every person in every town and village has the right to hear the good news that a Savior has come. There is a tendency to be selective and choose places that seem to be responsive or neighborhoods that are deemed to be the best prospects for church planting. But, in doing so, you will bypass many people that need to hear the gospel. Jesus died for all and wants all the people in every city and village to have hearts prepared to receive Him.

Why has God called you to the specific country or people, the place and assignment where you are going? It is because Jesus wants to be made known to the people there. He, in His providence, is already planning to touch the hearts and lives of people in Poland and Russia, in Mexico and Peru, in Tanzania and China, so He has called you to go before Him, to plant the witness and to touch the hearts of those that are lost. You don't actually precede Him for He goes with you, but the point is that He has chosen to manifest Himself and the good news of salvation through those called to be His witnesses, and He does not go there except as you and other missionaries are willing to go. You are being obedient, as the seventy; but unlike them Jesus goes with you. His indwelling presence will be evident in your life and witness.

YOU ARE BEING SENT TO TRUST GOD FOR YOUR EVERY NEED.

In verse 4 these seventy are told to "carry neither money bag, knapsack, nor sandals." In other words, they were not to base their going on material support. Now that may be a little radical. You would probably not be here were it not for the faithful support of Southern Baptists through the Cooperative Program and the Lottie Moon Christmas Offering. During the last few days you have already been briefed on the salary and cost of living provided by the International Mission Board. You have been advised about packing your household goods and making provision for shipping your freight to a foreign destination. Most likely you will be provided with an automobile for transportation and an adequate house in which to live. It may be small and not have all the amenities you are used to, but you are probably assuming those provisions go with your appointment and commitment to serve with the International Mission Board.

However, I would encourage you not to be under the illusion that going as a missionary does not entail sacrifice, for it does and always has. We do try to provide adequately for your needs, but if you ever become dependent on what the International Mission Board provides instead of on the spiritual resources God provides, you may continue on the field, but your effectiveness will be diminished. Determine right now that you are going to walk by faith. Realize that your security is in the Lord Jesus Christ and in His limitless resources, not in the International Mission Board.

YOU ARE BEING SENT TO IDENTIFY WITH THE PEOPLE WHERE YOU GO.

Also in this passage we are told, "Eat such things as are set before you." You will learn as I did on a recent trip to China that it is best not to ask what it is when some strange delicacy is placed before you. I recall encountering a new dish in Indonesia. It was some kind of stewed meat wrapped and steamed in a brown leaf. Upon inquiry our hostess told us what it was called and went on to explain that sometimes it was made with pork and sometimes with rats. I did not dare ask which had been used that day! However, I think that Jesus is not speaking so much of culinary habits as He is saying to identify with the culture and people to whom you are sent. Learn to eat what they eat, live as they live, speak their language; identify with them and win acceptance and a hearing for the gospel.

YOU ARE BEING SENT IN THE POWER AND AUTHORITY OF JESUS CHRIST.

But the advice which I think is most important for you to heed is found in verse 3 where Jesus says, "Go your way, behold, I send you out as lambs among wolves." You are being sent into the battlefield of spiritual warfare unlike you have ever known it. First John 5:19 says, "We are of God, but the whole world lies in the power of the evil one." You see, where Jesus is not known, the people and nations and cultures are in darkness and are Satan's dominion. You are venturing into his territory when you go to the Muslim countries of the Middle East and Central Asia. When you go to peoples with a godless heritage in Eastern Europe and hear the clanging gongs in Asian temples and see the fetishes of pagan superstition in Africa, you will find yourselves as lambs among wolves.

But as the seventy returned victorious, Jesus reminded them that "they had been given authority over all the power of the enemy." Never forget that the Great Commission is preceded by Jesus' claim, "All authority is given to Me in heaven and in earth" (Matt. 28:18). There is no power on heaven or earth that exceeds the power and authority of Jesus Christ, and He has promised to go with you. The seventy found that to be true as they returned from their mission exclaiming, "Even the demons are subject to us in Your name!" (Luke 10:17). Those who precede you on the mission field have found that to be true. There will be a hedge of protection; there will be an empowering that is not of yourself because you go in Jesus' name.

Satan is determined to thwart the advancement of God's kingdom. He uses government restrictions, religious deception, and cultural barriers—anything possible to keep the gospel from being heard and received. But we have seen that he cannot keep nations closed to a Christian witness as evidenced by those of you going to Russia and China and Central Asia, places that long prohibited a missionary witness. He cannot keep people groups, long isolated from an opportunity to hear the gospel, to remain unreached. So you need to be aware that if those tactics cannot succeed, then he will turn on you, the lamb among the wolves.

Satan will bring discouragement; he will inflict you with self-pity—feeling sorry for yourself in isolation and loneliness. He may even allow you unusual success in order to set you up for destructive pride. He will seek to destroy your walk with the Lord and rob you of the joy and victory Jesus has promised. He will lie and make you believe the people are resistant to the gospel, and there is no hope of response in spite of God's assurance to the contrary. If that doesn't work, he will bring conflict in interpersonal relationships with your colleagues and national coworkers; he will bring stress to your marriage and home. And Satan knows where we are really vulnerable—he will bring illness to your children and deprive them of perceived educational and social needs—anything he can do to destroy your faith, cause you to throw in the towel and turn your back on your calling, or at least erode the effectiveness of your witness.

That is why Jesus told us to be vigilant, to be alert and sober for "your adversary the devil walks about like a roaring lion seeking whom he may devour" (1 Pet. 5:8). That's why Jesus alerted the seventy to the opposition they would encounter, and I want you to be aware of the subtle tactics of the enemy as you go as lambs among wolves.

Note that the Scripture gives us another clue to victory in the spiritual warfare you will encounter. First John 5:4 tells us, "This is the victory that overcomes the world, even our faith." Hebrews 11:1 explains, "Faith is the substance of things hoped for, the evidence of things not seen." Faith is believing the promises of God when all the circumstances seem contrary to what God has said. God's Word has promised you victory. It says, "The earth shall be filled with the knowledge of the glory of God as the waters that cover the sea." (Hab. 2:14). It says, "All the ends of the earth shall turn to the LORD, and all the families of nations shall worship before you, for the kingdom is the LORD's and He rules over the nations" (Ps. 22:27–28). Jesus promises you victory that overcomes tribulation. He has promised to care for you and meet your every need according to His riches in glory. Claim the promises, believe them, and don't let Satan convince you otherwise.

Finally, the implications of all of this is to walk in absolute obedience to the instructions that Jesus has given His followers. Being sent on mission by God means total commitment to the Lord Jesus Christ who told you to take up your cross and follow him. If you are to claim the victory and live by faith, it will mean self-denial. It will mean a disciplined prayer time and nurturing your faith by feeding on God's Word. And you will find, as the seventy discovered, that even the demons are subject to you, the strongholds of Satan will crumble, and the very gates of hell will fall because you go in Jesus' name!

We are thrilled to be appointing these missionaries who are going in obedience to God's call, but for others I want to focus your attention on verse 2. Jesus had sent out the laborers. Not just twelve, but seventy went out as witnesses to the cities that Jesus might be made known. But even then He says, "Pray to the Lord of the harvest that He would send out laborers into His harvest." The seventy were not enough; others were needed, "for the harvest was plenteous, but the laborers were few." We have all been impressed with the large group of new missionaries being sent out tonight, but they are so few among the global fields of harvest. They join more than five thousand colleagues already on the field, but that averages about one missionary unit for every two million people. There would be hundreds of Baptist churches in a city of two million here in the United States plus many other evangelical churches.

Where are the laborers needed to be on mission with God as He accelerates the harvest in Africa? When the Lord of the harvest has opened an unprecedented door of opportunity in Eastern Europe, how can we fail to hear His call? How can one put a geographic restriction on a call to ministry and say, "I'm exempt from the fields of harvest except where I can enjoy the comfort and security of my American lifestyle"? Where is Jesus planning to go? Where does He desire to be made known? That's where He would call these and others.

In my recent trip to China, we met with strategy coordinators who are focusing on the harvest among people groups who have never before had access to the gospel. It is overwhelming to try to comprehend the massive challenge of reaching 1.2 billion people. Millions die every day and enter a Christless eternity not because they have rejected Christ or don't want the salvation He offers but because they have never heard. How many more will perish before someone responds to the call and says, like the seventy, "I will go"?

38

OVERCOMING OBSTACLES
IN THE NAME OF JESUS

Acts 4:10–31

God has called us to declare His glory to the ends of the earth. Those being sent as missionaries to the nations are simply the instruments through which the words of the psalmist will be fulfilled (Ps. 22:27): "All the ends of the earth shall turn to the Lord, and all the families of nations shall worship Him, for the kingdom is the Lord's and He rules over the nations." You are to go with a vision and passion for that day when every tribe and people and tongue and nation would sing glory and worship Him alone who is worthy of all worship and praise.

Those being sent out as we enter the twenty-first century are going into a world that is not unlike that in the first century when Christ sent the disciples to be His witnesses. I'll never forget my first visit to Yemen in the Middle East. As we drove the winding roads through villages of square, mud-walled homes built on that rocky terrain, we saw men in their flowing robes just like they had stepped out of a Christmas pageant at church; I felt we had gone back two thousand years to biblical times. However, the appearance of most of the places you go will be deceptive. The location of your assignment may be characterized by modern cities, Western dress, and a developing infrastructure; but it is not unlikely that you will encounter hostility and opposition just like the early disciples.

Encountering Poverty, Suffering, and Need

Like the early disciples you will encounter a world of suffering, of poverty, of overwhelming needs. In Acts 3:6 Peter and John were going to the temple, and they passed a man who was crippled. Peter said, "Silver and gold I do not have, but what I do have I give you; in the name of Jesus Christ of Nazareth, rise up and walk." You are going to encounter poverty, disease, and social problems that are overwhelming. With others you will try to minister as best you can. But like Peter you are not going with silver and gold and with an abundance of budget resources. What you do take with you as you go is the name of Jesus, that name above all names—a name that represents the power of God.

You may or may not experience a power encounter and see miracles of healing, though that is not uncommon in many parts of the world. But you will see people made whole as sinners are redeemed and people respond to the love of God, which you demonstrate and proclaim. You will be able to look on a congregation of believers saved out of bondage from the fear and superstition of their Hindu idols or those who now have eternal assurance after being delivered from the fatalistic perversion of Islam. May you be able to say with Peter in Acts 4:10, "Let it be known . . . that by the name of Jesus Christ of Nazareth whom you crucified, whom God raised from the dead, by Him this man stands here before you whole."

Dana Seale described her impressions during a visit she and her husband, Paul, had on a visit to a Yupka village high in the Andes Mountains of Venezuela. "I gazed at soft white clouds hovering over green velvety foothills. To my back, however, was a stark contrast: the Yupka village of Shirimi— fifteen thatched-roof huts with dirt floors; children with bellies swollen from parasites; a blind mother of five, who feels her way along rocky and sometimes slippery paths. One sweeping glance tells the story. Poverty, disease, lack of education, abuse, and neglect all take their toll.

> I leaned against the post of the open-air pavilion. No more
> time to meditate on life's injustices. Dirty bodies with glowing
> faces moved into action. Brown little naked bodies and shabbily
> dressed children lined up to sing for us. Offbeat clapping and loud,
> nasal, Yupka-style praise songs lifted to the heavens. Joy penetrated
> the air. We had hiked seven hours to get there for the medical
> outreach begun earlier, towing medicines, food, and school sup-
> plies on donkeys. But was joy the most valuable thing we brought?

Could that supersede the sorrows of infant mortality, stomachs that screamed with parasites, and blindness due to cataracts?

The chief stood and described the many improvements Southern Baptist volunteers had made to his village: "We have everything we need," he said. Everything? Dirt-floored huts? Campfires for stoves? A community faucet for a bath? Who had taught them to count their blessings instead of their woes? The Holy Spirit? It had to be. The gospel brought what we hoped it would—light and hope.

You will not be able to meet all the needs you encounter, but you carry something more valuable as you go in the name of Jesus—that which will bring joy in the midst of suffering and hope that transcends the temporal pain of this life.

ENCOUNTERING HOSTILE RELIGIOUS TRADITIONS

As I traveled in Northern Africa recently, I had the opportunity to talk with believers who had been arrested; they were harassed and lived under constant threats. A letter from a missionary in Bangladesh told of yet another Muslim convert who had been murdered. You will encounter religious strongholds all over the world. We watched multitudes streaming into the national mosque in Casablanca for the Friday day of prayer, but they were outnumbered by the crowds at the beach and in the markets of the city. You will encounter religious traditions, but for many religion is only a cultural stronghold.

I have seen many in Thailand and Sri Lanka who expressed a spiritual yearning, an emptiness, a search for something their self-help and works-based Buddhist devotion did not give them. But in Thailand, to be a Thai is to be a Buddhist. How can one be expected to deny their citizenship, their heritage, and family honor in order to abandon a hollow tradition that is nothing more than empty ritual?

The early believers confronted the hypocrisy and traditions of the Jewish faith and declared in Acts 4:12, "For neither is there salvation in any other, for there is no other name under heaven given among men whereby we must be saved." You are being sent to identify with the people among whom you live. You will respect their culture and their traditions and learn to speak their language. But the reason you go is to encounter religious traditions by boldly lifting up the name of Jesus and declaring that He is the way, the truth, and the life.

ENCOUNTERING THREATS AND RESTRICTIVE
GOVERNMENT POLICIES

Many of you are going to places where missionaries are not welcome, but the people need the Lord. You are going to places where Westerners, and Americans in particular, are considered the enemy because of actions or alliances of our government, but the people are lost and need the Lord. When you meet secretly to disciple a group of new believers, you never know if there may be an informant in the group. When you dare to share the plan of salvation with an inquiring friend, you may be in violation of restrictive laws against proselytizing. So what do you do—withdraw into a shell, bide your time waiting for the climate to change, decide presence instead of proclamation is why you are there?

When the New Testament believers were threatened, they recalled that David said (Acts 4:25–26), "Why did the nations rage, and the people plot vain things? The kings of the earth took their stand, and the rulers were gathered together against the Lord and against His Christ." It happened then; it has happened throughout history, and you can expect it to happen wherever you go today. You are venturing into Satan's territory and will be engaged in spiritual warfare. And in non-Christian societies it is often secular governments and rulers that will be rallied against the kingdom of God. They pass laws that prohibit the freedom of religion. They control visas and work permits. They intimidate and threaten just as they did Peter and John when they ordered them not to preach or teach in the name of Jesus.

So what did the early believers do? They prayed (Acts 4:29–30), "Now Lord, look on their threats and grant to Your servants that with all boldness they may speak Your word, by stretching out Your hand to heal, and that signs and wonders may be done through the name of Your holy Servant Jesus." They did not pray for the threats to cease. They did not pray for a change in government and religious authority. They did not plead for a new, open environment of peace in which they could serve the Lord. They prayed for boldness because this was an environment in which Jesus could demonstrate His power.

I just read an article in a mission magazine by Joseph Tson of Romania who was reflecting on the persecution that has escalated in India. He talked about the vitality and growth of the church in Romania under communism when pastors were arrested and public worship restricted. He said now that there was no significant persecution, growth had plateaued, but more serious than that, Christians had become complacent in their faith and witness.

You will encounter opposition, but our prayer is that you will respond like the believers in Acts. In Acts 4:31 we read, "And when they had prayed, the place where they were assembled together was shaken; and they were all filled with the Holy Spirit, and they spoke the word of God with boldness." There are those who advocate not going to restricted countries, but by what criteria should anyone be denied an opportunity to hear the gospel? Just like New Testament believers, you will encounter opposition. I once heard someone speculating on what it may have been like if someone had told the apostle Paul not to go to a closed, restricted country. Paul, who was called to the regions beyond, would have replied, "What do you mean closed to the gospel?" The speaker would have said, "You know, you might get arrested or beaten or deported." And Paul would have probably replied, "So? What's the point?"

You will encounter threats and opposition of government authorities wherever you go. You will confront a wall of resistance in the religious traditions of the people. You will be overwhelmed by poverty, suffering, and disease. But our prayer is that you will be filled with the Holy Spirit and with boldness will lift up the name of Jesus. May you be so filled with the love of God and His passion for all the peoples that, like the disciples, you "cannot stop speaking what (you) have seen and heard" (Acts 4:20).

How is it that the disciples could demonstrate such boldness and were blessed with such power in the face of threats and persecution? Acts 4:13 tells us that the religious leaders, "When they saw the boldness of Peter and John, and perceived that they were uneducated and untrained men, they marveled. And they realized that they had been with Jesus." Your education and training are valuable. The orientation and equipping you will undergo is important, but what will make a difference is spending time with Jesus. Nurture your time with Him. Pay the price in personal discipline to feed on His Word and spend time with Him in prayer until your life is no longer the same. Overflow with a sense of His presence and a compulsion to proclaim Him to a lost world. That is how you will overcome the obstacles and opposition you will encounter.

39

GOD WILL BRING YOU IN, OUT, AND THROUGH

Deuteronomy 8

With this appointment service we are seeing that missionaries are not just going to limited places where they are readily welcomed and received but to locations that would have been unthinkable just a few years ago. Their testimonies have truly given us a global perspective of how God is at work far beyond our provincialism and stateside perspective. We are reminded that the mandate of the Great Commission was to proclaim the gospel in all the world and disciple the nations. The task is similar to when God commissioned the tribes of Israel to go in and possess the land of Canaan. He has called us to go in and possess the lands for the kingdom of God. These missionaries are going to Kazakhstan, Uzbekistan, Indochina, to assignments in Northern Africa and the Middle East, Russia, and Eastern Europe. New and pioneer locations have been identified as the "last frontier" for fulfilling the Great Commission. Others have responded to God's leadership to join colleagues who are claiming the land for Jesus in Mexico, Peru, Brazil, Kenya, South Africa, and other historically traditional fields.

Where these new missionaries stand tonight in anticipation of fulfilling God's calling is not unlike the children of Israel as they prepared to enter the promised land. Moses was not able to accompany them, but the book of Deuteronomy records his exhortation and admonishment to them. I want to focus your attention tonight on chapter 8 where he tells them that (1) God will bring them in, (2) reminds them that God had brought them out, and (3) assures them that God will bring them through.

GOD WILL BRING YOU IN.

In Deuteronomy 8:7 Moses says, "For the LORD your God is bringing you into a good land." Wherever it is that God has called you, He will bring you in. You may not think of it as a "good land" in the terms that Moses described Canaan as a place of beauty, prosperity, and abundance as the land to which God is bringing you may actually be desolate, the people destitute, and you will be confronted with a deprived lifestyle. It may not be without problems or delays that He brings you in, but He will get you there. It may not be where you think you are going as it is not unusual for God to lead you to respond to a specific need that is an apparent match in order to simply position you through various circumstances to serve where He ultimately wants you. But you can have assurance He will bring you in because it is His desire for all the nations, including the one to which you go, to know Him and worship Him.

I often share the first-term experiences of Brian and Vicki Barlow who went to Liberia. Before they had been there a year, all the missionaries had to be evacuated because of the escalating warfare. The missionaries were dispersed throughout West Africa, and the Barlows went to Guinea only for the guerrilla fighting to disrupt their lives once again. They took a temporary assignment in Togo managing the Baptist Conference Center when a coup overthrew the government and the conference center was flooded with refugees. As things settled down, they returned to Liberia only to be evacuated again. I reflected on all this when they got home for furlough, and Brian smiled and said, "It was wonderful how God used these circumstances to place us where we needed to be to minister and share the love of Christ in times of turmoil."

It is amazing how God has called some of you with business skills or teachers, or out of some other vocational experience, to use that identity to meet a need in some developing country that does not yet welcome missionaries. This platform will allow you to go in and plant your life in an incarnational witness and begin to claim the land for Christ.

As you go to places where others have served, you will find the foundation has been laid, the logistical support is in place; and with relative ease you will ship your freight, set up your household, and go in. But for others, you are breaking new ground. There is no one in place to sponsor your visa. No local believers to welcome you or church fellowship to minister to your family. But God will work out the circumstances; He will bring you in because it is He that has called you to go in and possess the land.

GOD WILL BRING YOU OUT.

Realize that it is necessary for God to bring you out before He can bring you in! You must be willing to come out from your own land if He is to lead you in to another. Moses reminded the children of Israel that it was God who had brought them out of Egypt, the land of bondage. Lest they become proud and self-confident, he said in verse 14, "[Don't] forget the Lord your God who brought you out from the land of Egypt." It is not uncommon, even for missionaries, to take pride in what they are doing. Your church may put you on a pedestal, and people will comment on what a wonderful, sacrificial thing you are doing, and you will begin to believe it! Don't overlook the fact that you are here tonight because at some point in your life God delivered you from bondage to sin. You received Jesus Christ as your personal Lord and Savior, and God brought you out of a self-centered life of sin, separated from Him. But then, even as a child of God, you heard the call to give your life for others, to go and plant your life among those who do not have an opportunity to know Jesus, and God brought you out of bondage to personal ambition and self-serving plans to follow His call.

I've read your biographical material, and for some of you it is a struggle to leave. You were reluctant to leave behind a promising career or effective ministry. You thought of your family, their future, and their welfare. You wondered if you had what it takes to give up the comforts and security which we take for granted here. But God stirred your heart toward a world in darkness, waiting for someone to tell them of Jesus, and you said, "Lord, I am willing to give it up and for you to bring me out of my comfort zone."

Just last month my wife, Bobbye, and I were able to participate in a meeting of missionary personnel in Southeast Asia. It was a nostalgic experience of renewing fellowship with many of our colleagues from over twenty-three years of service in that part of the world. We had the privilege of presenting service pins to a number of those in Indonesia who were completing thirty years of service, among them, Ken and Mary Ellison. They have been able to continue to fulfill their calling there in spite of government restrictions because they, along with several others, said they were willing to give up their American passport and become Indonesian citizens. Now next to the presence and power of God, there is no greater security than your American passport. No matter what happens, you can always come home. As it happened, they did not have to give up their American passport; but in a willingness to do so, the Ellisons and others recognized it was God who had brought them out from America, and they were faithful to that purpose for which God had brought them out. Because it is God who is bringing you out from your family, your home, and familiar environment, He will give you grace for whatever it takes to leave.

GOD WILL BRING YOU THROUGH.

Just because you are being obedient to God's call to come out from your own country and follow Him as He brings you in to another country, there is no assurance that He will protect you from all harm, avert every danger and hardship, and transcend every trial. To the contrary, He does not guarantee a bed of roses. For, you see, He is sending you into Satan's territory; there is a spiritual warfare in possessing the land. You will encounter the adversary in trials and hardships, but God promises to bring you through. Moses reminded the people in verse 15, "He led you through the great and terrible wilderness," and goes on to describe the serpents, scorpions, barren desert, and hardships they endured. You are not exempt from trials and difficulties but will find these experiences as opportunities for growth and for God to demonstrate His power and sovereignty because He will bring you through them.

The Scripture says that it was the Lord your God who brought you through "that He might humble you and that He might test you" so that you might remember it is the Lord your God who gives you power (Deut. 8:16–18).

Last week Bobbye and I had the privilege of participating in a retirement recognition of Tom and Gloria Thurman who had served in Bangladesh for thirty-two years. Gloria's sister Martha shared a testimony of what it had been like to have family who were missionaries. She told about how it had changed their prayer life as they no longer simply prayed, "God bless the missionaries." When they saw a name on the prayer calendar, they were aware that each one had a family who was concerned about their physical health, their safety, their relationship with national coworkers and other needs. She said it broadened their understanding of the world beyond their South Alabama provincialism as they realized Bangladesh was included in the Great Commission, and having family as missionaries they began to understand God's heart for the world.

But finally, somewhat tongue in cheek, she said they found that missionaries in the family didn't necessarily consult other family members back home in making decisions, and in following God's will they often made poor decisions. For example, they should have come home when their boys were born, especially since Philip suffered from bronchial asthma and David from febrile convulsions, but they didn't. When Gloria was diagnosed with leprosy and Tom had hepatitis, they should have come home, but they didn't. When a tidal wave swept inland with a fierce force, then with a great surge rushed back to sea sweeping everything in its path out to sea and thousands died, they should have come home, but they didn't. When the war for independence came and their lives and their children's lives were in physical danger, they should have come home, but they didn't. She concluded by saying, "I had to learn to thank God for His faithfulness in all situations in bringing them through."

Tom had earlier given a testimony reflecting on their thirty-two years. He told of how they found no response in the first twelve years of ministry in that impoverished Muslim country. There were only twelve Baptist churches at the time. Now there are more than five hundred churches, 120 in the Gopalgonj area where the Thurmans served. He said, "In spite of the hardships and suffering, in spite of the lack of response, we stayed, and we saw God open the door!"

As you are commissioned tonight, you are aware that God has called you, and He is bringing you out. God will bring you in to the place to which He is leading that you may possess the land and claim the people for Him. And be assured that God will bring you through whatever hardship and challenge you face.

40

GOD'S DEPENDABILITY

Isaiah 51:15–16

In June 1970 my wife, Bobbye, and I were appointed for missionary service in Indonesia. In addition to us there were couples going to Uganda, Guatemala, Korea, the Philippines, Liberia, and two families who opened Southern Baptist work in Laos. For some reason we were asked to sing a contemporary mission song in closing. I don't know why; we weren't uniquely qualified as vocalists. In fact, I remember someone suggesting I stand away from the microphones! I don't know that I have ever seen that done again, but the emotion of that moment is still very real. Dr. Baker James Cauthen was president of the Foreign Mission Board at that time, and after his stirring challenge, those of us being appointed that night sang:

> *Here is my life. I want to give it.*
> *Here is my life. I want to live it,*
> *Serving my fellowman,*
> *Doing the will of God,*
> *Here is my life. Here is my life.*

There were only sixteen of us in that 1970 appointment service, the largest group to be commissioned that year. Now groups of sixty and seventy new missionaries are regularly sent out. It was amazing to us that, in the midst of the war in Indochina in 1970, Southern Baptist missionaries would be going to Laos, but not in our wildest imagination would we have dreamed that today we would be sending personnel to places such as Uzbekistan, Russia, Moldova, Romania, and Lithuania. It was beyond our most visionary plans

and strategies that others would be going to join in such an amazing harvest
of souls as we are seeing in Africa and Latin America today.

Like many missionaries being appointed, Bobbye and I had responded
many years before to a call to missions. We had finally completed the education and practical experience required for approval. Our adrenalin was
flowing, and we were ready to get to the field. But we found that we were ill
prepared for the journey of faith, the cross-cultural adjustments and spiritual warfare that we would face for the next twenty-three years of overseas
service. When we arrived on the field, God put us in a crucible of refining
and equipping from which one never graduates. I wish that I had time to
share with you all that we learned through those early years on the field, but
that would not necessarily be beneficial for you; you have to learn them for
yourself. But there were some anchors which we discovered to be essential not
only to success but survival on the mission field. God said in Isaiah 51:15–16,
"I am the Lord your God. . . . I have put My words in your mouth, and have
covered you with the shadow of My hand." We learned that God is dependable because of the reliability of His Word, the reality of His power, and the
resources of His grace.

THE RELIABILITY OF GOD'S WORD

The first discovery that we found to be absolutely essential is the reliability of God's Word. Now, like you, we truly believed that the Bible was God's
inspired, infallible Word, but we found God's promises to be true and His
Word to be dependable when we had nothing else to which to cling.

During my first term I had found a pocket of response in a rural
Muslim village and had been meeting with them for several weeks. As their
growing interest confirmed the convicting work of God's Spirit, I had given
them Bibles and encouraged them to read them. They did so with eagerness,
and each time I would meet with them, they would have many questions.
I recall someone asking a difficult question about an obscure passage. As
I heard myself explain that it was necessary to understand the historical
background and the context of the original language, I saw their demeanor
change, and God immediately checked my response. I was communicating
to these spiritually hungry, barely literate new believers that they really
couldn't understand God's Word without a great deal of education and
sophisticated knowledge.

From that day the focus of my ministry, and indeed my life, began to
change. I was in Indonesia to bear witness to a living Savior; but having

led people to Jesus Christ, my passion was to put in their hands the living Word of God and teach them to read it and, whatever they read, to believe and practice. I could not always be there to explain it and to teach them. Their faith, their growth, and their functioning as a church could not be dependent on my leadership but on the truth and reliability of God's Word.

An amazing thing began to happen! I began to see these new congregations growing in faith and boldness, praying with fervor, reminding God what He had said, and then believing Him to bring it about. I watched as they functioned as a *koinonia* fellowship with multiple, gifted leaders as a church ought to function. I saw them reach out in ministry to neighbors who were suffering because that's what God's Word taught them to do. I saw them pray for a miracle to end a drought, or for healing for those who were sick, and then rejoice as God did just what He said He would do.

Oh, I tried to mess it up occasionally. I had been meeting with a new church group on Tuesday evening and tried to persuade them to begin gathering and worshipping on Sunday; since it was the day of Christian worship, it would be a testimony to their Muslim village. They said they were already meeting on Sunday—and on Monday, Tuesday, Wednesday, Thursday, Friday, and Saturday. They had read in Acts 5:42 that the believers met daily in the temple and from house to house and "ceased not to teach and preach Jesus Christ." They asked if they should stop doing that and only meet on Sunday as a church. Not only did I realize that I could so easily lead others astray by my sophisticated rationalization and tradition; I began to discover how dependable God's Word was in my own life.

You will encounter many anxious situations, such as our missionaries who were abducted last week in Tanzania, but will discover the truth of God's Word which says, "The peace of God, which surpasses all comprehension, shall guard your hearts and your minds in Christ Jesus" (Phil. 4:7). God's word is reliable. Many of you are going to places that are resistant to the gospel. Remember, as you encounter obstacles and rejection, and doubts begin to fill your mind, that God's Word says, "The earth shall be filled with the knowledge of the glory of God as the waters that cover the sea" (Hab. 2:14).

THE REALITY OF GOD'S POWER

Another lesson we learned quickly on the mission field was the reality of God's power. If you haven't recognized it already, you will quickly discover that God hasn't called you because of your training and abilities but because He considers you a worthy channel of His Spirit and power. Yes, He will use your education and equipping; He has given you talents and gifts, but He also said in Acts 1:8, "You shall receive power when the Holy Spirit has come upon you and you shall be My witnesses." It thrills me to think how you are going to experience the reality of God's power in the diverse places you are going to witness.

I am still amazed when I think of Muslims coming to faith in Christ. It defies explanation, for they would often be rejected by their family, lose their job, be ridiculed in their community; sometimes their life would be threatened. Why would someone turn their back on their culture and religion and society to embrace a faith that had been introduced by a foreigner? Certainly it is not because of our wisdom and persuasive words trying to communicate in a language that is not natural. The only explanation is the power of God that indwells the message of the gospel. Remember as you go that "the gospel . . . is the power of God for salvation, . . . to the Jew first and also to the Greek" (Rom. 1:16).

In 1977 the Department of Religion in Indonesia said that missionaries could stay no longer than three years in the country. As we prayed, I happened to read Psalm 47:8 that says, "God reigns over the nations, God sits on His holy throne," and a few weeks later the head of the religion department was changed and that law was never implemented! The reality of God's power will be evident as He opens closed doors, as He stays the hand of Pharaoh, and as He manifests His power in signs and wonders that Christ might be lifted up and glorified.

My prayer is that which was prayed by Paul for the believers at Ephesus, "That [God] would grant you, according to the riches of His glory, to be strengthened with power through His Spirit in the inner man" (Eph. 3:16).

THE RESOURCES OF GOD'S GRACE

Finally, in addition to the reliability of God's Word and the reality of God's power, you need to be assured of the resources of God's grace. As John closed his gospel account and reflected on the life of Jesus, he said the world could not contain the books if all were written of what Jesus did and said. Neither could the world contain the testimonies of God's grace in the lives of missionaries overseas if they were all to be written down. You have the privilege of experiencing those resources as you follow His leadership to strange and distant places.

In the last few months we have had the privilege of traveling to China and East Asia, Romania, and throughout South America. We met missionaries who lived in remote locations without conveniences and social outlets they had thought to be so essential but testified to finding God's grace sufficient. We were with families experiencing debilitating illnesses or grieving over the loss of a parent far away in the States, but they shared how God had manifested His precious grace beyond what they had ever known before.

Bobbye and I have not had experiences nearly as difficult as many others, but early in our tenure overseas God taught us about the resources of His grace. We had just finished language study and begun our assignment in a one-family station, hours away from any of our missionary colleagues. We had been fighting staphylococcus infections breaking out all over our bodies, probably from our water supply. As we were eating a late Thanksgiving dinner, Bobbye and I both happened to notice at the same time that a boil on our two-year-old son's forehead was enlarged and a red streak extended down to his eye. Sensing intuitively the danger of the infection draining into his brain, we left our food on the table and left for our Baptist hospital, five hours away. When we got there a little before midnight, both of his eyes were swollen shut, and they told us later, after pumping him with antibiotics, that we would have lost him if we had not come that night. Since we were at the hospital, we all got a checkup and found that Bobbye needed major surgery. That delayed our return home, but we did get back a couple of weeks before Christmas, only for Bobbye and me both to come down with dengue fever. Now there is nothing you can do about dengue fever but let it run its course; it is sometimes called break-bone fever because you feel that your head and every bone in your body is breaking. That was a miserable Christmas—alone, far away from family and friends, wallowing in bed with a burning fever, Bobbye still recovering from surgery and having almost lost our son. Then the day after Christmas the phone rang, and our mission administrator called to say they had just gotten a call that Bobbye's parents had been in an automobile accident; her father had been killed, and her mother was in critical condition. Never had we felt so helpless. We held each other and cried. Other missionaries were notified, and soon they arrived to comfort and care for us; but in the midst of that time of trial God revealed Himself to us, and we experienced the presence of Jesus and an outpouring of God's grace as we had never known it before.

As you go to the mission field, you don't go on the condition that God is going to protect you from harm, deflect hardship and difficulty, and thwart every trial. But you have an opportunity to discover what Paul discovered when God did not remove his affliction. God said, "My grace is sufficient for you, for my power is perfected in weakness." And note Paul's response: "Most gladly therefore, I will rather boast about my weakness, that the power of

Christ may dwell in me" (2 Cor. 12:9). The resources of God's grace will be sufficient for whatever you face, and you will discover the reliability of God's Word and the reality of His power.

You have been commissioned and join more than five thousand Southern Baptist missionaries in making our Lord Jesus Christ known throughout the world. God has many lessons to teach you. You still have a lot to learn, but may you quickly discover the reliability of His Word, the reality of His power, and the resources of His grace.